Volume II

Spotlight ON READING

Shirley Russak Wachtel
Helena Swanicke

Middlesex County College

Kendall Hunt
publishing company

Dedication

*For our families
and in memory of our parents*

Brief Contents

Contents

UNIT 6   HOW CAN I EVALUATE WHAT I READ?   269
Spotlight on Donald Trump

Chapter 11   Bias   271

Chapter 12   Propaganda   299

About *Spotlight on Reading*

The primary goal for every college student should be to complete school as a "well educated" individual. Indeed, the basis for that education is a solid foundation in reading.

However, the path toward this goal is often not an easy one for students who struggle with the fundamentals of reading comprehension. *Spotlight on Reading* addresses students' concerns by providing instruction in basic skills along with an abundance of practice while motivating students to become readers on the road to becoming "well-educated" citizens.

We are proud to introduce *Spotlight on Reading, Volume II,* a unique text for the college student in need of secondary-level basic reading skills. The success of our many years in the classroom using the methods incorporated in the *Spotlight* texts has demonstrated that students can make significant strides in college-level reading skills when using an instructional text that provides motivational features, clearly explained pedagogy, and multifaceted practice exercises that reinforce learning.

Spotlight on Reading II contains many unique features, including intriguing biographies of students' favorite celebrities, as well as several articles written by and about spotlighted celebrities. For instructors, each chapter provides a comprehensive and manageable method that can be easily incorporated into any reading curriculum.

Rationale for *Spotlight on Reading*

Spotlight on Reading, Volume II is a college textbook that works for both teacher and student. It is unlike other texts that do a terrific job with one or more of the essential components in the instruction of reading. While one text focuses on teaching and practice of reading skills across the curriculum, another concentrates on intensive vocabulary training, and still another exposes students to notable works of fiction. Others take an "everything-but-the-kitchen-sink" approach, leaving to instructors the task of sorting out what to teach when, and delivering much more material than one course could possibly cover.

A Comprehensive Approach to Reading Instruction

Spotlight on Reading, Volume II has proven that students attain success when using a comprehensive text that provides the "big picture" while using a methodical, reader-friendly approach, but one that is at the same time manageable in terms of coverage and length. The text has garnered praise from teachers who appreciate its unit and chapter format and the variety of readings offered in the disciplines, as well as literary works. Several practice exercises along with diagnostic and assessment exams facilitate evaluation of skills.

Our hope is that adjuncts in particular, as well as any others assigned to courses without a great deal of preparation time, will enjoy the facility of presentation provided by *Spotlight on Reading*. Students will no longer feel overwhelmed, either by multiple texts, or by a single text the size and heft of a phonebook. This text offers ease of use for the instructor while providing a comprehensive, reader-friendly, and motivating apparatus for the college reading student.

Answering the Needs of All Students

This text is intended for use by the thousands of students in reading courses at colleges throughout the nation. Specifically, the book is aimed at the secondary-level reading class, which often includes a mix of native, international, learning disabled, and returning students, but also those students who need to "brush up" on skills before immersion into the college curriculum. These students typically lack or need review of comprehension skills and have scored just below norm on a school-administered basic skills reading exam. For many of these students, this text provides a means for easing them into the demands of the college classroom.

The goals for students of secondary-level reading classes include the ability to attain passing scores on the aforementioned exams, but, more importantly, to attain a basic understanding of literal reading skills with special emphasis on unlocking the meaning of vocabulary words and understanding the main idea. Additionally, the text helps students explore critical reading skills (including differentiation of fact versus opinion, inference, author's intent, attitude, and tone), through practice readings in various content disciplines. Recognizing that students need to have an understanding of controversial issues and current news, we also include work on understanding the newspaper, as well as essays that expound bold opinions. Finally, units promote affective skills through readings in poetry and short stories. Attainment of these skills will improve student comprehension of college textbooks, regardless of their major. Other long-range goals of this text are to: build a foundation for success in whatever career choice the student makes; teach an appreciation of and curiosity about literature; motivate students to explore issues that are relevant to their lives; and offer students a sense of satisfaction in mastering the essential skills of reading and, concurrently, writing.

How to Integrate Reading in Any Course

Sometimes students do not perform as well as they should because they struggle not with the subject, but with essential reading skills. The knowledgeable instructor can help these students by consistently reviewing homework, along with vocabulary unfamiliar to the student. Encourage students to follow the SQ3R plan when reading, which includes previewing, questioning material, highlighting, and reviewing. Make sure to reinforce readings by questioning and creating an open class atmosphere where students feel free to respond and air concerns. Connect the readings to real life experiences to inspire students to become successful in your class, and to become lifelong readers.

Features in the Text

Spotlight on Reading, Volume II contains the following features:

- **"Spotlight On"**—Each unit opens with a brief biography of an instantly recognizable celebrity, like Angelina Jolie, Avril Lavigne, Tommy Hilfiger, and Muhammad Ali. The "work" of each chapter is related to a motivating factor revealed in the celebrity's biography.

- **Readings**—Relevant material from across the curriculum and narratives that address topics related to the celebrity biographies in each unit are featured. Readings come from social science, humanities, science and math textbooks; popular sources (covering both timeless issues and current events); and literature. Once students attain basic comprehension strategies, they will be introduced to readings in literature by prominent and less-known authors that will inspire and empower. There is no need for students to purchase literature or other anthologies, since the text offers a plethora of reading selections.

- **Organization**—The progression of chapters in the book is based on the principle of scaffolding; that is, the skills taught in each chapter build, in obvious and practical ways, on skills mastered subsequently.

- **Units**—Ten major units, with two chapters per unit, each highlight a different skill and incorporate vocabulary, study skills, and inferential skills in comprehension exercises.

- **Chapters**—Based upon the principle of scaffolding, this chapter-by-chapter approach offers flexibility to those who wish to proceed at a faster or slower pace, but most importantly the skills taught in each chapter build, in obvious and practical ways, on skills mastered subsequently.

- **Exercises**—Comprehensive exercises are incorporated into each chapter to reinforce pedagogy and extend learning. Perforated pages allow students to submit work to the instructor.

- **"Your Turn, What Did You Learn?"**—These short quizzes check student comprehension.

- **"Comprehending Longer Selections"**—Comprehensive exercises included in eleven chapters are composed of activities that allow students to practice skills presented in the chapter. Activities based on the longer reading include:

  - two sets of vocabulary questions (one pre-reading and one post-reading);
  - multiple-choice and short-answer comprehension questions;
  - free writing journal suggestions;
  - individual and collaborative student activities;
  - and Web-based look-it-up research exercises.

- **Getting the Picture**—Pictures jump start guided freewrite activity at the end of every chapter.

- **SQ3R Cards**—Tear-out guide cards are included to assist students using this study system for select longer readings.

- **Chapter Previews and Highlights**—Presented before and after each chapter, these ensure that students see the progression of their skills, and the connection between what came before and what follows.

- **Content on Study Skills**—A unit on study skills is provided early in the text. The formula of SQ3R has proven effective in helping students succeed in college courses.

- **Content on Vocabulary**—The text includes two chapters of vocabulary instruction. Vocabulary skills are introduced early, as vocabulary comprehension is an essential tool in understanding the main idea and other reading concepts. Emphasis is given to meaning through context strategies as well as utilizing word parts and outside resources to promote understanding. Vocabulary is the basic building block to becoming a better reader and, as such, we stress the importance of word skills. Vocabulary skills are reinforced in conjunction with readings throughout the text, eliminating the need for a separate vocabulary textbook.

- **Assessment**—The text begins with a diagnostic reading test that will enable the student to identify skills which need work. The end of the book includes a post-test, which will serve as a review for the final exam for the course.

- For visual interest as well as comprehension practice, *Spotlight on Reading* includes a number of well-chosen **charts** and **photographs**.

- Each chapter reviews and provides practice for study skills, as well as specific **test-taking tips**, which deserve continual pedagogical reinforcement and which comprise an integral basis for college reading.

Spotlight on Reading, Volume II also contains these special **features** that specifically address the needs of college students in a secondary-level basic skills reading class:

- **An entire unit is devoted to understanding newspaper and news magazine articles**, with an explanation of the reporter's 5W's for easy comprehension. Besides articles that cover relevant issues, editorials, columns, and reviews are presented so the student may recognize opinion. These materials inspire students to learn more about society, including local, national, and international affairs.

- On this level, **two long readings with concurrent questions in vocabulary and comprehension are presented in each chapter.** Emphasis is given to meaning through context strategies as well as utilizing word parts and outside resources to promote understanding. Vocabulary is the basic building block to becoming a better reader and, as such, we stress the importance of word skills.

- Students hone critical thinking and reading skills as they **learn to recognize bias and propaganda**, as seen in advertising and several readings. The text devotes an entire unit to these skills.

- In order to **motivate and empower** students to explore literature, **short stories** by such notable writers as Alice Walker, Edgar Allan Poe, and William Carlos Williams are studied. **Poetry is demystified** through an explanation of figurative language, illustrated with several examples.

- It is our hope that students will be at ease not only when reading these poems and short stories, but that they will make the decision that reading can be inspiring and fun at the same time. Perhaps, and this is our ultimate goal, they will even become readers for life!

Acknowledgments

When we embarked upon this project five years ago, we could never have imagined its magnitude nor could we have anticipated the friends we would make along the way. First, thanks go to Sue Saad, our acquisitions editor who always had faith in our vision and made that vision a possibility. We owe gratitude to our developmental editor, Denise LaBudda, our permissions editor, Renae Horstman, and our production editor, Sheri Hosek. Their diligence and expertise are incomparable. We must also acknowledge our consultants Mark Gwiazdowski, Andrew Kistulentz, Elizabeth Swanicke Loonam, Lis Oliu, Georgiana Planko, Paul Swanicke, and Esther Young. We extend our gratitude as well to the English Department, especially our fellow reading instructors, Lucille Alfieri, James Bernarducci, Gertrude Coleman, Carol Fox, Leah Ghirardella, Barry Glazer, Marylou Kjelle, Renee Price, and Ellen Shur for their contributions and advice. We also wish to thank professors Elisabeth Altruda, Santi Buscemi, James Keller, and Iris Ramer for their support. Master teachers all, they inspire us each day.

Shirley Russak Wachtel is the author of *The Addison Wesley Longman Interactive Guide to Newsweek* (Longman Publishers, 1999), a supplementary guide for college students. Her book *The Story of Blima—A Holocaust Survivor* (Townsend Press, 2005) recounts the true story of her mother and is taught in classrooms throughout the nation. For her efforts, she has been recognized by the New Jersey Commission on Holocaust Education. The entire story of her mother's experience is narrated in Wachtel's acclaimed memoir, *My Mother's Shoes* (publ. 2011). She is also the author of five children's books, *What Would I Be? The Eight Days of Hanukkah, Charlie Wonder—Chef-Detective, Brad Sureshot—Coach-Detective, Howie Rocket—World Traveler-Detective;* and a book of poetry, *In The Mellow Light* (2009). Her poems and short stories have been featured in *Middlesex, A Literary Journal*. Dr. Wachtel received a Bachelor of Arts degree in English Literature from Brooklyn College, and a Master of Arts degree in English Literature from Long Island University. She earned a Doctor of Letters degree from Drew University. For the past twenty years, she has taught developmental reading and writing, freshman composition, and creative writing at Middlesex County College in Edison, New Jersey, where she has created several innovative combined reading/writing lessons. In 2006, Dr. Wachtel was awarded the Innovative Teaching Award presented by the League for Innovation in Community Colleges in conjunction with the *New York Times*. The award was given for the best use of the *New York Times* in a classroom nationwide. Dr. Wachtel is also a frequent presenter at professional conferences throughout New Jersey.

Helena Swanicke earned her Bachelor of Science degree in Elementary/Special Education from Rutgers College, Rutgers University, a Master of Arts degree in Reading Instruction from Concordia University, and a Master of Letters from Drew University. She is a certified reading specialist and has taught at the elementary, junior high, and community-college levels. For the past eighteen years, she has taught developmental reading and writing at Middlesex County College, Edison, New Jersey. Her creative works are published at Drew University. She has also been a presenter at college workshops and professional conferences. Swanicke is currently a candidate for the Doctor of Letters Degree at Drew University.

Name _____   Date _____

Diagnostic Test

Textbook Reading Comprehension
Time: Forty Minutes

Directions: This is a test of your ability to comprehend reading passages from textbooks used in a variety of college courses.

First, read each passage carefully. Then answer each question, selecting from the four possible answers the one that is best.

There are six passages and twenty-five questions. Although it is not necessary to finish the entire test to obtain a good score, try to finish the test within the forty-minute test time. If you finish before forty minutes have elapsed, reread as many passages as you can and check your responses. Remain seated and wait for further instructions.

Questions 1-4 are based on the following passage

As suggested by its name, the peripheral nervous system branches out from the spinal cord and brain and reaches the extremities of the body. Made up of long axons and dendrites, the peripheral nervous system encompasses all parts of the nervous system other than the brain and spinal cord. There are two major divisions, both of which connect the central nervous system with the sense organs, muscles, glands, and other organs. The somatic division specializes in the control of voluntary movements—such as the motion of the eyes to read this sentence or the hand to turn this page—and the communication of information to and from the sense organs. On the other hand, the autonomic division is concerned with the parts of the body that keep us alive—the heart, blood vessels, glands, lungs, and other organs that function involuntarily without our awareness. As you read now, the autonomic division of the peripheral nervous system is pumping the blood through your body, pushing your lungs in and out, overseeing the digestion of the meal you had a few hours ago, without a thought or care on your part. (Feldman 70)

1. The major topic for this selection is:
   a. somatic division of the nervous system.
   b. peripheral nervous system.
   c. brain and spinal cord.
   d. the autonomic division of the nervous system.

2. The peripheral nervous system includes all parts of the nervous system except the:
   a. brain.
   b. spinal cord.
   c. both A and B are excluded.
   d. neither A nor B is excluded.

3. The body functions that go on during sleep are controlled by what division?
   a. somatic
   b. autonomic
   c. peripheral
   d. all of the above

4. If you choose to stop reading this question voluntarily, this act is controlled by what division?
   a. peripheral division
   b. autonomic
   c. somatic
   d. all of these exert this control

Questions 5-8 are based on this passage

Another way for a firm to grow is by purchasing some other company. The purchase of one corporation by another is called a merger. (The term acquisition means essentially the same thing, but it is usually reserved for large corporations buying other corporations). The firm that is expanding simply buys the stock of the purchased corporation. (This is not always as simple as it sounds. In some cases, the management and stockholders of the firm targeted for acquisition are unwilling to let their company become a subsidiary of the purchasing firm. The results may be greatly inflated stock prices, legal battles, and—at the least—general ill will between the two firms.) The underlying reason for growth by merger is the supposition that the merged companies can produce benefits for the shareholders that the individual companies cannot offer on their own.

A horizontal merger is a merger between firms that make and sell similar products in similar markets. The purchase of Telecom USA by MCI Communications is an example of a horizontal merger. The rash of mergers between large American companies in the 1980s resulted in many horizontal mergers. This type of merger tends to reduce the number of firms in an industry—and thus may reduce competition. For this reason, each merger may be reviewed carefully by federal agencies before it is permitted. (Pride)

5. Compared to a merger, an acquisition differs in what?
   a. the size of the firm
   b. the shareholders
   c. the price of the stock
   d. the horizontal nature involved

6. What would be one example of a horizontal merger?
   a. McDonald's buys Wendy's
   b. McDonald's buys State Farm Insurance
   c. McDonald's buys McDonald's
   d. McDonald's buys Holiday Inn

7. One can conclude that mergers are:
   a. completed regardless of the federal government.
   b. accomplished quite easily.
   c. usually welcomed by both companies.
   d. made to benefit the companies and shareholders.

8. Mergers are one way for companies to:
   a. increase competition.
   b. grow.
   c. reduce ill will.
   d. inflate stock prices.

Questions 9-12 are based on this passage

Some individuals who survived a close brush with death have reported autoscopy (watching, from several feet in the air, resuscitation attempts on their own bodies) or transcendence (the sense of passing into a foreign region or dimension). Some see light, often at the end of a tunnel. Their vision seems clearer; their hearing, sharper. Some recall scenes from their lives or feel the presence of loved ones who have died. Many report profound feelings of joy, calm, and peace.

In recent years, the number of reports of near-death experiences has grown, thanks largely to advances in medical care. Most such experiences are remarkably similar, whether they occur in children or adults, whether the individuals actually are near death or only think they are. Less than 1% of those who've reported near-death experiences described them as frightening or distressing, although a larger number recall transitory feelings of fear or confusion. (Feldman)

9. Why are there more recent reports about this subject?
   a. People are living longer today.
   b. Emergency medical care is better today.
   c. More dying people are completing reports on this.
   d. Autoscopic and transcendent experiences have increased.

10. The majority of reports from persons near death:
    a. were generally not similar.
    b. differed greatly among various age groups.
    c. showed most were very frightened.
    d. were similar whether the person was near death or not.

11. One very important question not answered here is:
    a. Is there a rational explanation for this?
    b. Are these people telling the truth?
    c. Why does this only happen to people near death?
    d. Why is this happening so often today?

12. An appropriate way to describe these experiences is:
    a. frightening.
    b. questionable.
    c. unremarkable.
    d. mystical.

Questions 13-16 are based on this passage

Researchers have traditionally distinguished between different types of alcoholics. Type I alcoholics generally start heavy drinking, reinforced by external circumstances, after age 25. They can abstain for long periods of time but frequently feel a loss of control, guilt, and fear about their alcohol dependence. They also have characteristic personality traits: They tend to be anxious, shy, pessimistic, sentimental, emotionally dependent, rigid, reflective, and slow-tempered. Alcohol reduces their anxiety, and they rapidly develop tolerance and become dependent.

Type 2 alcoholics, on the other hand, typically become heavy drinkers before age 25; they drink regardless of external circumstances, have frequent fights and arrests, and experience guilt, fear, or a loss of control only infrequently. They're impulsive and aggressive risk takers, curious, excitable, quick-tempered, optimistic, and independent. Alcohol reinforces their feelings of euphoria and a sense of pleasant excitement. Often they abuse other substances besides alcohol. (Hales)

13. How is this information presented to the reader?
    a. cause-effect
    b. comparison-contrast
    c. process-sequence
    d. specific-general

14. According to this article, an adolescent alcoholic is:
    a. a Type I alcoholic.
    b. likely to have a criminal record.
    c. very popular in high school.
    d. a likely winner of a debate contest.

15. Type I alcoholics drink in order to:
    a. relieve anxiety.
    b. get high and have a good time.
    c. develop guilt.
    d. abuse others.

16. Type 2 alcoholics:
    a. are mostly males.
    b. are hiding their fears.
    c. begin drinking later in life.
    d. are likely to use other drugs.

Questions 17-20 are based on this passage

Researchers have suggested a variety of personal factors as reasons why individuals go into business. One that is often cited is the "entrepreneurial spirit"— the desire to create a new business. Other factors, such as independence, the desire to determine one's own destiny, and the willingness to find and accept a challenge certainly play a part. Background may exert an influence as well. In particular, researchers think that people whose families have been in business (successfully or not) are most apt to start and run their own business. Those who start their own businesses also tend to cluster around certain ages—more than 70% are between 24 and 44 years old. Women own 4.8 million businesses and are starting new businesses at twice the rate of men.

Finally, there must be some motivation to start a business. A person may decide she has simply "had enough" of working for someone else. Another may lose his job for some reason and decide to start the business he has always wanted rather than seek another job. Still another person may have an idea for a new product or a new way to sell an exciting product. Or the opportunity to go into business may arise suddenly, perhaps as a result of a hobby. (Pride)

17. Surprisingly, one reason not at all stressed for going into business is:
    a. the "entrepreneurial spirit".
    b. to control one's destiny.
    c. to make a lot of money.
    d. the role of the family history.

18. The best title for this selection would be:
    a. Getting Rich in Your Own Business.
    b. Getting Started in Your Own Business.
    c. The Psychology of Success in Small Business.
    d. Why People Start Their Own Businesses.

19. What does the selection tell us about women in small businesses?
    a. Women own more businesses than men.
    b. Women are more successful than most men in business.
    c. Women are starting more new businesses than men.
    d. Women are much younger than men in small businesses.

20. The article points out that the typical owner of a small business:
    a. probably inherited the business.
    b. makes more money than he might in a "regular" job.
    c. likes to accept a challenge.
    d. all of the above describes the typical small business owner.

Questions 21-25 are based on the following passage

Where, in all these theories of personality, is an explanation for the saintliness of a Mother Teresa, the creativity of a Michelangelo, the brilliance and perseverance of an Einstein? An understanding of such unique individuals—as well as more ordinary sorts of people who share some of the same attributes—comes from humanistic theory.

According to humanistic theorists, all of the theories of personality that we have previously discussed share a fundamental misperception in their views of human nature. Instead of seeing people as controlled by unconscious, unseen forces (as does psychoanalytic theory), a set of stable traits (trait theory), or situational reinforcements and punishments (learning theory), humanistic theory emphasizes people's basic goodness and their tendency to grow to higher levels of functioning. It is this conscious, self-motivated ability to change and improve, along with people's creative impulses, that makes up the core of personality.

The major representative of the humanistic point of view is Carl Rodgers. Rodgers suggests that people have a need for positive regard that reflects a universal requirement to be loved and respected. Because others provide this positive regard, we grow dependent on them. We begin to see and judge ourselves through the eyes of other people, relying on their values. (Feldman)

21. This selection is mostly about:
    a. creative and inventive people.
    b. psychological theories.
    c. humanistic theory.
    d. Carl Rodgers's theories.

22. Other personality theories, such as trait or learning theory:
    a. have been shown to be incorrect.
    b. are now disregarded by most psychologists.
    c. offer valid explanations for all personalities.
    d. cannot account for individuals like Einstein or Mother Teresa.

23. What aspect of personality is stressed by humanistic theory?
    a. our goodness
    b. our creativity
    c. our ability to change
    d. all of the above are stressed

24. The humanistic theory of personality stresses the role of:
    a. self-motivated improvement and change.
    b. unconscious forces.
    c. reinforcements and punishments.
    d. stable traits.

25. The theory that best views human nature is:
    a. psychoanalytic theory.
    b. learning theory.
    c. humanistic theory.
    d. trait theory.

STOP

**IF YOU FINISH BEFORE TIME IS CALLED,
GO BACK AND CHECK YOUR WORK.**

WHAT ARE MY READING SKILLS?

CHAPTER 1 What Kind of Learner Are You?
CHAPTER 2 Active Reading and Active Learning

Before you begin learning reading skills, it is important to understand the learning style that is best for you. In this unit, you will find out how to determine your learning style and how to become an active learner.

Spotlight on

Tommy Hilfiger (1952–)

Tommy Hilfiger, one of the hottest designers in the world, is best known as the fashion mogul with the blue-white-red rectangular logo. Considered the innovator of "urban fashion" in sportswear during the 1990s, Hilfiger opened for business in upstate New York in 1969, and made New York City his base in the late 1970s. In 1982, Tommy Hilfiger, Inc., was started, and in1984 he began a collection of jeans and men's sportswear, adding women's clothing, eyewear, jewelry, fragrances and home products by the mid-90s. Hilfiger's products have generated billions in annual worldwide retail sales. In May, 2010, the company was sold for $3 billion to clothing conglomerate Phillips-Van Heusen. Hilfiger has four children with his first wife, and a son with his second wife, Dee Ocleppo. Besides being a fashion mogul and receiving numerous awards from the fashion industry, Hilfiger is actively involved in a number of causes, charities, and hosted a CBS reality show called "The Cut," where sixteen style-savvy contestants competed for a chance to design their own line of clothing under the Tommy Hilfiger label. However, it seems remarkable that Tommy Hilfiger's professional triumphs were achieved in spite of a learning handicap, dyslexia.

© Dziekan/Retna Ltd./Corbis

Chapter 1

WHAT KIND OF LEARNER ARE YOU?

Do you know your learning style? It is important that we recognize our learning styles so that we can find which method of learning works best for us. Researchers Colin Rose and Malcolm J. Nicholl have investigated the process of learning and concluded: "[T]he left brain specializes in academic aspects of learning—language and mathematical processes, logical thoughts, sequences, and analysis. The right brain is principally concerned with creative activities utilizing rhyme, rhythm, music, visual impressions, color, and pictures. It's our metaphorical mind, looking for analogies and patterns" (Rose and Nicholl). However, both the left and right brain hemispheres are involved in almost all thinking. Hence, thinking and learning are related.

To better understand how you prefer to learn and process information, consider the work of Bandler, Grinder, and Grinder. These researchers have identified three distinct communications and leaning styles: visual, auditory, and kinesthetic.

Visual learners learn through seeing. **Auditory learners** learn through hearing. **Kinesthetic learners** learn through physical activities and through direct involvement. According to Bandler, Grinder and Grinder, 70% of learners will be able to cope, regardless of how a lesson is presented; 10% will be unable to learn, no matter what method is employed; and 30% will only be able to learn

"Want to hear something scary? This is the third time this week I've gotten off the bus and still remember what I learned."

in either a visual, auditory, or kinesthetic way (Bandler, Grinder, and Grinder). Knowing your own learning style allows you to focus your studying on methods that are most effective for you. Clearly, *all* students can benefit from knowing their learning style preference(s). What is your learning style?

Exercise   **1.1**   # What Is Your Learning Style?

Take the Learning Style Inventory to better understand how you prefer to learn and process information.

Directions: Place a check in the appropriate space after each statement below. Then use the scoring procedures at the end to evaluate your responses. Use what you learn by your scores to better develop learning strategies that are best suited to your particular style. This 24-item survey is not timed. Respond to each statement as honestly as you can.

	Often	Sometimes	Seldom
1. I can remember best about a subject by listening to a lecture that includes information, explanations, and discussion.			
2. I prefer to see information written on a chalkboard and supplemented by visual aids and assigned readings.			
3. I like to write things down or to take notes for visual review.			
4. I prefer to use posters, models, or actual practice and other activities in class.			
5. I require explanations of diagrams, graphs, or visual directions.			
6. I enjoy working with my hands or making things.			
7. I enjoy looking at maps and charts.			
8. I can tell if sounds match when presented with pairs of sounds.			
9. I remember best by writing things down several times.			
10. I can easily understand and follow directions on maps.			

11. I do best in academic subjects by listening to lectures and tapes.			
12. I play with coins or keys in my pockets.			
13. I learn to spell better by repeating words out loud than by writing the words on paper.			
14. I can understand a news article better by reading about it in the newspaper than by listening to a report about it on the radio.			
15. I chew gum, smoke, or snack while studying.			
16. I think the best way to remember something is to picture it in your head.			
17. I learn the spelling of words by "finger spelling" them.			
18. I would rather listen to a good lecture or speech than read about the same material in a textbook.			
19. I am good at working and solving jigsaw puzzles and mazes.			
20. I grip objects in my hands during learning periods.			
21. I prefer listening to the news on the radio rather than reading about it in the newspaper.			
22. I prefer obtaining information about an interesting subject by reading about it.			
23. I feel very comfortable touching others, hugging, handshaking, etc.			
24. I follow oral directions better than written ones.			

SCORING PROCEDURES

Directions: Place the point value on the line next to the corresponding item below. Add the points in each column to obtain the preference score under each heading.

OFTEN   = 5 points
SOMETIMES   = 3 points
SELDOM   = 1 point

VISUAL		AUDITORY		TACTILE or KINESTHETIC	
No.	Pts.	No.	Pts.	No.	Pts.
2	____	1	____	3	____
4	____	5	____	6	____
7	____	8	____	9	____
10	____	11	____	12	____
14	____	13	____	15	____
16	____	18	____	17	____
19	____	21	____	20	____
22	____	24	____	23	____
VPS = ____		APS = ____		TPS = ____	

VPS = Visual Preference Score

APS = Auditory Preference Score

TPS = Tactile Preference Score

Adapted from Penn State Learning Style Inventory

How Can You Study Best?

If you are a visual learner, by all means be sure that you look at all study materials. Use charts, maps, filmstrips, notes, videos, and flash cards. Practice visualizing or picturing words and concepts in your head. Write out everything for frequent and quick visual review.

If you are an auditory learner, you may wish to use tapes. Tape lectures to help fill in gaps in your notes. But do listen and take notes—and review your notes frequently. Sit in the lecture hall or classroom where you can hear well. After you have read something, summarize it and recite it aloud. Talk to other students about class material. Some machines can help you by reading your class text aloud. Check with your instructor to see if these are available at your college. **If you are a tactile or kinesthetic learner,** trace words as you are saying them. Facts that must be learned should be written several times. Keep a supply of scratch paper on hand for this purpose. Taking and keeping lecture notes is very important. Make study sheets. Associate class material with real-world things and occurrences. When appropriate, practice role playing.

Different Learning Styles

Everyone is born different and learns in different ways. We have seen that not everyone has the same learning style. However, no matter what their learning style, many people who are quite smart and successful may have struggled with learning at some point in their lives. Some of the celebrities you will meet in this book fall into this category. Diagnostic categories for learning disabilities and/or Attention-Deficit/Hyperactivity Disorder were not always in use; therefore, successful celebrities whether suspected of or diagnosed with having a learning disabilities and/or Attention-Deficit/Hyperactivity Disorder directed their academic frustration and energies toward other avenues, sometimes discovering hidden talents.

Celebrity Questionnaire

1.2   *Exercise*

The following famous and successful people struggled with learning disabilities. **See if you can match the personal descriptions to the names below:**

a. Albert Einstein
b. Walt Disney
c. Nelson Rockefeller
d. F.W. Woolworth
e. Winston Churchill
f. Hans Christian Andersen
g. George Patton
h. Tom Cruise

1. _____ As a child, he was labeled as slow. He clerked in a village grocery store. He suggested putting slow-moving merchandise on a counter and selling it for five cents. This venture was so successful that it continued with new goods. He became the principal founder of a chain of five and ten cent stores.

2. _____ When he was twelve years old, he could not read, and he remained deficient in reading all of his life. However, he could memorize entire lectures, which is how he got through school. He became a famous general during WWII.

3. _____ He was slow in school work and did not have a successful school experience, but later became a well-known movie producer and cartoonist.

4. _____ This noted Englishman had much difficulty in school. He later became a national leader and an English Prime Minister.

5. _____ This young boy had difficulty reading but was able to write some of the world's best-loved stories.

6. _____ This boy could not talk until the age of four. He did not learn to read until he was nine. His teachers considered him to be a mentally slow, unsociable dreamer. He failed the entrance examination for college. Ultimately, he developed the theory of relativity.

7. _____ He is a famous movie star. He learns his lines by listening to a tape. He suffers from dyslexia.

8. _____ This young man had much difficulty reading and throughout his life was unable to read well. However, he was the governor of the state of New York for four terms and later won congressional approval to be appointed vice president of the United States.

Answers to the Celebrity Quiz
1. d, 2. g, 3. b, 4. e, 5. f, 6. a, 7. h, 8. c.

Adapted from LearningDisabilityForum.com

Getting the Picture

The Tommy Hilfiger brand is known worldwide largely due to good publicity and advertising. Look at the photo. Would you buy these suits because they look good on display? Explain how advertising influences the products you buy.

_____

_____

_____

_____

_____

© Roberto Chicano, 2010. Used under license from Shutterstock, Inc.

_____

_____

_____

_____

_____

_____

_____

_____

_____

_____

_____

_____

_____

Chapter Highlights

What Have We Learned?

1. A particular method of learning that is best for you is called a **learning style**.

2. It is important to know your own learning style because it helps you decide **how to learn best**.

3. A **visual** learner learns best by reading or seeing information.

4. An **auditory** learner learns best by listening to information.

5. A **kinesthetic** learner learns best by manipulating materials physically or incorporating movement.

Chapter 2

ACTIVE READING AND ACTIVE LEARNING

Active Reading: The Three Levels of Comprehension

Being a successful reader means being an active reader who can interact with text in three major areas of reading comprehension: *literal, critical,* and, *affective.*

The triangle below illustrates these three areas of comprehension. At the base of the triangle is the most basic level of comprehension, *literal comprehension.*

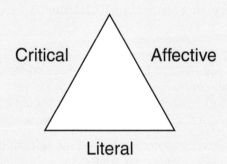

Literal Comprehension

The skills associated with literal comprehension include (1) vocabulary, (2) main idea, (3) rhetorical modes, and (4) study techniques.

- **Vocabulary:** Vocabulary knowledge constitutes the building blocks of reading comprehension. Understanding the meaning of words is most often attained through the *context.* (That's why people who read a lot often know an abundance of words!) In addition to learning words from *context,* you may also learn words through an understanding of word parts (prefix, suffix, root) and by looking up the words in a *dictionary.*

To check your understanding of vocabulary knowledge, read the following sentences, define the italicized word, and explain how you were able to determine the word's meaning (choose "context," "word parts," or "dictionary").

1. The freight truck set out from New York and traveled *interstate* to California.

   interstate means: _____

   How I found it (context, word parts, dictionary) _____

2. Pigeons are a *ubiquitious* sight in the city.

   ubiquitious means: _____

   How I found it (context, word parts, dictionary) _____

3. When Scottie hit his brother, he was committing a *malicious* act.

   malicious means: _____

   How I found it (context, word parts, dictionary) _____

You will learn how to improve your vocabulary in Unit 3: Chapter 5 focuses on vocabulary in context and Chapter 6 focuses on word parts and dictionary skills.

- **Main Idea:** Finding the main idea of a reading selection is probably the most essential reading skill you need to know. If you can understand the main idea (also known as *main point, controlling idea, central thesis,* or *gist*), you will be able to grasp the meaning of the material. The main idea should not be confused with the topic, which is the general subject and is often represented in a title or headline.

   The *main idea,* or *topic sentence,* of a reading selection always (1) is a complete sentence, (2) conveys a message, and (3) says something about the topic. The topic sentence may be found anywhere in a paragraph, or it may even be implied. The main idea of an entire article or essay is called the *thesis.*

   The *major details* support the main idea directly, while *minor details* (sometimes in the form of quotes or responses), indirectly support the main idea. Students are sometimes confused by what they read because many complicated details may cloud the meaning. However, once you are able to locate the main idea, you can attain a basic understanding of anything you read.

   Together, the topic, main idea, and details form an article or essay. Each work has an *introduction*, which introduces the reader in a clear, sometimes imaginative way, to the material. The *body* contains the details that support the thesis or main idea. Finally, the *conclusion* summarizes the major points, often leaving the reader with "food for thought."

   To check your understanding of main idea, read the paragraph below and answer the following questions.

   Zeus was a powerful god in many ways. First, he was intelligent. When Zeus was born, his mother, Rhea, hid him because his father, Kronos, had eaten all Zeus's sisters and brothers and he wanted to eat Zeus, too. Zeus was smart enough to trick his father into disgorging (throwing up) his brothers and sisters. Together, they overthrew their father. Second, Zeus was also the acknowledged leader, and he made key decisions as to who should be punished or rewarded and what the punishment or rewards should be. For instance, Zeus decided that Prometheus, who gave humans fire, should be chained to a rock forever so that an eagle could eat out his liver for eternity. Finally, Zeus was strong. He was so powerful that he could affect the weather. Thus, he is often associated with a thunderbolt. All of these characteristics combined to make Zeus a powerful leader. (Long 6)

Topic: _____

Main Idea: _____

Three Details: _____

    1. _____

    2. _____

    3. _____

© dpaint, 2010. Used under license from Shutterstock, Inc.

Powerful Zeus

You will learn how to improve your literal comprehension in Unit 4: Chapter 7 focuses on the main idea, topic, and details.

- **Rhetorical Modes:** Patterns in which a writing selection's details are organized are called *rhetorical modes*. These patterns include the following:

Illustration or example
Definition
Comparison/contrast
Sequence of events
Cause and effect
Description
Narration

You will learn more about patterns of organization in Unit 4: Chapter 8 focuses on rhetorical modes.

- **Study Techniques:** A popular method of study is the **SQ3R** approach, which can be applied to articles, essays, and just about any college discipline.

"S" Stands for Survey. To get a general sense of the article/essay/text, preread the headline, subheadings, words written in boldface or italics, and the introductions and conclusions.

"Q" Stands for Question. To maintain interest in the reading, turn a statement into a question. For example, the statement "An important scientific discovery was made last week" might be converted to "What was the important scientific discovery made last week?" The process makes sense; once you pose a question, you will read on to attain the answer.

"R" Means Read. After you have surveyed and questioned, you can now read the article/essay/text word for word, focusing on words in groups to get meaning from the context.

The Second "R" Means Recite. It is an important but often overlooked aspect of the study process. Until this stage, you have been absorbing the material. But recitation or practice is needed if you are to "give back" that material in the form of a research paper, discussion, or exam. This step may take the form of oral recitation, annotation, taking notes, or creating more formal outlines, maps, or summaries.

The Third "R" Means Review. In this stage, you skim through the selection and answer questions immediately after the reading and prior to the exam.

You will learn more about fact and opinion in Unit 6: Chapter 14 focuses on opinions in the news.

Critical Comprehension

Once you have achieved a literal comprehension of a reading selection, you are ready for the next step: gaining an understanding on a critical level. *Critical comprehension* is simply the ability to interpret what is read. Skills incorporated in critical reading include: (1) distinguishing fact from opinion; (2) recognizing the writer's intent, attitude, and tone; (3) recognizing inference and drawing conclusions; and (4) understanding bias.

Fact versus Opinion

A *fact* is anything that can be proven. For example, a statement such as "this room measures 20-by-30 feet" may be proven true simply by measuring the room. If the room measurement does not agree with the statement, then the statement is incorrect. An *opinion* is a statement that can be disputed. For example, the sentence "This is a comfortable room" would be considered an opinion because the statement is an observation that can be disputed.

You will learn more about fact and opinion in Chapters 9 and 14. Chapter 14 focuses on opinions in the news.

Intent, Attitude, and Tone

A well-crafted persuasive essay or news story uses intent, attitude, and tone to add shades of meaning to the piece.

The writer's intent is simply his or her purpose for writing the article or essay. For example, the intent may be to educate, entertain, or argue a point. An understanding of intent is important because it determines how the writer approaches the material.

The writer's attitude shows how he or she feels about the subject.

The writer's tone is reflected in how the writer expresses himself or herself, and often is what makes a piece memorable.

Irony is a popular device used in expressing tone; it is an outcome which is contrary, or opposite, of what is expected. For example, it is ironic when someone who always remembers an umbrella forgets it on the day it rains.

Recognizing Inference and Drawing Conclusions

Inference is meaning that is received indirectly, or hinted at in the text. Using literal reading skills and then applying critical skills, readers are able to *infer* a deeper meaning from the language. For example, if a writer describes a house that is ornate and has servants' quarters, a tennis court on premises, and a magnificent swimming pool, the writer may then infer that the person living there is rich. The adept reader also draws *conclusions* from essays/text that present facts and opinions.

Bias

Bias is a prejudice, or a slanted view of something. Writings that exhibit bias are said to be *subjective*. Those that do not reveal bias are *objective*. The astute reader learns how to recognize bias while evaluating an article/essay/text, and then comes to his or her own conclusions. Sometimes, the presence of bias is quite clear, as in *editorials,* which are by definition slanted toward one particular opinion. In other instances, bias can be found in unlikely sources, such as history textbooks that present only one side of an event or omit the accomplishments of a particular group. Although such bias may not be intended, it is important that the reader realize that a complete, balanced picture is not being presented.

You will learn more about inference in Unit 5: Chapter 9; intent, attitude, and tone in Unit 5: Chapter 10; and bias in Unit 6: Chapter 11.

Affective Comprehension

The highest order of comprehension is *affective comprehension,* and it can be attained only with both a literal and a critical understanding of the material. Simply stated, affective comprehension *reflects how the reader is "affected"* by articles, essays, pictures, or even ads. It is an emotional or intellectually charged reaction to the work. Whenever anyone cries, laughs, or becomes angry or frightened by a reading, then affective comprehension is attained. Everyone wants to be moved or stimulated by material, and that is exactly why people enjoy reading!

By practicing your reading skills, you can move from literal comprehension to critical comprehension and affective comprehension. Read a variety of materials to expand your knowledge and experience with different kinds of print. Make reading a habit. In fact, if you read fifteen minutes each day, you will read approximately twenty books a year. We do not neglect to nourish our bodies, and we cannot neglect to nourish our minds, so Read! Read! Read!

You will learn more about affective comprehension in Unit 6: Chapter 12, focusing on propaganda; Unit 8: Chapter 15, focusing on comprehending narratives; and Unit 9: Chapter 17, focusing on analogies and figures of speech, and Chapter 18, focusing on poetic figures of speech and imagery.

Your Turn—What Did You Learn ?   2.1   *Exercise*

1. Reading is a/an _____ process.

2. The least sophisticated level of comprehension is the _____ level.

3. You must first achieve _____ comprehension before you are ready for _____ comprehension.

4. The highest order of comprehension is the _____ level.

5. The best thing you can do to improve your comprehension ability is to _____.

Exercise   **2.2**   # Identifying Levels of Comprehension

Directions: Carefully read "Dependence on Nicotine." It is a selection from a college psychology textbook. Concentrate on the general topic—what the selection is about. After that, you will be asked to read specific questions about each paragraph. **Do not answer** the questions. **Instead**, decide if the questions relate to literal comprehension, critical comprehension, or affective comprehension. Before each question write L for literal, C for critical, or A for affective.

Dependence on Nicotine

1. Nicotine has a much more powerful hold on smokers than alcohol does on drinkers. Whereas about 10% of alcohol users lose control of their intake of alcohol and become alcoholics, as many as 80% of all heavy smokers have tried to cut down on or quit smoking but cannot overcome their dependence.

2. Nicotine causes dependence by at least three means:

   1. It provides a strong sensation of pleasure.

   2. It leads to fairly severe discomfort during withdrawal.

   3. It stimulates cravings long after obvious withdrawal symptoms have passed.

© robertopalace, 2010. Used under license from Shutterstock, Inc.

3. Few drugs act as quickly on the brain as nicotine does. It travels through the bloodstream to the brain in seven seconds—half the time it takes for heroin injected into a blood vessel to reach the brain. And a pack-a-day smoker gets 200 hits of nicotine a day—73,000 a year.

4. After a few years of smoking, the most powerful incentive for continuing to smoke is to avoid the discomfort of withdrawal. Generally, ten cigarettes a day will prevent withdrawal effects. For many who smoke heavily, signs of withdrawal, including changes in mood and performance, occur within two hours after smoking their last cigarette.

5. Smokeless tobacco users also get constant doses of nicotine. However, absorption of nicotine by the lungs is more likely to lead to dependence than absorption through the linings of the nose and mouth. As with other drugs of abuse, continued nicotine intake results in tolerance (the need for more of a drug to maintain the same effect), which is why only 2% of all smokers smoke just a few cigarettes a day, or smoke only occasionally. According to the Addiction Research Foundation in Canada, tobacco smokers say cigarettes are harder to abandon than other drugs, even when they find them less pleasurable than their preferred drug of abuse. (Hales 375–376)

Write L, C, or A in front of each question.

_____ 1. What is the topic or general subject of this selection?

_____ 2. Why do smokers continue to smoke?

_____ 3. Is it harder to quit smoking cigarettes than other drugs?

_____ 4. Explain why anyone can become very dependent on nicotine.

_____ 5. How do you feel about being seated next to smokers in a restaurant?

Active Learning: You and the Material

Each time you sit down to study, two forces meet—**you** and the **material**. Examining these forces will help you understand *how* to study. One way to become a better learner is to practice **metacognition.** Metacognition is defined as "knowing about your knowing" (Rudell), or becoming aware of how much you already know in order to learn more. Let's take a look at how you can use the metacognition process.

It's about You...

Schema is the *"you"* part, or the information we store inside our brains. Another word for schema is *prior knowledge*. It is easy to find out the size of your schema. Do you enjoy cooking? If you do, then your schema on this subject is large. If you never cook, your schema would be small. Have you ever worked as a camp counselor? If you have, then your schema on this subject is large; if you have never worked as a counselor, then your schema is small. Simply stated, we all have varying-size schemas depending on our experiences and what we have learned.

Why is an understanding of our own schema important when it comes to learning? Whenever we begin to learn new material, it is important that we test our schema. For example, if you are attending a football game for the first time, then your schema on this subject is small. You realize that you need to pay more attention to the game and ask questions in order to enlarge your schema. Your friend, on the other hand, may be a big fan of football. His schema in this area is large; therefore, he doesn't have to do nearly as much work in understanding the game as you would. This idea may apply to any subject you need to study: science, mathematics, even poetry.

We have learned that the smaller our schema, the more work we need to do to enlarge it. This process of adding new information is called **assimilation.** Another word for assimilation is *learning*. Suppose Mary and Sam need to write a paper for a class in world history. Mary, who is a history major, has a larger schema than Sam in this area; therefore, her learning process, or *assimilation*, will be shorter than Sam's, who is not a history major. On the other hand, when Mary and Sam need to write a paper for their computer studies class, Sam, who knows a lot about computers and has a greater schema than does Mary, would have to do less work, or require less *assimilation*. In other words, the greater your **schema** (knowledge), the less **assimilation** (learning) is needed. Conversely, the smaller your **schema**, the more **assimilation** is needed.

Each day, we are learners. We are constantly testing our **schema,** or what we know, and then learning new information, the process of **assimilation.** How can knowing about schema and assimilation help you when you are taking a reading comprehension test? First, you skim the passage you are about to read to get a general idea of the topic. You will get an idea about it relatively quickly. At this point, you can test your schema. For example, you find that the first reading passage is about rock music, which happens to be a hobby of yours. You realize that your *schema on this topic is large, so your assimilation, or learning process, will take a short time.* Therefore, you can read the passage at a relatively fast pace in order to gain a basic understanding. However, the next passage concerns the works of Theodore Roethke, a poet whom you have never studied. Your *schema, therefore, is small, so your assimilation process will be longer.* Therefore, you will have to concentrate and focus more fully on the passage.

It's about the Material....

Now for the second element you need when studying—the **material.** No new knowledge can take place without something to study. This "something," or the *material,* can be in the form of a textbook, notes, an essay, or even a lecture. Just as we test our schema to see what we know about a topic, we need to get a basic idea of what we are reading before we actually begin to read and absorb the work. To comprehend why this is important, let us compare the idea of reading to going swimming. Most of us would place our hands or feet into a pool before diving in in order to get a "feel" for the temperature of the water. In the same way, we need to get a cursory, or superficial "feel" for the material before we actually begin reading.

Most of us, at some point, need to study the material in a textbook. Therefore, it would be a good idea to examine our textbooks and their basic elements before we begin assignments. Familiarize yourself with these basic elements of most textbooks:

1. Title page—this page provides basic information about the text, including title, author, and edition.
2. Copyright page—this page tells you the name of the publisher and date of publication as well as previous dates of publication. This information is important to help you see how up-to-date your textbook is, and, in the case of a book that has undergone many editions, implies that the book is of good quality. A book in its first publication may offer a new slant on the material.
3. Preface—the author states the purpose and goals of the textbook, and provides acknowledgments, or thanks, to those who helped with the book.
4. Table of Contents—an outline that shows how the book is organized.
5. Index—located in the back of the book, this alphabetized list helps you find specific terms, or concepts, as well as individuals.
6. Glossary—some books may contain this small dictionary in the back of the text. It contains key words found in the textbook and their definitions.
7. Appendix—like the appendix in the human body, the appendix of a book is not essential. It does, however, provide supplemental, or extra, information to aid the reader. This may include charts, graphs, lists of books or authors, quizzes, or other helpful information.

Your Turn—What Did You Learn?

1. _____ is "knowing about your knowing."

2. Stored knowledge is called _____.

3. Another word for the process of learning is _____.

4. Everybody has _____ (the same, different) types of schema.

5. If someone has a small amount of stored knowledge, then the process of learning must be _____ (longer, shorter).

6. The _____ is the outline of a textbook which shows how it is organized.

7. Another name for a dictionary within a textbook is _____.

8. A _____ states the goals of a textbook.

9. A _____ contains supplemental, or extra, information.

Identifying Parts of a Textbook

Respond to the following questions about your textbook by locating the part of the book where you can find your answer. Indicate the letter of the section where you found your answer. Be careful, this book may not contain each section listed.

a. title page
b. copyright page
c. preface
d. table of contents
e. index
f. glossary
g. appendix

1. When was this book published? _____

   Answer location _____.

2. On what page can I find information about the main idea? _____

   Answer location _____.

3. Who are the authors of this book? _____

   Answer location _____.

4. On what page can I find information about theme? _____

   Answer location _____.

5. Why was this textbook written? _____

   Answer location _____.

6. Which unit contains information on propaganda? _____

   Answer location _____.

7. What is the edition of this book? _____

   Answer location _____.

8. Which page contains the definition of a simile? _____

   Answer location _____.

Getting the Picture

Tommy Hilfiger has emerged as an icon in the world of fashion, but it takes more than a brand name to be successful. Look at the picture of a fashion model. Discuss how you are influenced by what other people wear. Would you buy something because you see others wearing it? Discuss your answer.

© mashe, 2010. Used under license
from Shutterstock, Inc.

_____

_____

_____

_____

_____

_____

_____

_____

_____

_____

_____

_____

_____

_____

_____

_____

_____

_____

_____

_____

Chapter Highlights

What Have We Learned?

1. Your interaction with the writer's words is influenced by these four things: **prior knowlege, previous experiences, reason(s) for reading, and concentration with the topic.**

2. Being a successful reader means being an active reader.

3. An **active reader** interacts with text at the **literal, critical,** and **affective** levels of reading comprehension.

4. First you have to comprehend at the literal level, for the critical and affective levels are more sophisticated.

5. Practicing your reading skills should be a lifelong pursuit, so read every day, and read a variety of materials to expand your knowledge and experience with different kinds of print.

6. The two forces that come together whenever we study are YOU and the **material.** When beginning to read new material, you must test your **schema** (knowledge) of the topic to determine how much **assimilation** (learning) needs to be done. Familiarize yourself with the material, and in the case of textbooks, examine the various sections that aid knowledge (**title page, copyright page, preface, table of contents, index, glossary, appendix**).

HOW CAN I LEARN BETTER?

CHAPTER 3   Study Skills—SQ3R
CHAPTER 4   Summaries, Outlining, Maps

You now know what your reading skills are, what kind of learner you are, and what skills you need to become a successful reader. In Unit 2 you will find out how you can become a better learner.

Spotlight on
Christopher Reeve (1952–2004)

Christopher Reeve is considered an iconic figure not only as an actor, but as someone who demonstrated heroism after a serious accident. Reeve attended the Juilliard School of Performing Arts and shot to stardom when he starred in the *Superman* films beginning in 1978. However, in 1995, Reeve received a severe injury when he severed his spinal cord after falling off a horse during a riding competition held in Charlottesville, Virginia. The injury paralyzed Reeve from the neck downwards, confining him to a wheel-chair and in need of a respirator to assist his breathing. Ironically, although his body was incapacitated, Reeve became active in campaigns supporting handicapped children and paraplegics, and founded the Christopher Reeve Paralysis Foundation in 1998 to promote research into spinal cord injuries. Christopher Reeve was a tireless lobbyist for stem-cell research and an advocate for improving the lives of the disabled. He even testified before a Senate subcommittee in favor of federal funding for stem cell research. Reeve did not abandon his acting, and his work included a television production of *Rear Window* (1998). He also directed two television films, *In the Gloaming* (1997) and *The Brooke Ellison Story* (2004). His autobiography *Still Me* was published in 1998. Christopher Reeve died from cardiac arrest on October 10, 2004. He was survived by his wife Dana and son William, as well as his two children, Matthew and Alexandra from his previous relationship. His wife Dana, an actor who was devoted to his recovery, died of cancer in March 2006.

© Patrick Robert/
Corbis Sygma

Chapter 3

STUDY SKILLS—SQ3R

The Study System— Understanding SQ3R

Now that you understand the two forces at work when you study—*you* and the *material*—let's examine how the two come together with an effective study system.

© Francesco Ridolfi, 2010. Used under license from Shutterstock, Inc.

Why Is a Study System Important?

Studying is different from simply reading for pleasure or because you are bored. You might pick up a magazine while waiting in a doctor's office because the photo or topic on the cover interests you. As you read the articles, you simply read for a basic understanding. You know that you do not need to study the material because you will not be tested on it in any way. However, when you read material from a college textbook, you will be asked to demonstrate your knowledge by taking a test, writing a paper, or perhaps making a presentation. Therefore, your approach to the reading must be focused and organized. To succeed, you need a study system!

In the early 1940s, Professor Francis P. Robinson developed a unique method, or formula, for studying. Since then, this method, or formula, has gained in popularity for its simplicity and effectiveness. The study technique is **SQ3R.** Let's see how it works.

"S" Stands for Survey. To get a general sense of an article or chapter, preread the headings, subheadings, words written in boldface or italics, and the introduction and conclusion. Skim through the material for length to see how long it will take you to complete the reading. Your process for this step should take only about a minute.

"Q" Is for Question. We have learned that in order to be successful, you must be an active reader. You can accomplish this by turning a heading or topic sentence into a question. For example, the statement "There were many causes for the American Revolution" could be changed to "What were the causes for the American Revolution?" The process makes sense; once you pose a question, you will actively read on to attain the answer.

"R" Means Read. After you have surveyed and questioned, you can now read the material, focusing on words in groups to get meaning from the context. Don't worry about the meaning of individual words, but focus on the main idea.

The Second "R" is Recite, or Practice the Material. Reciting is an important but often overlooked aspect of the study process. Almost everyone has had the panicky feeling of "freezing up" when confronted with an exam, even if you have studied for it intensively! Skipping this step can be the reason for this frightening feeling. Until this stage, you have been absorbing the material. But recitation, or practice, is needed if you are to "give back" the information you learned in the form of a research paper, discussion, or exam. This step may be "informal," taking the form of oral recitation, annotation (highlighting or marking the text), taking notes,* or it may be more "formal" in outlines, maps, or summaries (which we will review in the next lesson).

The Third "R" Means Review. In this stage, you skim through the selection and answer questions immediately after the reading and prior to an exam.

Exercise   **3.1   Your Turn—What Did You Learn?**

1. Whenever you study, the two forces that come together are _____ and the _____.

2. A successful study system invented by Prof. Francis Robinson is _____.

3. The five parts of this study system are _____, _____, _____, _____, and _____.

4. The most overlooked part of this study system, in which we practice "giving back" the material, is called _____.

---

*A Note about Annotating: Be careful about annotating your text. Highlighting every line of an essay serves no useful purpose, because you will need to read the entire article or chapter again during a review. Highlight only *key ideas* that will focus and simplify your studying.

*An Additional Note about Note Taking: Note taking is essential when studying a textbook or class lectures. One popular method for taking notes is the Cornell Method, in which an important term is written in the margin and is defined or explained in the body of the paper. However, you may devise your own method for note taking, using abbreviations or other shortcuts that you can understand.

Practicing the SQ3R Method

3.2   *Exercise*

Christopher Reeve was truly a "superman," not only because of his extra-ordinary acting abilities, but mostly because of his determination and strength after the accident that paralyzed him. Christopher Reeve never lost his motivation to walk again and to aid others through example. The follow-ing essay, "Intrinsic and Extrinsic Motivation," which appears in Benjamin B. Lahey's Psychology: An Introduction, *explores the idea of motivation and its consequences.*

Directions: Use the SQ3R method to prepare for a short quiz on this essay.

1. **SURVEY**—Skim the essay for length, headings, boldface words, information in the margins, lists, to get a general idea of the essay. Test your schema: What do you already know about this subject? How much assimilation (learn-ing) will you need?

   Answer: What do I already know about this topic?

   _____.

   Answer: What would I like to know about this topic?

   _____.

   Answer: How long will it take me to read this essay?

   _____.

2. **QUESTION**—Turn the headings, beginnings of paragraphs, and topic sen-tences into questions so that you can begin actively reading. Use the following lines for your questions.

   Questions: _____

   _____

   _____

   _____

3. **READ**—Remember to read words in groups in order to understand the main idea. Read at a steady pace. Do not stop at words you do not know.

4. **RECITE**—Use informal recitation. As you read, feel free to annotate the text with highlighter and a pen. Circle items, place asterisks (*) next to important terms; write notes and questions in the margins. You may use a separate sheet of paper if you wish to use the Cornell Method for note taking.

5. **REVIEW**—Read over your notes and what you have highlighted. Be sure you can answer the "questions" you posed in the "Q" step of SQ3R.

When you have completed all the steps in the SQ3R study method, you will be prepared to take the short quiz that follows this reading.

Intrinsic and Extrinsic Motivation
By Benjamin B. Lahey

Intrinsic (in-trin'sik) Motivation. Human motives stimulated by the inherent nature of the activity or its natural consequences. **Extrinsic (eks-trin'sik) Motivation.** Human motives activated by external rewards.

*It is important to distinguish between intrinsic and extrinsic motivation. We speak of **intrinsic motivation** when people are motivated by the inherent nature of the activity, their pleasure of mastering something new, or the natural consequences of the activity. For example, the monkeys that we mentioned earlier who will take apart mechanical puzzles for no reward other than getting them apart are intrinsically motivated to solve puzzles. People who read nonfiction books that are recognized are intrinsically motivated. **Extrinsic motivation,** on the other hand, is motivation that is external to the activity and not an inherent part of it. If a child who hates to do arithmetic homework is encouraged to do so by payment of a nickel for every correct answer, he is extrinsically motivated. That is, he works for the external payment rather than because of an intrinsic interest in math. Similarly, a person who works hard to be a good employee because she wants to be admired by others—rather than because of a genuine interest in the work—is extrinsically motivated. People who are intrinsically motivated tend to work harder and respond to challenges by working even harder. They enjoy their work more and often perform more creatively and effectively than people who are extrinsically motivated (National Advisory Mental Health Council, 1995b). Intrinsic motivation is shaped by our learning experiences. For example, children from families who emphasize the joys and importance of learning have more intrinsic motivation to learn in school (Gottfried, Fleming, & Gottfried, 1998).*

Perhaps the most significant issue concerning the distinction between intrinsic and extrinsic motivation is the question of when extrinsic rewards should be supplied by parents, teachers, and employers in an effort to increase motivation. When is it wise to use extrinsic motivation in the form of positive reinforcement to increase the frequency of some behavior (such as completing homework, delivering packages on time, and so on)? Considerable evidence suggests that if a behavior occurs infrequently—and its intrinsic motivation can be assumed low for that individual—then extrinsic motivation can be successful in increasing the frequency of occurrence of the behavior. Children who hate to do their math homework often will do it diligently if rewarded with additional allowance money. On the other hand, if the individual is already intrinsically motivated to perform an activity, adding extrinsic motivation may detract from the intrinsic motivation. For example, when young children who like to draw pictures in school were given certificates for good drawing, they drew pictures less often than did children who had not received certificates (Lepper, Greene, & Nisbett, 1973). This study, and many subsequent studies (Ryan & Deci, 2000; Tang & Hall, 1995), suggest that we must be careful to avoid squelching intrinsic motivation by providing unnecessary extrinsic rewards.

What about praise? When we pat a child on the back for a job well done—whether it be homework or reading a book—does our praise increase the child's intrinsic motivation? Psychologists Jennifer Henderlong and Mark Lepper (2002) suggest that it depends on what we say and how we say it. (Lahey)

Praise increases intrinsic motivation when the praise:

1. Implies that the child was successful because of his or her effort and not because of the child's natural talent or abilities.

2. Is sincere and does not imply that the adult is controlling the child.

3. Does not compare the child to other children.

4. Implies that the adult has standards for the child's behavior that the child believes that he or she can attain with effort.

In contrast, praise that focuses on the child's abilities rather than effort, seems controlling rather than sincere, compares the child to others, or implies that he or she must reach standards in the future that seem impossible (or too low), may undermine intrinsic motivation according to Henderlong and Lepper (2002).

For example, if a child writes a clever poem for her teacher, Henderlong and Lepper (2002) suggest that this might be effective praise that would increase the child's intrinsic motivation to write:

> "I really like this poem! I especially like the way you found ways to compare leaves and songs. That must have taken a lot of thought!"

On the other hand, praise like this might reduce the child's intrinsic motivation:

> "This is brilliant! I told you that you were the only genius in Mrs. Long's class. If you just write, write, write every night like your mother told you, you'll be great! Soon Harvard and Yale will be fighting over you."

For many years, it was assumed that another good way to increase intrinsic motivation was to give people choices. When people have options, they will choose activities that they are intrinsically motivated to perform, and performing them will further enhance their intrinsic motivation. Recent findings suggest that this is true, but only in individualistic Western societies (Iyenger & Lepper, 1999). American children of European ancestry show more intrinsic motivation for school tasks and other activities that they choose themselves. In contrast, Asian American children from collectivistic cultures that place greater emphasis on the well-being of the group than on the well-being of the individual have more intrinsic motivation for activities that were selected for them by trusted authority figures or friends (Iyengar & Lepper, 1999). As in many aspects of psychological life, sociocultural factors are important in motivation. (Lahey 381)

Have you completed this reading using the SQ3R method? Make sure you have successfully completed studying before taking the quiz on the next page. Don't look back to find answers.

Quiz: Intrinsic and Extrinsic Motivation

1. People who have intrinsic motivation are motivated by _____ _____, while those who have extrinsic motivation are motivated by _____.

2. Those who have _____ motivation find their accomplishments more rewarding.

3. True or False: It is a good idea to provide extrinsic motivation to individuals who are already intrinsically motivated.

4. Choose one answer: Extrinsic motivation is a good idea for behaviors that occur: (a) frequently (b) infrequently.

5. There are four ways that praise increases motivation. One of the ways is by using praise that _____.

6. Choose one answer: Overly praising a child's efforts often has a (a) good (b) bad result.

7. True or False: Giving children choices generally motivates all children.

8. People who are in the _____ profession might be most interested in reading this essay.

Answers to Quiz: Intrinsic and Extrinsic Motivation

1. the activity—something outside the activity
2. intrinsic
3. False
4. b
5. Any version of one of the following answers is correct: (a) is about the effort, not talent (b) is sincere (c) doesn't make comparisons with others (d) shows the parent's standards for behavior attained with effort
6. b
7. False
8. teaching (*managing* or *parenting* are also acceptable answers)

If you answered all eight questions correctly, then you deserve congratulations. You have mastered the SQ3R method! If you answered a few of the questions incorrectly, take time to review SQ3R. On the next page you will see how one student followed the SQ3R steps to attain success.

Joe Follows the SQ3R Method

S—Survey Okay, this is about two kinds of motivation and seems to be about helping children succeed at some tasks. My schema knows that when I was a swim instructor last summer, I tried to praise and encourage the young kids. I bought ice cream cones for the kids who were able to float or start swimming on their own. But I never read any books about this subject, so I will really have to focus. I think this essay will take me about 10 or 15 minutes to read.

Q—Question Here are some of the questions I can try to find the answers to as I read:

What is meant by intrinsic and extrinsic motivation?

How are they different?

When should extrinsic rewards be supplied by parents, teachers, and employers?

How can extrinsic motivation detract from intrinsic motivation?

In what ways can praise increase a child's intrinsic motivation?

What is the difference between praise that focuses on ability and praise that focuses on effort?

What is the difference between good and bad praise?

Does giving people choices always increase intrinsic motivation?

R—Read Now I'm ready to read and find the answers to these questions, and I will try not to stop at words I'm not familiar with.

R—Recite Take a look on the next page to see how I have annotated and taken notes in the margins. If I am alone, I can recite some of the main points aloud.

R—Review I think that I am ready for a fast review of my notes, annotations, and answers to my questions. Now I should be able to answer all the questions on the quiz.

Joe's Work

Intrinsic and Extrinsic Motivation
By Benjamin B. Lahey

Intrinsic (in-trin′sik) Motivation. Human motives stimulated by the inherent nature of the activity or its natural consequences. **Extrinsic (eks-trin′sik) Motivation.** Human motives activated by external rewards.

What is the meaning of intrinsic and extrinsic motivation?

*It is important to distinguish between intrinsic and extrinsic motivation. We speak of **intrinsic motivation** when people are motivated by the inherent nature of the activity, their pleasure of mastering something new, or the natural consequences of the activity. For example, the monkeys that we mentioned earlier who will take apart mechanical puzzles for no reward other than getting them apart are intrinsically motivated to solve puzzles. People who read nonfiction books that are recognized are intrinsically motivated. **Extrinsic motivation,** on the other hand, is motivation that is external to the activity and not an inherent part of it. If a child who hates to do arithmetic homework is encouraged to do so by payment of a nickel for every correct answer, he is extrinsically motivated. That is, he works for the external payment rather than because of an intrinsic interest in math. Similarly, a person who works hard to be a good employee because she wants to be admired by others—rather than because of a genuine interest in the work—is extrinsically motivated. People who are intrinsically motivated tend to work harder and respond to challenges by working even harder. They enjoy their work more and often perform more creatively and effectively than people who are extrinsically motivated (National Advisory Mental Health Council, 1995b). Intrinsic motivation is shaped by our learning experiences. For example, children from families who emphasize the*

Like something outside— a reward?

Does intrinsic motivation provide more inner satisfaction?

difference?

Look up?

when we use extrinsic
motivation

when we do not use it

Need to look up

Sometimes it works

What kind works?

when praise does not
work

Examples

joys and importance of learning have more intrinsic motivation to learn in school (Gottfried, Fleming, & Gottfried, 1998).

Perhaps the most significant issue concerning the (distinction) between intrinsic and extrinsic motivation is the question of when extrinsic rewards should be supplied by parents, teachers, and employers in an effort to increase motivation. When is it wise to use extrinsic motivation in the form of positive reinforcement to increase the frequency of some behavior (such as completing homework, delivering packages on time, and so on)? Considerable evidence suggests that if a behavior occurs infrequently—and its intrinsic motivation can be assumed low for that individual—then extrinsic motivation can be successful in increasing the frequency of occurrence of the behavior. Children who hate to do their math homework often will do it diligently if rewarded with additional allowance money. On the other hand, if the individual is already intrinsically motivated to perform an activity, adding extrinsic motivation may detract from the intrinsic motivation. For example, when young children who like to draw pictures in school were given certificates for good drawing, they drew pictures less often than did children who had not received certificates (Lepper, Greene, & Nisbett, 1973). This study, and many subsequent studies (Ryan & Deci, 2000; Tang & Hall, 1995), suggest that we must be careful to avoid (squelching) intrinsic motivation by providing unnecessary extrinsic rewards.

What about praise? When we pat a child on the back for a job well done—whether it be homework or reading a book—does our praise increase the child's intrinsic motivation? Psychologists Jennifer Henderlong and Mark Lepper (2002) suggest that it depends on what we say and how we say it. (Lahey)

Praise increases intrinsic motivation when the praise:

1. Implies that the child was successful because of his or her effort and not because of the child's natural talent or abilities.

2. Is sincere and does not imply that the adult is controlling the child.

3. Does not compare the child to other children.

4. Implies that the adult has standards for the child's behavior that the child believes that he or she can attain with effort.

In contrast, praise that focuses on the child's abilities rather than effort, seems controlling rather than sincere, compares the child to others, or implies that he or she must reach standards in the future that seem impossible (or too low), may undermine intrinsic motivation according to Henderlong and Lepper (2002).

For example, if a child writes a clever poem for her teacher, Henderlong and Lepper (2002) suggest that this might be effective praise that would increase the child's intrinsic motivation to write:

"I really like this poem! I especially like the way you found ways to compare leaves and songs. That must have taken a lot of thought!"

On the other hand, praise like this might reduce the child's intrinsic motivation:

"This is brilliant! I told you that you were the only genius in Mrs. Long's class. If you just write, write, write every night like your mother told you, you'll be great! Soon Harvard and Yale will be fighting over you."

For many years, it was assumed that another good way to increase intrinsic motivation was to give people choices. When people have options, they will choose activities that they are intrinsically motivated to perform, and performing them will further enhance their intrinsic motivation. Recent findings suggest that this is true, but only in individualistic Western societies (Iyenger & Lepper, 1999). American children of European ancestry show more intrinsic motivation for school tasks and other activities that they choose themselves. In contrast, Asian American children from collectivistic cultures that place greater emphasis on the well-being of the group than on the well-being of the individual have more intrinsic motivation for activities that were selected for them by trusted authority figures or friends (Iyengar & Lepper, 1999). As in many aspects of psychological life, sociocultural factors are important in motivation. (Lahey 381)

When do choices help?

notes!

Have you completed this reading using the SQ3R method? Make sure you have successfully completed studying before taking the quiz on the next page. Don't look back to find answers.

5. Compare the responses of the Bush administration to the Obama administration to this issue.

_____

_____

_____

Journal Suggestion

In your journal, define the different types of stem cell research being conducted. Which diseases or health problems have most benefited from this research? Which diseases have potential for treatment?

Individual/Collaborative Activity

Discuss the pros and cons of embryonic cell treatment. Debate the issue with those in your group.

Look It Up

1. Using the Internet, research what is being done to treat spinal cord injuries or one of the other serious diseases mentioned in the article you just read. Which treatments are being used? How can stem cell research potentially find an answer? Write a paper discussing your results.

2. Research both sides of the ethical question of using embryonic stem cells to treat health problems. Write a paper advocating one position and present it with another student who will advocate the opposing position.

5.   reminisce about Harvard Square and the houses in which you

   lk   c. remember fondly
   gue   d. laugh

6.   **initial** reaction to this situation was usually one of confusion or
   e degree of disbelief.
   artling   c. first
   nsteady   d. unusual

7   began to realize that our **conspicuousness** was not such a bad
   g.
   knowledge   c. fear
   concern   d. being readily visible

   were a very visible **affirmation** that Harvard was a diversified com-
   nity where all people were accepted no matter what they looked
   , what they believed in, or whom they chose to go to bed with.
   difference   c. truth
   confirmation   d. sign

   e were a very visible affirmation that Harvard was a **diversified** com-
   unity where all people were accepted no matter what they looked
   e, what they believed in, or whom they chose to go to bed with.
   . varied   c. accepting
   . outstanding   d. unusual

   However, I dare say that once that diploma has been matted,
   ramed, and put on the wall the memories that it will **evoke** will not be
   of what it took to get it.
   a. create   c. make disappear
   b. imagine   d. call to mind

stions on "Brooke Ellison's Graduation Speech"

   Why was Brooke concerned about entering Harvard?

   _____

   _____

   _____

2. According to Brooke, what is the "beauty of the Harvard experience"?

   _____

   _____

   _____

3. What does Brooke say students will most remember about Harvard?

   _____

   _____

   _____

4. Who are the people who have helped her?

   _____

   _____

   _____

5. What is her advice to the students?

_____

_____

_____

Journal Suggestion

Brooke Ellison certainly serves as an inspiration to everyone. Write a letter to Brooke responding to her graduation speech. Which details most impressed you? What have you learned from her speech?

Collaborative Activities

Some of us have physical disabilities while others have mental or emotional issues with which we need to cope. List some of your "handicaps" (laziness, nervousness, stubbornness, etc.) and how you have overcome or plan to overcome them. Discuss what you have written with others.

Look It Up

1. Read *Miracles Happen* by Brooke Ellison and *Still Me* by Christopher Reeve. Write a report comparing and contrasting the two books and the message in each.

2. After reading *Miracles Happen* by Brooke Ellison, find and view *The Brooke Ellison Story,* which was directed by Christopher Reeve. Write a report comparing and contrasting the book and movie. Which device was most effective in portraying Brooke's story? Which did you prefer? Discuss your conclusions with others.

3. Brooke Ellison's graduation speech suggests that Harvard University made accommodations for her. Research the accommodations your institution has provided for those with physical and/or mental disabilities. Write an essay discussing your findings and suggestions for improvement.

Getting the Picture

This photo shows Brooke Ellison with Christopher Reeve during the filming of *The Brooke Ellison Story*. What kind of relationship do you think these two had during the filming?

_____

_____

_____

_____

Courtesy of Brooke Ellison

_____

_____

_____

_____

_____

_____

_____

_____

_____

_____

_____

_____

_____

_____

_____

_____

_____

_____

Chapter Highlights

What Have We Learned?

1. Studying material is different from other types of reading because when we study we need an organized **study system** so that we can later demonstrate our knowledge.

2. SQ3R is a successful study system which includes **survey** (skim selection, read headings, etc.), **question** (turn headings into questions), **read** (read words in groups), **recite** (say aloud, annotate, take notes), **review** (answer questions you posed earlier).

Chapter 4

SUMMARIES, OUTLINING, MAPS

Now that you know the SQ3R method will help you approach college reading assignments in a focused and organized manner, Chapter 4 will teach you how to summarize, outline, and map material you must learn. Moreover, these are valuable skills for everyday life, especially if Superman can't come to your rescue!

Why Is Summarizing Important?

College students need to master summarizing to write papers, give reports, study lecture notes, and prepare study sheets on textbook reading assignments.

Understanding Summaries

You don't have to be Superman to understand how to summarize. It doesn't require extraordinary mental power, for it is something people do often in everyday life. For instance, when asked what kind of day you had, don't you summarize? Instead of relating every detail about your day you probably say something brief and specific or more detailed. If you said, "I had a busy day," your summary statement is specific, but not as detailed as if you said, "I had a busy day. After three morning classes, I spent three hours in the library doing homework. Then I grabbed a sandwich, which I ate on the way to my waitress job. After classes, homework, and a job, I collapsed on my bed." It is obvious from this example that a summary of college reading material can be defined as the reduction of a large amount of information to its most important points or main ideas. Identifying the important points is easy if you follow these suggestions:

1. **Read** carefully to determine the author's purpose so you can distinguish between more important and less important information. The more important information includes the main points and major supporting details.
2. **Reread, label, and underline.** As you reread, focus on the author's paragraphing and label each important thought. Underline key ideas and terms.
3. **Write** one-sentence summaries (in other words, the shortest summary possible) of each stage of thought. Use paper or the computer to do this.
4. **Write a thesis—a one-sentence summary of the entire passage.** The thesis should express the main ideas of the entire passage, based on the preceding steps 1, 2, and 3. The thesis you write will depend on the type of reading material. For example, if the passage is persuasive, the thesis can be created from the author's conclusion. If the passage is descriptive, the thesis should indicate the subject of the description and its key features. If the thesis is stated in the original passage, you may want to quote it directly.

5. **Write the first draft of your summary** by keeping in mind the following important points:

   a. A summary should never include more than one statement of the main idea or thesis, and the thesis should be the first sentence of the summary.

   b. The length of a summary depends on your purpose. For instance, an article can be reduced to a paragraph; an entire textbook chapter might be reduced to three or so pages of notes. The summary should be about one-fourth as long as the original passage.

   c. Depending on your purpose, a summary can be the words of the author, or in your own words, or a combination of the two. If you are summarizing textbook material or a class lecture, you might think about using the author's words or the instructor's words, especially if there are important terms you must know. If you are summarizing a story or article as part of a written report, you are expected to use your own words.

   d. Understanding the different patterns of organization or rhetorical modes authors use can help you summarize material. For example, if a selection is mainly a narrative, then your summary will briefly narrate a series of events. If a selection is a series of definitions and examples, then your summary will provide both, but the examples will be condensed.

   e. Check your summary against the original passage, checking for accuracy and completeness.

   f. Revise your summary, making use of transitional words and phrases to ensure coherence.

   g. Check your style. Avoid short, choppy sentences by combining sentences for a smooth, logical flow of ideas.

   h. Check for grammatical correctness, punctuation, and spelling.

Exercise   **4.1   Your Turn—What Did You Learn?**

1. A _____ is a way of condensing all the main ideas an author has presented in a longer selection such as an essay or article or a section of a chapter.

2. The shortest possible summary is a _____.

3. Good summaries are about _____ of the length of the original.

4. College students need to master summarizing in order to _____, _____, _____, and _____.

Writing the Summary

Directions: Read the following paragraphs used in Elizabeth Cloninger Long's *Resources for Writers*. Underline the topic sentence. Then write in your own words a summary of each paragraph. **Hint:** Use the title in your topic sentence. Make the topic sentence the first sentence. The summary should be one-fourth the length of the original passage.

Aphrodite's Affairs

Aphrodite, who was the Greek goddess of love and desire, had many love affairs. The cause of these affairs was her great beauty, which led almost everyone to fall in love with her. Her most famous love affair was with the war god, Ares. Aphrodite and Ares loved each other and continued their relationship even though Aphrodite was married to Hephaestus, the god of fire and metalworking. A second love affair of Aphrodite's came from her connection to Adonis, an extremely handsome human. Though Adonis was very young, Aphrodite fell in love with him and took him as a lover. Third, Aphrodite had a love affair with the mortal man Anchises. This union, though based on love and desire, produced the war hero Aeneas. Aphrodite also had an affair with Dionysus, the god of wine, and with the Olympian god Hermes, though Hermes tricked her into having an affair with him. Each of these unions was different in nature, but they all stemmed from Aphrodite's great beauty and her powers of love. (Long 3)

Summary:

_____

_____

_____

_____

_____

_____

_____

_____

_____

_____

_____

Nutritious Chocolate

Many myths surround chocolate. One myth is that chocolate is made up only of fat. Really, chocolate provides different types of calories. In one ounce of milk chocolate, people get one gram of protein and fifteen grams of carbohydrates. Of course, they also get nine grams of fat, but regular exercise will take care of that. Another myth surrounding chocolate is that it's unhealthy. This isn't true. Chocolate contains zinc, iron, and other nutrients that make it a good part of people's diets. Milk chocolate also contains calcium, so it helps build strong bones. The most significant myth is that chocolate makes you fat. There are 140 calories in an ounce of semisweet chocolate and 150 calories in an ounce of milk chocolate. That might sound like a lot, but it's low compared with the number of calories in a bottle of sweetened iced tea. People get fat only if they eat too much chocolate. Overall, the myths are not true and chocolate is healthier than people realize. (Long 3)

© chris May, 2010. Used under license from Shtterstock, Inc.

Summary:

_____

_____

_____

_____

_____

_____

_____

_____

_____

_____

_____

Peer Editing

Working with classmates is one of the best ways to improve your writing. Share your summaries with a classmate. Read each other's summaries out loud. When peer editing, make sure the directions were followed and your feedback is honest and specific. If the suggestions make sense to you, then you should consider revising your summary writing.

Revised Summary of "Aphrodite's Affairs"

_____
_____
_____
_____
_____
_____
_____
_____
_____
_____

Revised Summary of "Nutritious Chocolate"

_____
_____
_____
_____
_____
_____
_____
_____
_____
_____
_____

More Practice in Summary Writing   4.3   *Exercise*

Directions: Now that you have practiced summarizing paragraphs, reread the psychology selection from Chapter 3, "Intrinsic and Extrinsic Motivation." Having read this selection using SQ3R, you are ready to summarize it. Look back at Understanding Summaries if you need to refresh your memory about writing a textbook summary. Don't forget to start your summary with a thesis. Then support the thesis with major supporting details. Write draft one. Peer edit draft one. Write draft two. Peer edit draft two.

Intrinsic and Extrinsic Motivation
By Benjamin B. Lahey

Intrinsic (in-trin'sik) Motivation. Human motives stimulated by the inherent nature of the activity or its natural consequences. **Extrinsic (eks-trin'sik) Motivation.** Human motives activated by external rewards.

*It is important to distinguish between intrinsic and extrinsic motivation. We speak of **intrinsic motivation** when people are motivated by the inherent nature of the activity, their pleasure of mastering something new, or the natural consequences of the activity. For example, the monkeys that we mentioned earlier who will take apart mechanical puzzles for no reward other than getting them apart are intrinsically motivated to solve puzzles. People who read nonfiction books that are recognized are intrinsically motivated. **Extrinsic motivation,** on the other hand, is motivation that is external to the activity and not an inherent part of it. If a child who hates to do arithmetic homework is encouraged to do so by payment of a nickel for every correct answer, he is extrinsically motivated. That is, he works for the external payment rather than because of an intrinsic interest in math. Similarly, a person who works hard to be a good employee because she wants to be admired by others—rather than because of a genuine interest in the work—is extrinsically motivated. People who are intrinsically motivated tend to work harder and respond to challenges by working even harder. They enjoy their work more and often perform more creatively and effectively than people who are extrinsically motivated (National Advisory Mental Health Council, 1995b). Intrinsic motivation is shaped by our learning experiences. For example, children from families who emphasize the joys and importance of learning have more intrinsic motivation to learn in school (Gottfried, Fleming, & Gottfried, 1998).*

Perhaps the most significant issue concerning the distinction between intrinsic and extrinsic motivation is the question of when extrinsic rewards should be supplied by parents, teachers, and employers in an effort to increase motivation. When is it wise to use extrinsic motivation in the form of positive reinforcement to increase the frequency of some behavior (such as completing homework, delivering packages on time, and so on)? Considerable evidence suggests that if a behavior occurs infrequently—and its intrinsic motivation can be assumed low for that individual—then extrinsic motivation can be successful in increasing the frequency of occurrence of the behavior. Children who hate to do their math homework often will do it diligently if rewarded with additional allowance money. On the other hand, if the individual is already intrinsically motivated to perform an activity, adding extrinsic motivation may detract from the intrinsic motivation. For example, when young children who like to draw pictures in school were given certificates for good drawing, they drew pictures less often than did children who had not received certificates (Lepper, Greene, & Nisbett, 1973). This study, and many subsequent studies (Ryan & Deci, 2000; Tang & Hall, 1995), suggest that we must be careful to avoid squelching intrinsic motivation by providing unnecessary extrinsic rewards.

What about praise? When we pat a child on the back for a job well done—whether it be homework or reading a book—does our praise increase the child's intrinsic motivation? Psychologists Jennifer Henderlong and Mark Lepper (2002) suggest that it depends on what we say and how we say it. (Lahey)

Praise increases intrinsic motivation when the praise:

1. Implies that the child was successful because of his or her effort and not because of the child's natural talent or abilities.

2. Is sincere and does not imply that the adult is controlling the child.

3. Does not compare the child to other children.

4. Implies that the adult has standards for the child's behavior that the child believes that he or she can attain with effort.

In contrast, praise that focuses on the child's abilities rather than effort, seems controlling rather than sincere, compares the child to others, or implies that he or she must reach standards in the future that seem impossible (or too low), may undermine intrinsic motivation according to Henderlong and Lepper (2002). For example, if a child writes a clever poem for her teacher Henderlong and Lepper (2002) suggest that this might be effective praise that would increase the child's intrinsic motivation to write:

"I really like this poem! I especially like the way you found ways to compare leaves and songs. That must have taken a lot of thought!"

On the other hand, praise like this might reduce the child's intrinsic motivation:

"This is brilliant! I told you that you were the only genius in Mrs. Long's class. If you just write, write, write every night like your mother told you, you'll be great! Soon Harvard and Yale will be fighting over you."

For many years, it was assumed that another good way to increase intrinsic motivation was to give people choices. When people have options, they will choose activities that they are intrinsically motivated to perform, and performing them will further enhance their intrinsic motivation. Recent findings suggest that this is true, but only in individualistic Western societies (Iyenger & Lepper, 1999). American children of European ancestry show more intrinsic motivation for school tasks and other activities that they choose themselves. In contrast, Asian American children from collectivistic cultures that place greater emphasis on the well-being of the group than on the well-being of the individual have more intrinsic motivation for activities that were selected for them by trusted authority figures or friends (Iyengar & Lepper, 1999). As in many aspects of psychological life, sociocultural factors are important in motivation. (Lahey 381)

Draft One:

Draft Two:

Why Is Outlining Important?

College students need to master outlining to write papers, give reports or written responses, study lecture notes, and prepare study sheets on textbook reading assignments. An outline provides you with a shortened form of the main ideas. If you think back to grade school, you were introduced to formal outlines. However, a scratch outline is all you need for most college assignments. It is a simple way of ordering or planning the information you read, say, or write. In fact, when using SQ3R, outlining is one way to recite what you read, say, or write.

Think of a scratch outline as a series of stacked boxes. The first box is the **introduction,** which includes the main idea or thesis. **Support** for the main idea or thesis is a series of body paragraphs with topic sentences related to the thesis. Like the introduction, the **body paragraphs** are stacked boxes arranged in logical order. The last box is the **conclusion,** which is often a summary and final thought, or a prediction and recommendation, or a thought-provoking question. A scratch outline, like a blueprint or x-ray, helps readers or writers visualize what they are reading or where they are heading in their writing.

Introduction with thesis

First Body Paragraph
Main Point: **Support:**   (1)   (2)   (3)

Second Body Paragraph
Main Point: **Support:**   (1)   (2)

Third Body Paragraph
Main Point: **Support:**   (1)   (2)   (3)

Conclusion

Sample Scratch Outline

Thesis (Last sentence in the Introduction): Full-time work, college, and family responsibilities have made my life stressful.

First Body Paragraph (Topic Sentence):	1. Full-time work makes studying difficult.
First Paragraph (Supporting Details):	a. Skimming textbook readings b. Barely studying for tests c. Not rewriting papers
Second Body Paragraph (Topic Sentence):	2. There is little time to socialize at college.
Second Paragraph (Supporting Details):	a. Between classes b. After classes
Third Body Paragraph (Topic Sentence):	3. Family responsibilities prevent personal pleasures.
Third Paragraph (Supporting Details):	a. No time for favorite TV shows b. Cannot watch Sunday football games c. Impossible to date

Conclusion

Exercise **4.4** ## Your Turn—What Did You Learn **?**

1. A(n) _____ provides you with a shortened form of the main ideas.

2. An outline can help a student _____, _____, _____, and _____.

3. Writing an outline is a part of the _____ process in the SQ3R system.

Exercise **4.5** ## Writing the Scratch Outline

Directions: Read the following essays and create a scratch outline for each essay. Hint: Read each essay at least twice. On the second reading, identify the main point or topic sentence of each paragraph. Below the main point of each paragraph, identify the details directly supporting the main point. Decide what the thesis is after identifying the main points and details of each paragraph. Keep in mind that the essay title is the topic of the essay and it should be part of the thesis statement.

Celebrating My Graduation
By Harriet Smith

For my graduation from high school, my parents asked me what I wanted as a gift. Since I will be going out of state to college, I asked for a party with family and friends. With a large family and lot of friends, my parents expect me to choose the fire house in town. However, I want to celebrate my graduation at home. For me, a home party has more advantages than a firehouse party.

For one thing, going to the firehouse means the party must be indoors and it can only be three hours on a Sunday afternoon. My family would not mind this arrangement, but my friends would. If my party was at home, it can be indoors and outdoors, the time can be extended to more than three hours, and the day does not have to be a Sunday afternoon. Instead, I would prefer Saturday starting in the evening and ending midnight.

Another reason for wanting a home party is the entertainment factor. Unlike the firehouse, which is limited to conversation, music and dancing, my home can accommodate indoor and outdoor activities. An Olympic size pool and tennis

courts are outside. Inside, the finished basement offers an array of activities such as pool and ping pong tables, a huge flat screen TV, karaoke equipment, and several pin ball machines. I don't have to worry about my friends having a fun time at my house.

Finally, the most important difference between a home and firehouse party is the cost. Besides a fee to use the firehouse, it will cost money to rent tables and chairs. Because my home is free and there are plenty of tables and chairs, the cost of the party will be less.

So, for my graduation celebration, I prefer a home party. Clearly, my friends are guaranteed a great time if I can have my desired day, party hours and indoor and outdoor activites. Most importantly, it will cost less. I can only hope my graduation wish is granted, especially if my friends and I help with the party setup and cleanup.

Now that you have read this essay, reread the directions before making a scratch outline of the essay. You may not use all the letters for details.

Thesis (in your own words): _____

Paragraph 1: Main Point: _____

      a. _____

      b. _____

      c. _____

      d. _____

      e. _____

Paragraph 2: Main Point: _____

      a. _____

      b. _____

      c. _____

      d. _____

      e. _____

Paragraph 3: Main Point: _____

      a. _____

      b. _____

      c. _____

      d. _____

      e. _____

Paragraph 4: Main Point: _____

      a. _____

      b. _____

      c. _____

      d. _____

      e. _____

Paragraph 5: Main Point: _____

    a. _____

    b. _____

    c. _____

    d. _____

    e. _____

Your scratch outline should look something like this.

Scratch Outline

Thesis (in your own words)

A home graduation party has more advantages than a firehouse party.

Par. 1: Main Point: For Smith, a home party has more advantages than one in a firehouse.

    a. The party is a graduation gift.
    b. Family and friends will be included.

Par. 2: Main Point: A home graduation party would be better for my friends.

    a. The party can be indoors and outdoors.
    b. The party time can be longer than three hours.
    c. The party can be on a Saturday.

Par. 3: Main Point: My home can accommodate indoor and outdoor activities.

    a. outside Olympic size pool
    b. outside tennis courts
    c. pool and ping pong tables inside
    d. flat screen TV inside
    e. karaoke equipment inside
    f. pin ball machines inside

Par. 4: Main Point: A home party is less expensive.

    a. No facility rental fee
    b. No need to rent tables and chairs

Par. 5: Main Point: I prefer a home party. (Restatement of the main idea in the conclusion)

    a. My friends are guaranteed a great time.
    b. I can have my desired day, party hours, and indoor and outdoor activities.
    c. It will cost less.

Creating a Scratch Outline

Directions: Often, college students feel that summer does not last long enough, that they don't accomplish all they have planned, especially when the days are beautiful and inviting. It may surprise you that college professors often feel the same way about summers when days seem to rush by. Read and annotate the following essay by the author of this textbook, and then create your own scratch outline.

When Summer Goes Too Fast
By Shirley Russak Wachtel

There is a saying, "time flies." This statement is probably most accurate during the summer. And no one feels it more acutely than teachers who during those waning days of spring set detailed plans for doctors' appointments, tire rotations, and garage sweep-ups only to find, alas, it's mid-August and time to start writing lesson plans again.

As an English professor at a local college, I too had grandiose ideas for those precious summer days. Among other things, I needed to write an outline for a textbook, contact literary agents for a novel I recently completed, enter a few poetry contests, and somehow find the time to clean out my home office where stacks of knee-high papers mocked me daily. And, that first week off when incessant rain splattered against the window panes, all of it seemed quite "do-able." That is, until the one thing none of us had factored into our serious intentions interfered. The sun came out.

So, during a string of days when I should have been sitting at the computer or stacking old clothes for the rummage sale, I was, instead, lounging at Avon Beach, breathing in the alluring scent of surf and sand. On lazier days, I would content myself with a short drive to the local swim club where I ignored the whines of toddlers and the screams of diving campers, plopped into a large tube, and closed my eyes as a soft current carried me around the cooling river. Other times I would vary my destination and partake in several street fairs and carnivals or browse the shops in Flemington or Princeton, stopping briefly with friends for a ladies' luncheon or perusing local perfume and soap shops. On sun-drenched weekends I found more excuses to procrastinate, and bribed the youngest of my three sons who, at 19 and away at college during cooler months, is only occasionally not embarrassed to be seen with his mother. We would drive to Point Pleasant where he could squander twenty dollars for a chance at a two-dollar rubber duck as I sat on a hot bench, my face tilted upwards. Or we would grab our bikes and ride through Bicentennial Park and return sweaty and exhilarated to cap off the day with family sitting outside Old Man Rafferty's

© Kushch Dmitry, 2010. Used under license from Shutterstock, Inc.

in New Brunswick eating salads and burgers and sipping long cold glasses of iced tea.

If all else failed and I couldn't find anyone to accompany me on these weekend excursions (my husband for some unknown reason prefers the comfort of air conditioning as he sits in his armchair, eating nachos and watching the Yankees), I would step outside into my backyard. There, I would tune to an oldies station, slather on tanning lotion and, positioning my lounge chair at just the right angle, lie down and contemplate the white clouds weaving their way around the face of the sun. As I lay there, each cloud took on the shape of a memory of summers past. The round one, a giant volleyball my college friends and I pounded over a net, a smaller shell-like cloud became the face of my child sleeping nearby in the stroller. Outside too I could open my eyes and see my future.

Graduations, weddings, vacations—I pinned each wish to the multitude of still-green leaves which patiently vacillated from above. So you see, work became no match for each beautiful outdoor day. In fact, the compulsion became so bad, nights I found myself watching the forecasts hoping for some sign of rain; even a hurricane would have been acceptable (well, almost).

With more fair-weather days in sight, though, I have finally reached what I think is an effective compromise. Hauling my son's old laptop outdoors, I begin to work, spitting out page after page. There is only one drawback, though. Hold on a minute—here comes the sun.

Now that you have read this essay, reread the directions before making a scratch outline of the essay. You may not use all the letters for details.

Thesis (in your own words): _____

Paragraph 1: Main Point: _____

      a. _____

      b. _____

      c. _____

      d. _____

      e. _____

Paragraph 2: Main Point: _____

      a. _____

      b. _____

      c. _____

      d. _____

      e. _____

Paragraph 3: Main Point: _____

    a. _____

    b. _____

    c. _____

    d. _____

    e. _____

Paragraph 4: Main Point: _____

    a. _____

    b. _____

    c. _____

    d. _____

    e. _____

Paragraph 5 and Paragraph 6: Main Point: _____

    a. _____

    b. _____

    c. _____

    d. _____

    e. _____

Why Is Mapping Important?

Besides outlining, mapping is another strategy college students can use to write papers, give reports or written responses, study lecture notes, and prepare study sheets on textbook reading assignments. If you like to do your thinking in a visual way, mapping uses lines, boxes, arrows, and circles to show relationships among the ideas and details that you encounter in printed materials, or that occur to you as you generate material for a paper. Maps may be time lines in which events are organized according to when they occurred. You may compose a map by hand or using a computer.

Mapping is a way to think on paper. It can show how ideas and details relate to one another. For example, map the sample scratch outline about juggling a job, college, and family responsibilities. In the center of a blank sheet of paper is the essay's main idea or thesis: Full-time work, college, and family responsibilities have made my life stressful. Put a circle around it. Next, find the details that directly support the main idea. Organize this material into categories, write down a short description for each category, and put circles around your descriptions. Now use lines to connect these circles to your category circles. What you end up with is a logical, graphical summary of the material.

Exercise **4.7   Your Turn—What Did You Learn?**

1. _____ is a visual way of organizing material.

2. A _____ is a type of map that is organized by the time in which events occurred.

3. You may compose a map by using _____, _____, and _____.

Creating the Map

4.8   Exercise

Directions: Reread the student essays "Celebrating My Graduation" and "When Summer Goes Too Fast." Then create a map of each essay. What you will end up with is a logical, graphical summary of the material.

Map #1: Celebrating My Graduation

Map #2: When Summer Goes Too Fast

Getting the Picture

In this chapter, you learned how to summarize, outline, and map material you must learn. Summarize the photo and briefly explain who you think the person in the photo is, and what he is doing.

© Richard Hamilton Smith/CORBIS

_____

_____

_____

_____

_____

_____

_____

_____

_____

_____

_____

_____

_____

_____

_____

_____

_____

_____

_____

_____

_____

_____

_____

_____

Chapter Highlights

What Have We Learned?

1. College students need to master **summarizing, outlining,** and **mapping** to write papers, give reports or written responses, study lecture notes, and prepare study sheets on assignments.

2. A **summary** is the reduction of a large amount of information to its most important points or main ideas.

3. An **outline** provides you with a shortened form of the main ideas.

4. If you like to do your thinking in a **visual** way, **mapping** uses lines, boxes, and circles to show relationships among the ideas and details that you encounter in printed materials or material you generate for a paper.

HOW CAN I IMPROVE MY VOCABULARY?

CHAPTER 5   Vocabulary in Context
CHAPTER 6   Word Parts and Dictionary Skills

You have learned the basic study skills. You are now ready for the basic tools to become a good reader. Let's start with vocabulary.

Spotlight on

Jon Stewart (1962–)

© Azzara Steve/Corbis Sygma

Jon Stewart, born Jonathan Stewart Leibowitz, is best known as host of Comedy Central's comedy and news show, *The Daily Show with Jon Stewart*, which has been on the air since 1999. The show dubs itself "the most trusted name in fake news." The witty Stewart is the anchorman and the show's co-executive producer. He has become the most outspoken critic of Washington and the "status quo." In addition to *The Daily Show*, Stewart has appeared in numerous other venues. He has hosted award shows, including the Grammy Awards in 2001 and 2002, and the Academy Awards in 2006 and 2008. A graduate of William and Mary, Stewart was invited to speak at the commencement ceremonies of his Alma Mater where he was presented with an honorary Doctor of Arts degree. The same year, he was the Class Day keynote speaker at Princeton University, and in 2008 he was the guest speaker at Hamilton College. The Emmy winning Stewart is also a two-time recipient of the Peabody Award, and in 2005, was named by *Time Magazine* to its annual list of 100 of the most influential people of the year. Stewart's work has been published in several magazines, including *The New Yorker* and *Esquire*. His first book was *Naked Pictures of Famous People* (1998), a collection of essays written in a satirical style. His next book, written with Ben Karlin and David Javerbaum, *America (The Book): A Citizen's Guide to Democracy Inaction* (2004), became a bestseller. *Earth (The Book): A Visitor's Guide to the Human Race* was released in 2010. Stewart married Tracey McShane in 2000, and they have a son, Nathan Thomas, and a daughter, Maggie Rose.

Chapter 5

VOCABULARY IN CONTEXT

Jon Stewart has earned his reputation as a funnyman because his audiences understand his jokes. They comprehend the punch line, knowing that the words in context imply different tones such as irony, parody, satire, and sarcasm. But how do most students and adults learn words? If you think they look up words in a dictionary, you are incorrect, because students and adults are most likely to figure out an unknown word from context. That is, they use the words surrounding the unknown word to decipher its meaning. Unfortunately, a word's context will provide only a general idea of its meaning and no help with pronunciation. Knowing the correct pronunciation is important if you don't want to embarrass yourself when you speak with other people. Therefore, learning new words from context may require using a dictionary to make sure of a word's meaning and pronunciation. And when you look up a word, go beyond reading the first definition. Note the secondary meanings, the different parts of speech, the pronunciation, and the etymology (a word's history) to see whether the word is related to other words you know.

A good vocabulary is developed by reading well-written newspapers, magazines, and books. To achieve this end, looking up every word you do not know can interfere with your comprehension or understanding of the text. So, try to get the general meaning from context and continue reading. Sometimes you may need to stop your reading to work on a word's meaning. An effective approach for constructing word meaning is the four-step interactive process W.S. Gray labeled CSSD—Context, Structure, Sound, and Dictionary (Gray). According to the process outlined by Gray, when you come to a word you do not know, here's what to do:

Step 1: Use context clues. Read to the end of the sentence. Can you guess the meaning? Are there any clues in the surrounding sentences or paragraphs? If you have a good idea of the meaning and it makes sense, keep on reading. If not, go to Step 2.

Step 2: Look at the parts of the word. Can you identify a word's prefix, root, suffix, or inflections (plurals, past tense, etc.) along with context information to arrive at a meaning? If you arrive at a meaning, keep on reading. If not, go to Step 3.

Step 3: Try to pronounce the word. When you sound out the word, is it a word you know? If not, look and say the letters or letter combinations along with context information to arrive at a meaning. If you arrive at a meaning, keep on reading. If not, go to Step 4.

Step 4: Look up the word in a glossary or a dictionary. Combine the word meaning with information from context. It should make sense. (Gray)

Contextual Hints

When using context to figure out a word's meaning, look for different types of context clues, such as **contextual hints, signal words, contextual examples,** and **definition clues.** Doing this can often result in understanding a word's meaning, thus eliminating the need to look at the parts of the word, the need to pronounce the word, or the need to use a glossary or a dictionary.

To understand **contextual hints,** read the following sentence:

> The cacophonous sound of the jackhammer made the pedestrians wish they had earplugs.

The word *jackhammer* and the phrase "wish they had earplugs" give clues to the meaning of the word *cacophonous*—having a harsh or unpleasant sound.

Exercise **5.1** ## Practice Contextual Hints

Directions: Define the italicized words in the following sentences, and explain the contextual hints. The first and second sentences are examples.

1. Monica *abjured* walnuts for several days after eating a quarter pound and breaking out in hives.
   a. *abjured* means <u>refrained from</u>
   b. The clue is <u>eating a quarter pound and breaking out in hives.</u>

2. The hurricane struck the city with *dire* consequences; nearly every building was destroyed, and there was no food, water, or shelter for its inhabitants.
   a. *dire* means <u>disastrous</u>
   b. The clue is <u>every building was destroyed, and there was no food, water or shelter for its inhabitants.</u>

3. When Matt saw his dog chew up his favorite loafers, he became *livid*, and he restrained himself from hitting the dog.

   a. *livid* means _____

   b. The clue is _____.

4. Winter seemed *interminable*; the weather started getting cold in early September and it didn't warm up until late April.

   a. *interminable* means _____

   b. The clue is _____.

5. In the *melee* of shoppers trying to enter the store for a midnight madness sale, an employee was seriously injured.

   a. *melee* means _____

   b. The clue is _____.

6. My sister is saving her journals for *posterity*; she hopes that her children and grandchildren will enjoy reading them.

   a. *posterity* means _____

   b. The clue is _____.

Signal Words

To understand **signal words**, read the following sentence:

> After my sister's engagement ended, she became *morose;* however, a month later she seems her happy self again.

The word *however* signals that a change is to occur. *Morose* means sad or sullen, and the signal word *however* contrasts the way my sister feels a month after her engagement ended.

Some **signal words** to help you unlock the meaning of an unfamiliar word are these:

but	while	in spite of	in contrast	however	despite	rather
although	nevertheless	even though	yet	instead		

Practice Signal Words   5.2 *Exercise*

Directions: Define the italicized words in the following sentences, and explain the signal word. The first and second sentences are examples.

1. Some people can study with other people around, but I need total *seclusion*.
   a. *seclusion* means aloneness
   b. signal word(s): <u>but</u>

2. The doctor paid *meticulous* attention to his patients, rather than giving them a quick examination.
   a. *meticulous* means <u>careful about details; fussy</u>
   b. signal word(s): <u>rather</u>

3. Although the family was *indigent*, they managed to have shelter, food, and clothing.

   a. *indigent* means _____

   b. signal word(s): _____

4. Even though Frank satisfied the *marginal* requirements for the job, he was worried that he didn't have more experience.

   a. *marginal* means _____

   b. signal word(s): _____

5. Tamara is usually *vivacious*; however, since she found out that she lost her job, she now doesn't feel like doing anything.

   a. *vivacious* means _____

   b. signal word(s): _____

6. The cabin was *remote*; however, we could not find one that was closer.

   a. *remote* means _____

   b. signal word(s): _____

Contextual Examples

To understand **contextual examples**, read the following sentence:

> Stanley was very frugal. Even though he earned a lot of money, he saved most of his salary and rarely ate at restaurants, shopped at malls, or entertained friends.

The word *frugal* means thrifty. The contextual examples that help define the word *frugal* are the phrases "saved most of his salary, rarely ate at restaurants, rarely shopped at malls," or "rarely entertained friends."

Exercise **5.3**   # Practice Contextual Examples

Directions: Define the italicized words in the following sentences, and explain the contextual examples. The first and second sentences are examples.

1. My friend Cindy doesn't try to leave *innuendos* about gifts, for she always tells me that she likes money, jewelry, or books.
   a. *innuendos* means <u>sly hints</u>
   b. example clue: <u>she always tells me that she likes money, jewelry, and books.</u>

2. My neighbor's *hubris* is annoying; she is always claiming to have the best lawn in the neighborhood, the cleanest house, and the smartest children.
   a. *hubris* means <u>excessive pride</u>
   b. example clue: <u>she is always claiming to have the best lawn in the neighborhood, the cleanest house, and the smartest children.</u>

3. My little brother's actions are so *impertinent;* he is always talking back to our parents, throwing temper tantrums, and yelling at his teacher.

   a. *impertinent* means _____

   b. example clue: _____

4. We could tell the fluid in the specimen was *contaminated* because it was cloudy and had a bad smell.

   a. *contaminated* means _____

   b. example clue: _____

5. Julio was *discreet* about his promotion—he didn't brag, answer any questions, and never brought it up in conversation with his friends.

   a. *discreet* means _____

   b. example clue: _____

6. Paula has some peculiar *mannerisms:* she always scratches her head, wrings her hands, and grinds her teeth.

   a. *mannerisms* means _____

   b. example clue: _____

Definition Clues

To understand **definition clues,** read the following sentence:

> Jon Stewart's *sarcastic* political jokes, which say *the opposite of what he means,* help his audience understand American politics.

The word *sarcastic* is defined right in the sentence itself. The words *the opposite of what he means* actually define the word *sarcastic.*

Now that you know context clues—contextual hints, signal words, contextual examples, and definition clues—you can unlock the meaning of unfamiliar words and use them; they appear frequently as an aid for figuring out a word's meaning by its context. Also, one helpful way to learn words that give you trouble is to make vocabulary flash cards.

Practice Definition Clues   5.4 *Exercise*

Directions: Define the italicized words in the following sentences, and explain the contextual definitions. The first and second sentences are examples.

1. Mark referred to his children as "the *menagerie*" because his children acted like animals.

    menagerie means <u>a collection of animals</u>

2. The dessert was *gratis*, or free of charge, because it arrived at our table late.

    gratis means <u>free of charge</u>

3. The tourists waited patiently in long *queues*, while citizens pushed to the head of the line.

    queues means _____

4. The designers *toiled*, working hard past midnight nearly every night for a month to meet the manufacturer's deadline.

    toiled means _____

5. The city's crumbling *infrastructure* resulted in the city council's decision to increase taxes to repair deteriorating highways, bridges, public buildings, and other public resources.

    infrastructure means _____

6. The politician's most obvious feature is her *charisma*, or magnetic charm.

    charisma means _____

Exercise **5.5   Your Turn—What Did You Learn?**

1. Most students and adults use _____ to unlock the meaning of an unfamiliar word.

2. In order to pronounce a word correctly, you should use _____.

3. Four types of context clues are _____, _____, _____, and _____.

Exercise **5.6   Practice Context Clues**

Can American politics according to Jon Stewart be taken seriously? If you are gullible, you will believe Stewart's "fake" news is "authentic" news. On the other hand, the following exercises reflect "real" American political news.

Directions: The following essay profiles former U.S. Secretary of Labor Robert Reich. After reading each segment of the profile, decide the meaning of the highlighted word and indicate which type of context clue you used: **contextual hints, signal words, contextual examples,** or **definition clues.**

The Wisdom of Robert Reich
By Mark Henricks

© Jonathan Ernst/Reuters/Corbis

*The fact that Robert Reich will even talk to you is comforting. After all, this guy quit his job as U.S. Secretary of Labor, where he presumably had the ear of President Bill Clinton, because he had better things to do. He's got enough Establishment clout to have commanded a private dinner with Bill Gates, and enough countercultural (1) **chutzpah** to recommend that Windows software be given away for free, as a public resource too valuable to be (2) **sequestered** in private hands. He's a professor at Brandeis University—he left Harvard to join the Clinton Cabinet—and his eight books include the bestsellers Locked in the Cabinet and The Work of Nations (which has been translated into 22 languages). OK, so the publicity campaign for his new book, The Future of Success (Knopf, $26), is the reason he's giving interviews. Still, to have him listen to your questions and give thoughtful-sounding answers suggests that maybe you are, if not actually important, not such a lightweight.*

From American Way, February 1, 2001 by Mark Henricks. Copyright © 2001 by American Way. Reprinted by permission.

1. The word *chutzpah* means:
   a. nerve; audacity
   b. a desert
   c. obedience

   The clue: _____

2. The word *sequestered* means:
   a. bought
   b. justified
   c. removed or set apart for private use

   The clue: _____

"As Secretary of Labor, my goal was to try to get more jobs and better wages for Americans, and after working hard at that role for a number of years, you can't help but feel jobs and wages are everything," Reich observes, setting himself up. "But, obviously, (3) **intrusiveness** of work—almost 24 hours a day, given cell phones and e-mails and faxes—and with the two tracks that are emerging, the fast and the slow track and the absences of (4) **gradations** between; given all that, it's not simply a matter of having a job or even having decent pay. (Henricks)

3. The word *intrusiveness* means:
   a. apathetic
   b. invading
   c. passiveness

   The clue: _____

4. The word *gradations* means:
   a. a system of academic evaluation
   b. evidence
   c. a series of gradual, successive stages

   The clue: _____

"We've gotten to the point where even though we are very (5) **prosperous** overall as a nation, we are remarkably poor in terms of the quality of our lives outside work," Reich continues. "That's what the book is about. It tries to explain that (6) **paradox**." (Henricks)

5. The word *prosperous* means:
   a. well-off, rich
   b. close to poverty level
   c. highly educated

   The clue: _____

6. The word *paradox* means:
   a. a seemingly contradictory statement that may nonetheless be true
   b. a theory or hypothesis
   c. an order

   The clue: _____

The *Future of Success* does that well—maybe too well. Reich's (7) **depiction** of a steadily tightening noose, in the form of rising expectations, global competition, ever-wiser marketers, and ever-better communications technology, begins to assume the (8) **guise** of inevitability after a while. That's not an image he does much to dispel. He discounts the more obvious time-management tools, as well as the whole movement toward simplification. Recounting his efforts to pursue these routes to achieving a more manageable success, he concludes they simply don't work. *(Henricks)*

7. The word *depiction* means:
   a. characterization or portrayal
   b. construction
   c. a lie or falsehood

   The clue: _____

8. The word *guise* means:
   a. honesty
   b. illusion
   c. method of simplification

   The clue: _____

Whew. Reich does not temper his visions with too much (9) **pragmatism**, as even he admits. "We wouldn't want to rush wholesale into any of these without more experiments," he allows. "I offer them as a set of starting points for a conversation we ought to be having in this country." *(Henricks)*

9. The word *pragmatism* means:
   a. a practical, matter-of-fact-way of solving problems
   b. bravery
   c. impracticality

   The clue: _____

But before you start dusting off your watercolors and working on your stage presence, Reich cautions against trying to emulate the success of anyone else. He acknowledges no hero of success in his own life. "I don't know that we can pattern our lives after any individual person," he says. "But self-awareness is the first step toward achieving a better set of priorities. And I'm trying to be quite self-aware." Reich even goes so far as to provide tips for entrepreneurs. For instance, he advises small firms to link up with giants, in the way that tiny online retailers affiliate with Amazon.com. "People simply can't remember more than three to five brands in any field," he says. "But these big brands are going to be contracting with hundreds of thousands of small businesses that actually produce the products and services." Want some ideas for fields to start a new business in? In his book, Reich provides seven he calls the (10) **insatiables**: industries from entertainment to financial planning that provide products and services people can't get enough of.

10. The word *insatiable* means:
   a. satisfaction
   b. something that people can't get enough of
   c. a commodity

   The clue: _____

More Context Clue Practice

5.7 *Exercise*

Jon Stewart's satirical comedic style is evident in the "local news" excerpt you will read from his book *Naked Pictures of Famous People*. After reading the excerpt, see how many words you can identify by using context clues. Remember to look for different types of context clues, such as **contextual hints, signal words, contextual examples,** and **definition clues.**

Well-Known Taco Bell Chihuahua Killed in Bar Fight

ANAHEIM (AP): Señor Jangles, the four-legged star of the Taco Bell commercials, died last night following a physical (1) **altercation** at an adult entertainment establishment in Anaheim. He was forty-nine years old. Jangles, whose real name was Shaky Pete, was beloved by audiences for being a cute dog that could talk. Today, Senor Jangles was described by (2) **distraught** friends as a fine actor and a good boy.

Jangles broke into acting in 1993 at the age of fourteen when a representative of the William Morris Agency discovered the talented Chihuahua talking to himself on a Los Angeles street corner. Jangles found steady commercial work soon after the (3) **fortuitous** meeting, and in 1995 the chatty Chihuahua booked the role of Pepe the Mexican Laddie in the animated Disney film Oh My God, Our Appliances Can Talk! But it was Jangles's role in the Taco Bell campaign that would bring his greatest (4) **notoriety.**

Jangles attained great fame and wealth through the Taco Bell campaign, but friends of the star reported he had grown (5) **despondent** in recent months. Sources close to Jangles claim he began to view his commercial role as (6) **degrading** and spoke often of what he perceived as Hollywood's closed-mindedness toward Latino actors. Jangles would also speak of the (7) **hypocrisy** of a society that allowed him to sell food he would never be allowed to eat off the table. The tensions came to a head three weeks ago when Jangles reportedly walked off the set during the filming of a Taco Bell spot after refusing to (8) **don** a sombrero and serape. Jangles's publicist refused comment but did say Jangles was suffering from hip (9) **dysplasia** and had been taking prescribed painkillers at the time of the (10) **alleged** work stoppage.

The alleged incident leading to Jangles's death occurred around one in the morning. Authorities say Jangles had been in the adult (11) **establishment** drinking for hours and had been repeatedly warned about licking his crotch. Around midnight, James MacPherson, forty-three, entered the bar and soon thereafter became involved in an argument with the four-legged pitchman. While details of the incident are still unclear, Diamond, a dancer at the popular adult nightspot, believes MacPherson, an unemployed long-haul trucker, took offense at comments Jangles made about his tipping. Others report the (12) **brouhaha** was touched off when Jangles, hackles raised, pointed at MacPherson and shouted [an obscenity]. Witnesses do agree on two points. Only one punch was thrown and Señor Jangles's last words were "Ay caramba" (Oy Vey).

Excerpts from pp. 61-3 and 107-8 from Naked Pictures of Famous People by Jon Stewart. Copyright © 1998 by Jon Stewart.

© Annette Shaff, 2010. Used under license from Shutterstock, Inc.

> MacPherson's lawyers denied reports that their client (13) **instigated** the attack on the popular canine. They insisted that MacPherson acted only in self-defense after an enraged and (14) **inebriated** Jangles ignored numerous pleas to sit and stay. Tonight MacPherson is in custody awaiting (15) **arraignment** on second-degree murder charges.
>
> "It's such a shame," said Diamond. "Mr. Jangles told me he was through with Taco Bell and was going to head to New York and Broadway—to play Rizzo in Grease. His whole body was shaking and he seemed really excited . . . or cold."
>
> Senor Jangles is survived by his mother, Pretty Peggy, of San Diego. The identity of his father is unknown, and he had no children due to a childhood operation. (Stewart 61-63)

Directions: Define the fifteen boldfaced words using context clues and explain the type of context clue.

1. **altercation** means _____

   The clue is _____

2. **distraught** means _____

   The clue is _____

3. **fortuitous** means _____

   The clue is _____

4. **notoriety** means _____

   The clue is _____

5. **despondent** means _____

   The clue is _____

6. **degrading** means _____

   The clue is _____

7. **hypocrisy** means _____

   The clue is _____

8. **don** means _____

   The clue is _____

9. **dysplasia** means _____

   The clue is _____

10. **alleged** means _____

    The clue is _____

11. **establishment** means _____

    The clue is _____

12. **brouhaha** means _____

    The clue is _____

13. **instigated** means _____

    The clue is _____

14. **inebriated** means _____

  The clue is _____

15. **arraignment** means _____

  The clue is _____

Getting the Picture

In this chapter, you learned about vocabulary and context clues. Jon Stewart usually satirizes the political parties. The symbol of the donkey represents the Democratic Party while the Republican Party is represented by the elephant. Survey the cartoon and briefly explain its context, noting what it implies.

© Robert F. Balazik, 2010. Used under license from Shutterstock, Inc.

_____

_____

_____

_____

_____

_____

_____

_____

_____

_____

_____

_____

_____

_____

_____

_____

_____

_____

_____

Chapter Highlights

What Have We Learned?

1. Most students and adults **learn words from context**, or the words surrounding the unknown word, to decipher its meaning.

2. Learning new words from context may require **using a dictionary** to make sure of a word's meaning and pronunciation.

3. **A good vocabulary** is developed by reading well-written newspapers, magazines, and books. To achieve this end, try to get the general meaning of the unknown word from context when you approach an unfamiliar word. If this is not effective, look at the parts of the word, or try to pronounce the word before looking it up in a glossary or a dictionary (Gray's four-step interactive process labeled CSSD).

4. When using context to figure out a word's meaning, **look for types of context clues,** such as contextual hints, signal words, contextual examples, and definition clues.

Chapter 6

WORD PARTS AND DICTIONARY SKILLS

In Chapter 5 you read Jon Stewart's excerpt, "Well-Known Taco Bell Chihuahua Killed in Bar Fight." If you had trouble understanding what is comical about this piece, you probably did not comprehend unfamiliar words from context. Sometimes context may not help unlock the correct meaning of a word, so you must use other strategies, such as looking at a word's structure or turning to a dictionary, to understand what the word means.

If context clues are not enough to decipher a word's meaning, look at the parts of the word, along with context information, to understand how the word is used.

A root or stem or base word is a word from which other words are formed either by adding parts in front of it or at the end of it. **To find the root,** you simply take away the parts that have been added. When you cannot take away any more parts and still have a word related in meaning, you probably found the word's root. A word part that can be added to the beginning of a word to change its meaning or to form a new word is called a **prefix.** Words made up of a root word plus one or more prefixes are called **derivatives** because they are derived from, or formed from, another word. A word part that is added to the end of a root word is called a **suffix.** Words containing a root word and one or more suffixes are also called **derivatives.** But remember that sometimes the addition of a certain suffix changes the spelling of the root word, such as dropping a final *e*, changing final *y* to *i* or f to *v*, or doubling the final consonant. Or, there is the **rare instance calling for other changes** such as in the word *fifteen—five* + teen = fifteen. A prefix or a suffix is called an **affix** when added to a base word.

Included below are comprehensive lists of roots, prefixes, and suffixes to help you break down words to find their meaning:

Identifying Roots

Cited below is a list of roots (base words) to help you break down words for better understanding.

Lists of Roots		
Base or Root	**Meaning**	**Origin**
act	to act	Latin
acu, acr, ac	needle	Latin
alt	high	Latin
anima, anim	life, mind	Latin
ann, enn	year	Latin
anthrop	man	Greek
aqua	water	Latin
arch, archi	govern, rule	Greek
arm	army, weapon	Latin
arbitr, arbiter	to judge, consider	Latin
art	craft, skill	Latin
arthr, art	segment, joint	Greek
aud	to hear	Latin
bell	war	Latin
biblio, bibl	book	Greek
bio	life	Greek
capit, cipit	head	Latin
caus	cause, case, lawsuit	Latin
cede	to go, yield	Latin
cele	honor	Latin
cell	to rise, project	Latin
cent	one hundred	Latin
cept, capt, cip, cap, ceive, ceipt	to take, hold, grasp	Latin
cert	sure, to trust	Latin
cess, ced	to move, withdraw	Latin
cid, cis	to cut off, be brief, to kill	Latin
circ, circum	around	Latin
civ	citizen	Latin
claud	close, shut, block	Latin
clin	to lean, lie, bend	Latin

Base or Root	Meaning	Origin
cog	to know	Latin
column	a column	Latin
comput	to compute	Latin
cont	to join, unite	Latin
cor, cord, cour, card	heart	Latin
corp	body	Latin
cosm	world, order, universe	Greek
crac, crat	rule, govern	Greek
cred	believe, trust	Latin
crit, cris	separate, discern, judge	Latin
culp	fault, blame	Latin
curs, curr, corr	to run	Latin
custom	one's own	Latin
dem	people	Greek
dent, odon	tooth	Latin
derm	skin	Greek
dic, dict	to say, to speak, assert	Latin
duct, duc	to lead, draw	Latin
dur	to harden, hold out	Latin
ego	I	Latin
ethn	nation	Greek
equ	equal, fair	Latin
fac, fic, fect, fact	to make, to do	Latin
famil	family	Latin
fen	to strike	Latin
fer	to carry, bear, bring	Latin
fid	trust, faith	Latin
fin	to end	Latin
flu	to flow	Latin
form	shape, form	Latin
fort	chance, luck, strong	Latin
frig	cool	Latin
fum	smoke, scent	Latin
gam	marriage	Greek
gen	race, family, kind	Latin
geo	earth	Greek
gno, kno	to know	Greek
grad, gred, gress	step, degree, rank	Latin
graph, gram	write, draw, describe, record	Greek

(continued)

Base or Root	Meaning	Origin
grat	pleasure, thankful, goodwill, joy	Latin
grav, griev, grief	heavy	Latin
gymn	naked	Greek
hab	to have, hold, dwell	Latin
hom	man, human	Latin
hosp	guest, host	Latin
host	enemy, stranger	Latin
hydro	water	Greek
hygiene	the art of health	Greek
hypno	sleep	Greek
init	to begin, enter upon	Latin
jur, jus, jud	law, right	Latin
juven	young	Latin
labor, lab	work	Latin
lat	lateral, side, wide	Latin
laud	praise	Latin
leg, lig	law, to chose, perceive, understand	Latin
lev	to make light, raise, lift	Latin
liber, liver	free	Latin
lingu, langu	tounge	Latin
lith	stone	Greek
loc	place	Latin
locu, loqu	word, speak	Latin
log	idea, word, speech, reason, study	Greek
luc, lum	light	Latin
man	hand	Latin
mar	sea	Latin
med, medi	middle	Latin
medic	physician, to heal	Latin
memor	mindful	Latin
men, min, mon	to think, remind, advise, warn	Latin
ment	mind	Latin
meter, metr	measure	Greek
migr	to move, travel	Latin
mim	copy, imitate	Greek
mit, mis	to send	Latin
mor	fool, manner, custom	Greek
morph	form	Greek
mort	death	Latin

Base or Root	Meaning	Origin
mov, mob, mot	to move	Latin
mus	little mouse	Latin
mut	change, exchange	Latin
necess	unavoidable	Latin
neur, nerv	nerve	Greek
noc, nox	night, harm	Latin
nomen, nomin	name	Latin
null, nihil, nil	nothing, void	Latin
nym, onym, onom	name	Greek
opt	eye	Greek
ord, ordin	order	Latin
ortho	straight	Greek
par, pair	arrange, prepare, get ready, set	Latin
part, pars	portion, part	Latin
ped, pes	foot	Latin
pend, pond, pens	to weigh, pay, consider	Latin
phe, fa, fe	speak, spoken about	Greek
phil	love	Greek
phon	sound, voice	Greek
photo	light	Greek
pler	to fill	Latin
plic	to fold	Latin
plur, plus	more	Latin
pneu	breath	Greek
polis, polit	citizen, city, state	Greek
port	to carry	Latin
pos	to place, put	Latin
pot	powerfull	Latin
prim, prin	first	Latin
priv	separate	Latin
prob	to prove, test	Latin
psych	mind, soul, spirit	Greek
pyr	fire	Greek
reg, rig, rect, reign	government, rule, right, straight	Latin
respond	to answer	Latin
rupt	break, burst	Latin
sacr, secr, sacer	sacred	Latin
sat	to please	Latin
sci	to know	Latin

(continued)

Base or Root	Meaning	Origin
scope	to see	Greek
scrib, script	to write	Latin
sed, sid, sess	to sit, to settle	Latin
sent, sens	to feel	Latin
sequ, secut	to follow, sequence	Latin
simil, simul, sembl	together, likeness, pretense	Latin
sol, soli	alone, lonely	Latin
solus	to comfort, to console	Latin
somn	sleep	Latin
son	sound	Latin
soph	wise	Greek
spec, spect, spic	to look at, behold	Latin
spond, spons	to pledge, promise	Latin
tac, tic	silent	Latin
techn	art, skill	Greek
temp	time	Latin
ten, tain, tent	to hold	Latin
tend, tens	to give heed, stretch toward	Latin
term	boundary, limit	Latin
test	to witness, affirm	Latin
the, them, thet	to place, put	Greek
theatr	to see, view	Greek
theo	god	Greek
topo	place	Greek
tract	to pull, draw	Latin
trib	to allot, give	Latin
vac	empty	Latin
ven	to come	Latin
ver	truth	Latin
vers, vert	to turn	Latin
vest	to adorn	Latin
vestig	to track	Latin
via	way, road	Latin
vir	manliness, worth	Latin
vis, vid	to see, to look	Latin
viv, vit	life	Latin
voc, vok	voice, call	Latin

Identifying Prefixes

Cited below is list of prefixes (which appear at the beginning of words) to help you break down words for better understanding.

List of Prefixes		
Base	**Meaning**	**Origin**
ab	away	Latin
acro	top, tip, end	Greek
ad, ac, at, as, ap, am, an, ar, ag, af	to, toward, at	Latin
ambi	around, both	Latin
amphi	both, of both sides, around	Greek
ant, anti	against	Greek
ante	before	Latin
apo, ap, aph	away from, off	Greek
archa, arshae	old, ancient	Greek
auto	self	Greek
ben, bon	good, well	Latin
bi	two	Latin
co, con, com	together, with	Latin
contra, contro	against	Latin
de	from, away, off	Latin
deca, dec, deka	ten	Greek
di, dis	two, twice	Greek
dia	through, across	Greek
dis, dif	apart, away, not, to deprive	Latin
du	double, two	Latin
dys	difficult, bad	Greek
e, ex, ec	out, beyond, from, out of, forth	Latin
ecto	outside of	Greek
en	in give [intensifier]	Latin
endo, ento	within	Greek
ep, epi	upon, at, in addition	Greek
eu	good, well	Greek
extra	beyond	Latin
fore	before	Anglo-Saxon
hemi	half	Greek
hetero	various, unlike	Greek
hier	sacred	Greek
holo	whole	Greek

(continued)

Base	Meaning	Origin
homo	same	Greek
hyper	above, beyond	Greek
hypo, hyp	under, less than	Greek
ideo, idea	idea	Greek
in, ir, im, il	not, without	Latin
in, im	in, on, upon, into, toward	Latin
inter	between	Latin
intro	within	Latin
iso	equal	Greek
kilo	thousand	Greek
macro	long, large	Greek
magn, mag, meg, maj	great	Latin
mal	bad, ill	Latin
mega	great	Greek
met, meta, meth	among, with, after, beyond	Greek
micro	small	Greek
migr	to move, travel	Latin
mill	thousand	Latin
mis	less, wrong	Latin
mono	one	Greek
multi	many, much	Latin
neo	new	Greek
non, ne	not	Latin
o, ob, oc, of, op	against, toward	Latin
omni	all	Latin
paleo	long ago, ancient	Greek
pan, panto	all, every	Greek
para	beside, beyond	Latin
penta	five	Greek
per	through	Latin
peri	around, about	Greek
pre	before	Latin
pro	before, forward, forth	Latin
pronto	first	Greek
poly	many	Greek
post	after	Latin
pseudo	false, counterfeit	Greek
quad, quart	four	Latin
re	again, anew, back	Latin
retro	back, backward, behind	Latin
se, sed	apart, aside, away	Latin
semi	half	Latin

Base	Meaning	Origin
sover	above, over	Latin
sub	under, below, up from below	Latin
super, supra	above, down, through	Latin
syn, sym, syl	together, with	Greek
tele	far off	Greek
trans	over, across	Latin
tri	three	Latin
un	not	Latin
uni	one	Latin

Identifying Suffixes

Cited below is a list of suffixes (which appear at the end of words) to help you break down words for better understanding.

Noun-forming Suffixes		
Suffix	**Meaning**	**Origin**
age	belongs to	Latin
ance	state of being	Latin
ant	thing or one who	Latin
ar	relating to, like	Latin
ary	relating to, like	Latin
ence	state, fact, quality	Latin
ent	to form	Latin
ic	like, having the nature	Latin & Greek
Ine	nature of (feminine ending)	Latin
Ion, tion, ation	being, the result of	Latin
ism	act, condition	Latin & Greek
Ist	one who	Latin
Ive	of, belonging to, quality of	Latin
ment	a means, product, act, state	Latin
or	person or thing that	Latin
ory	place for	Latin
ty	condition of, quality of	Latin
y	creates abstract noun	Greek & Anglo-Saxon

Adjective-forming Suffixes

Suffix	Meaning	Origin
able	capable of being	Latin
al	like, suitable for	Latin
ance	state of being	Latin
ant	thing or one who	Latin
ar	relating to, like	Latin
ary	relating to, like	Latin
ate	to become associated with	Latin
ent	to form	Latin
ial	function of	Latin
ible	capable of being	Latin
ic	like, having the nature of	Latin & Greek
ine	nature of (feminine ending)	Latin
ive	of, belonging to, quality of	Latin
ory	place for	Latin
ous	characterized by, having quality of	Latin
y	quality, somewhat like	Greek & Anglo-Saxon

Verb-forming Suffixes

Suffix	Meaning	Origin
ate	to become associated with	Latin
fy	make, do	Latin
ise, ize	to become like	Latin

Adverb-forming Suffixes

Suffix	Meaning	Origin
ic	like, having the nature of	Latin & Greek
ly	like, to extent of	Latin

Your Turn—What Did You Learn?

1. The base of a word is called a _____.
2. The beginning of a word is called a _____.
3. The end of a word is called a _____ .
4. Derivatives are formed from _____ and _____.
5. A prefix or a suffix is called a(n) _____ when it is added to a base word.

Word Meanings Using Word Parts

Directions: Use the lists of roots, prefixes, and suffixes to identify the meanings of the words listed.

1. submarine _____
2. homicide _____
3. malicious _____
4. pretest _____
5. convene _____
6. mobility _____
7. monogamy _____
8. semicircle _____
9. mortuary _____
10. transcribe _____
11. descend _____
12. spectacle _____
13. certify _____
14. revive _____
15. microscope _____

Exercise   **6.3**   **Word Parts Practice**

Directions: From the words below, choose one for each of the following sentences and write it in the blank. If you are not sure of all the meanings, do those you know first.

graceless   disgrace   gracefully   ungracious   gracing

1. The gymnast somersaulted _____ over the raised balance beam while the audience cheered loudly.

2. The customer was rude and _____ to the novice waiter.

3. On a French marble antique table, _____ the foyer, stood an enormous Japanese flower arrangement.

4. The teenager's pregnancy brought _____ to her prominent family.

5. The young aspiring model seems too clumsy and _____ to ever make runway modeling a reality.

    a. What word forms a part of each word listed? _____

    b. How many parts are added before this word? _____

    c. How many parts are added after? _____

    d. In which two words is the spelling changed when an ending is added? _____

When a word is made up of several parts, and you want to get the meaning of the word, remove the parts in your mind and see if you can find a word you recognize. Then check to see if the word you find has anything to do with the meaning of the sentence. Is this what you did to find *grace*? Then did you think of the various meanings *grace* could have depending on its context? Now go back to the five numbered sentences. In which numbered sentence(s) are the words related in some way to the possible meanings of *grace*? _____

Identifying Word Parts in an Essay

6.4 *Exercise*

Directions: Read the following excerpt from Jon Stewart's book *Naked Pictures of Famous People*. In the passage, selected words with prefixes and suffixes are boldfaced. Write the words below. Next, circle each prefix and suffix. Then give the meaning of each prefix and the part of speech of each word with a suffix. Do not forget to use the comprehensive lists of roots, prefixes, and suffixes to help you break down words.

The Devil and William Gates
By Jon Stewart

It's a story they tell in the Pacific Northwest, where Washington State meets up with what is left of the Wilderness Provinces formerly known as Canada.

Yes, William Gates is dead and **buried**—or at least he died. Folks say they **converted** his remains into **binary** code and shot him out over the World Wide Web. Some say it was the work of his most **committed** disciples, others that his remains just **reverted** back to their natural state of being. Whichever school of thought you go by, most folks agree that he still haunts almost every **transaction** of business takin' place. They say when you go to the ATM and it tells you you ain't got sufficient funds, or if you swipe your personal ID cyberpass, the one built into your eyeball, into your front door and it still denies you access, you can stop and take a listen . . . and you'll hear ol' Billy gigglin' and wipin' his runny nose on the sleeve of his all-weather **reversible** Lands' End parka. And they say you can visit his Web site at BillGates.com and type in "Bill Gates . . . Billy Gates!" and sure enough the keyboard'll start to shiverin' and the screen will jump to life and a kind of **annoyed**, not very deep voice will answer—if you have the model with the voice actualizer—"Hey, neighbor, how stands the Microsoft Union?" And you better answer that "She stands as she stood, innovative, dominant and up one and an eighth per share" or a **smallish**, soft-skinned hand is liable to shoot out of the screen and **delete** you. At least that's how they told it to me as a boy. (Stewart 107-8)

Excerpts from pp. 61–3 and 107–8 from Naked Pictures of Famous People by Jon Stewart. Copyright © 1998 by Jon Stewart.

1. _____

2. _____

3. _____

4. _____

5. _____

6. _____

7. _____

8. _____

9. _____

10. _____

Why Is It Important to Read a Dictionary?

When context, sound, and structure do not give you enough help to understand an unfamiliar word, you may need to go to a dictionary. Thumb through a dictionary and you will discover it is more than a book about words. A dictionary is a spelling book, a guide to pronunciation, a source of historical information, and a vocabulary aid.

Learning about Dictionary Word Entries

Here is a typical dictionary word entry from an online dictionary:

Main Entry:

bib·lio·phile

Pronunciation:

\\bi-blē-ə-ˌfī (-ə)l\

Function:

noun

Etymology:

French, from *bibli-* + -phile

Date:

1824

: a lover of books especially for qualities of format ; *also* : a book collector

bib·lio·phil·ic \ˌbi-blē-ə-ˈfi-lik\ *adjective*
bib·li·oph·i·lism \-ˈä-fə-ˌli-zəm\ *noun*
bib·li·oph·i·ly \-lē\ *noun*

Source: *Merriam-Webster Online*

In print and online dictionaries, the main word or entry word appears in bold type and is divided into syllables by dots. The syllable divisions help you pronounce a word and also show you where to hyphenate a word as needed when writing a paper—**bib·lio·phile.**

Two major rules for dividing words into syllables:

1. Divide between double consonants: mes/sage, dis/tance, fun/gus
2. Divide before a single consonant: lo/cal, bla/tant, fru/gal

(Pronunciation hint: The vowel before a division at a single consonant usually has a long sound).

Always divide compound words between the words that form the compound.

whole/sale   ever/green   news/print

Divide between prefixes and suffixes.

head/ing   dis/content   sub/merge

Following the word *bibliophile* are the pronunciation symbols—ˈbi-blē-ə-ˌfī (-ə)l. To help you pronounce the word, a pronunciation key in a print dictionary is usually located in the front of the dictionary and at the bottom of every other page. However, in an online dictionary, you will most likely click on the words *pronunciation key,* which will link you to the pronunciation symbols. For example, the *Merriam-Webster Online* pronunciation key is shown below.

Pronunciation Symbols

\ə\ as **a** in <u>a</u>but	\g\ as **g** in <u>g</u>o	\r\ as **r** in <u>r</u>ed
\ˈə͜ə\ as **u** in <u>a</u>but	\h\ as **h** in <u>h</u>at	\s\ as **s** in le<u>ss</u>
\ᵊ\ as **e** in kitt<u>en</u>	\i\ as **i** in h<u>i</u>t	\sh\ as **sh** in <u>sh</u>y
\ər\ as **ur/er** in furth<u>er</u>	\ī\ as **i** in <u>i</u>ce	\t\ as **t** in <u>t</u>ie
\a\ as **a** in <u>a</u>sh	\j\ as **j** in <u>j</u>ob	\th\ as **th** in <u>th</u>in
\ā\ as **a** in <u>a</u>ce	\k\ as **k** in <u>k</u>in	\th\ as **th** in <u>th</u>e
\ä\ as **o** in <u>mo</u>p	\ḵ\ as **ch** in i<u>ch</u> dien	\ü\ as **oo** in l<u>oo</u>t
\au̇\ as **ou** in <u>ou</u>t	\l\ as **l** in <u>l</u>i<u>l</u>y	\u̇\ as **oo** in f<u>oo</u>t
\b\ as in <u>b</u>a<u>b</u>y	\m\ as **m** in <u>m</u>ur<u>m</u>ur	\v\ as **v** in <u>v</u>i<u>v</u>id
\ch\ as **ch** in <u>ch</u>in	\n\ as **n** in ow<u>n</u>	\w\ as **w** in a<u>w</u>ay
\d\ as **d** in <u>d</u>i<u>d</u>	\ŋ\ as **ng** in si<u>ng</u>	\y\ as **y** in <u>y</u>et
\e\ as **e** in b<u>e</u>t	\ō\ as **o** in g<u>o</u>	\yü\ as **you** in <u>you</u>th
\ˈē͜ē\ as **ea** in <u>ea</u>sy	\ȯ\ as **aw** in l<u>aw</u>	\y\ as **u** in c<u>u</u>rable
\ē\ as **y** in eas<u>y</u>	\ȯi\ as **oy** in b<u>oy</u>	\z\ as **z** in <u>z</u>one
\f\ as **f** in <u>f</u>i<u>f</u>ty	\p\ as **p** in <u>p</u>e<u>pp</u>er	\zh\ as **si** in vi<u>si</u>on

Source: *Merriam-Webster Online*

Use the pronunciation key as a guide to pronouncing different vowel sounds (a, e, i, o, u). Furthermore, accent marks (ˈbi-blē-ə-ˌfī (-ə)l—the accent mark is before the first syllable) show where the stress or accent should be when saying a word. In other words, the accented syllable is said with more force than the unaccented syllables. Knowing which syllable is accented or stressed makes the word easier to pronounce.

Additionally, the word's third and last syllables have a symbol that looks like an upside-down e. This symbol is called a schwa, and it stands for the unaccented sound in words such as *ago, item, edible, gallop, and circus.* More approximately, it stands for the sound of *uh*—like the "uh" sound speakers may make when they hesitate in their speech—ə. Finally, because there are probably more words in your listening vocabulary than in your sight vocabulary, you will recognize more spoken words than written ones. Learning how to sound out and pronounce unfamiliar words will help narrow any gap between your listening and sight vocabularies. Knowing the pronunciation will help you to recognize and say the word correctly.

Below the pronunciation symbols is the word's function or part of speech. If abbreviations are used, *n* means noun, *adj.* means adjective, and *vb* means verb. The word *bibliophile* is a noun. Knowing what part of speech a word is will help you use it correctly.

Next shown is the word's etymology. Etymology is the history of a word. Many words have origins in foreign language such as Greek (GK) or Latin (L). Such information is usually enclosed in brackets in a print dictionary. Because the most common and helpful roots, prefixes, and suffixes in English come from Latin and ancient Greek, becoming familiar with some word parts can help you figure out the meaning of a word (refer back to the "Reagan Latin and Greek Roots and Affix" list at the beginning of the chapter). This can help you understand and remember a word's meaning. The origin of the word *bibliophile* is French, 1824.

After the word's etymology is the word's definition or meaning. The word *bibliophile* means a lover of books especially for qualities of format; *also:* a book collector. When there is more than one meaning to a word, the meanings are numbered in the dictionary. In many dictionaries, the most common meanings are presented first. The introductory pages of your dictionary will explain the order in which meanings are presented.

Exercise   **6.5   Your Turn—What Did You Learn?**

1. When you are unable to find the meaning of a word through context or structure (word parts), you should use a _____.

2. The pronunciation will help you to _____.

3. The etymology of a word gives you its _____.

4. After the etymology of a word, you will find its _____.

Word Meaning in Textbooks

Directions: The paragraph below comes from the textbook *Sociology: A Brief Introduction* by Richard T. Schaefer. First, read the paragraph. Then look up the boldfaced words *census* and *mortality*. For each word do the following: Write each word's second spelling or pronunciation; write each word in syllables; state each word's origin; state each word's part of speech; define each word as it is used in the context of the paragraph.

> Social class is clearly associated with differences in morbidity and **mortality** rates. Studies in the United States and other countries have consistently shown that people in the lower classes have higher rates of mortality and disability. A study published in 1998 documents the impact of class on mortality. The authors concluded that Americans whose family incomes were less than $10,000 could expect to die seven years sooner than those with incomes of at least $25.000 (Bureau of the **Census** 2000a:135). (Schaefer)

Census:

Pronunciation: _____

Syllabication: _____

Origin: _____

Part of Speech: _____

Definition (Use context clues): _____

Use the word in a sentence: _____

Mortality:

Pronunciation: _____

Syllabication: _____

Origin: _____

Part of Speech: _____

Definition (Use context clues): _____

Use the word in a sentence: _____

Getting the Picture

In this chapter, you learned about word parts and dictionary skills. Using the alphabet photo, make up nine words with three or more syllables. Write each word. Then separate each word into syllables. For example, the first word is done for you.

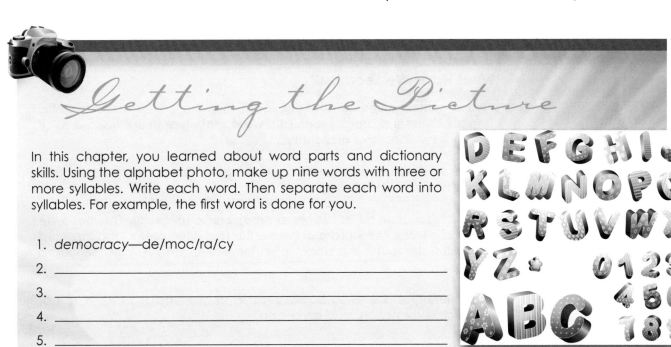

© AKaiser, 2010. Used under license from Shutterstock, Inc.

1. democracy—de/moc/ra/cy

2. _____

3. _____

4. _____

5. _____

6. _____

7. _____

8. _____

9. _____

10. _____

Chapter Highlights

What Have We Learned?

1. **When context clues do not help** you unlock the correct meaning of a word, use other strategies such as a **word's structure** to understand what the word means, or a **dictionary.**

2. **A word's structure** along **with context information** will help you understand how the word is used.

3. A word's structure refers to a word's **root, prefix,** and **suffix.** The **root** is the **base of a word.** The **word part before the root** is the **prefix,** and the **word part after the root** is the **suffix.** Together prefixes and suffixes are called **affixes.**

4. A **dictionary** is a spelling book, a guide to pronunciation, a source of historical information, and a vocabulary aid.

WHAT'S IT ALL ABOUT? GETTING THE MAIN IDEA

CHAPTER 7 The Main Idea
CHAPTER 8 Rhetorical Modes

Now that you know how to improve your vocabulary through context, word parts, and dictionary skills, you will learn in Unit 4 how to determine the main idea and details.

Spotlight on

Muhammad Ali (1942–)

Known as "The Greatest," heavyweight boxing champion Muhammad Ali was an outspoken and charismatic heavyweight fighter of the 1960s and 1970s. Famous for his sharpness and speed in the ring, Ali won the world heavyweight title on three separate occasions over a span of fifteen years. Born Cassius Clay, he came into the public eye after winning a gold medal at the 1960 Olympics in Rome. Four years later, he won his first title by defeating Sonny Liston in 1964. Once Clay joined the Nation of Islam, he changed his name to Muhammad Ali. After Ali was called to serve in the U.S. military during the war in Vietnam, he refused to fight, citing his Islamic faith. As a result, his title was revoked and he was sentenced to five years in prison for draft evasion. (The United States Supreme Court reversed the conviction in 1971.) His rival, heavyweight Joe Frazier, was a popular opponent with whom he traded both barbs and punches in three fights. Ali lost the first match in 1971, but won rematches in 1974 and 1975. Ali also defeated George Foreman in the famous 1974 "Rumble in the Jungle" held in Kinshasa, Zaire. Ali retired in 1981. In 1996, Ali lit the ceremonial flame at the Summer Olympics in Atlanta. Years later, the movie *Ali* (2001), which depicts the fighter's rise and stars the actor Will Smith, sparked renewed interest in this legendary athlete. Ali suffers from Parkinson's disease, a motor-skills illness which has slowed his movement and impaired his speech.

© Rick Maiman/Sygma/Corbis

THE MAIN IDEA

The Importance of Getting the Main Idea

As a boxer, Muhammad Ali understands the importance of training in order to be successful. Similarly, in order to fully understand what you read, learning and practice are important keys in gaining success. Whether reading material from a textbook, newspaper, or journal, understanding the main idea is essential. Once you grasp the meaning of the main idea, you will then be able to have a basic understanding of the material you read, no matter how complicated it may appear to be. Understanding the main idea will also help you annotate and take notes more effectively and respond to what you have read. Finally, comprehension of the main idea will improve your summaries of the material and your ability to score well on reading exams. In this chapter, you will learn how to break down the elements of a paragraph, apply the formula for identifying and locating the main idea, as well as how to identify and locate the thesis statement in longer readings.

The **main idea** is the author's main point about a topic. In a paragraph, it is a *complete sentence* that *states the topic* and *says something about the topic.*

To understand **main idea,** think of the main idea as the hub, or center of the wheel. Without the hub, a wheel cannot function; similarly, without a main idea or topic sentence, you don't have a paragraph. The spokes of the wheel may be compared to the **details** of the paragraph; they help support the main idea or topic sentence. The "wheel" analogy below illustrates the concept.

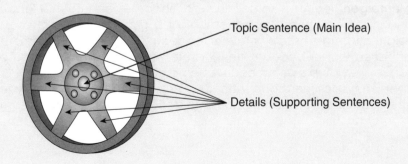

Topic Sentence (Main Idea)

Details (Supporting Sentences)

When attempting to comprehend a paragraph, you must also consider the questions: *Who or what is this paragraph about?* And then, *what is the author saying about the topic?*

The answer to the first question will enable you to find the **topic** or **subject** of the paragraph. The answer to the second question will enable you to find the paragraph's **main idea,** which is expressed in a single sentence called a **topic sentence.**

Read the following paragraph from a communications textbook, and see if you can determine what it is about and what the writer is saying about the topic.

Leadership

© JupiterImages Corporation

1. In small groups, two types of leaders are designated and emergent. 2. A **designated leader** is someone who has been appointed or elected to a leadership position (e.g., chair, team leader, coordinator, or facilitator). 3. An **emergent leader** is someone who becomes an informal leader by exerting influence toward achievement of a group's goal but who does not hold the formal position or role of leader. 4. Groups benefit from having a designated leader because designated leaders add stability and organization to the group's activities. 5. An emergent leader can be any group member who helps the group meet its goals. 6. Groups work best when all members contribute skills and leadership behaviors on behalf of the group. (Pearson et al. 217)

This paragraph, as the title indicates, is about *leadership.* This is the **topic** or **subject.** Specifically, what the author says about leadership is:

In small groups, two types of leaders are designated and emergent.

This is the **main idea** or **topic sentence.**

The details supporting the main idea are the five sentences following the main idea or topic sentence, which is the first sentence of the paragraph. The outline below specifically illustrates the topic, main idea, and supporting details:

Topic or subject: Leadership

Main idea (*a single sentence which is called the topic sentence*): In small groups, two types of leaders are designated and emergent. This is the first sentence of the paragraph.

Supporting details:

1. A **designated leader** is someone who has been appointed or elected to a leadership position (e.g., chair, team leader, coordinator, or facilitator).
2. An **emergent leader** is someone who becomes an informal leader by exerting influence toward achievement of a group's goal but who does not hold the formal position or role of leader.
3. Groups benefit from having a designated leader because designated leaders add stability and organization to the group's activities.
4. An emergent leader can be any group member who helps the group meet its goals.
5. Groups work best when all members contribute skills and leadership behaviors on behalf of the group.

General Topic or Subject

The outline above illustrates that the topic or subject, *leadership,* is a **general topic or subject,** but it has a specific focus or main idea: *In small groups, two types of leaders are designated and emergent.* So when you are asking the question "Who or what is the paragraph about?", to identify the topic or subject of a paragraph, your answer must be a general topic or subject. It cannot be too general or too specific. And a general subject must be included in the main idea or topic sentence. Specifically, when you ask the question "What is the author saying about leadership?", the general topic or subject, *leadership,* is stated in the main idea or topic sentence: *In small groups,* **two types of leaders** *are designated and emergent.* Notice how the topic or subject, *leadership,* is imbedded in the main idea or topic sentence.

Main Idea

In the wheel analogy, the main idea or the topic sentence is like the hub of the wheel, essential to the paragraph. It is the most important part of the paragraph. It is a sentence that conveys the author's message and says something about the topic or subject. Specifically, in regard to leadership, the writer is saying that there are two types of leaders, designated and emergent.

NOTE: While the main idea is the first sentence of this paragraph, this is not the case in every paragraph.

Details

In the wheel analogy, the **details** may be considered the "spokes" of the wheel. While the hub of the wheel is essential for it to function, the spokes help the wheel to run. Similarly, supporting details aid in developing the author's main idea. Sentences #1 and #2 explain the definitions for designated and emergent leaders. Sentences #3 and #4 provide more information about these two types of leaders. Sentence #5 provides a suggestion concerning leadership. All of these details concern the topic or subject, leadership, and provide support that further explains the writer's main idea that there are two types of leaders, designated and emergent. As you can see, while the details take up most of the paragraph, the main idea (the most important part of a paragraph) is usually only *one* sentence.

Identifying The Topic

We have learned that the topic is the general subject of the paragraph. Everything in the paragraph should have something to do with the topic. The topic may be found as the title or a heading of a paragraph, or it might merely be implied in the body of the paragraph. You can locate the topic by simply skimming through the reading for a repeated general idea. However, you should also make sure that the topic is neither too general nor too specific. For example, the subject "hunger" would be considered too broad for a paragraph. It is difficult to understand what type of hunger the writer is referring to. Does the paragraph deal with the biological urge that is hunger? Is it about the emotional "hunger" some people have for power? Or does the topic concern the problem of hunger within the United States? On the other hand, the topic of a paragraph should not be too specific. The example of Mr. Richard's application for food stamps is considered much too specific to be a topic. However, "The U.S. Hunger Problem" is an appropriate topic because it is neither too general nor too specific.

See if you can determine the topic in the following paragraph.

© JupiterImages Corporation

Adolescents and their parents are often at odds over the acquisition of bodily decorations. For the adolescent, piercing or tattoos may be seen as personal and beautifying statements, while parents may construe them as oppositional and enraging affronts to their authority. Distinguishing bodily adornment from self-mutilation may indeed prove challenging, particularly when a family is in disagreement over a teenager's motivations. (Martin)

_____ The topic of this paragraph is:
- a. Self-mutilation
- b. Acquisition of bodily decorations
- c. Decorations

Answer (a), "Self-mutilation," is a paragraph detail and too specific to be a topic. Answer (c), "Decorations," does not quite tell what the paragraph is about when you ask the question "Who or what is the paragraph about?" It is still too broad to be a topic. Answer (b) is the correct answer to the question "Who or what is the paragraph about?" *Acquisition*

the design of its elevator (by the American Elisha Otis), which at the lowest level had to ascend in a curve. (Adams 769)

1. _____ What is the best topic for this example?
   a. the magnificent Eiffel Tower
   b. the beauty of art
   c. the work of Alexandre-Gustave Eiffel

2. _____ Write the number of the sentence that states the main idea or topic sentence.

D. Journalism

1. It is impossible to write for the public unless you understand what you are writing about. 2. Comprehension precedes clarity. 3. You cannot "be wholly clear about something you don't understand," says John Kenneth Galbraith, the Harvard economist whose books and articles about what is called "the dismal science" of economics are models of clarity. (Mencher 144)

1. _____ What is the best topic for this example?
   a. writing for the public
   b. writing and comprehension
   c. the wisdom of John Kenneth Galbraith

2. __1__ Write the number of the sentence that states the main idea or topic sentence.

E. Business

1. The successful salesperson is an individual who loves selling, finds it exciting, and is strongly convinced that the product being sold offers something of great value. 2. Of the eight work characteristics for sales success, love of selling is clearly number one. 3. Love is at the center of success. 4. It has been said that if you find a job you love, you will never work again. (Futrell 20)

1. _____ What is the best topic for this example?
   a. the love of selling
   b. how to be a good salesperson
   c. finding a job you love

2. __2__ Write the number of the sentence that states the main idea or topic sentence.

Placement of the Stated Main Idea

You have learned that the main idea or topic sentence is the most important part of a paragraph. It is essential that the author's main idea or topic sentence states the general topic and something about the topic. Now that you know the three characteristics of the main idea, the question becomes *Where is it located?* The answer to the question is that it may be found anywhere in the paragraph, or it may even be unstated (you will learn about this in a later chapter).

Stated Main Idea at the Beginning

Most often, the main idea or topic sentence appears as the first sentence of a paragraph. The base of an equilateral triangle below illustrates how an author might use *deductive reasoning,* moving from a stated main idea or topic sentence that is supported by specific details. Remember that, like the hub of a wheel, the paragraph has only one main idea. The rest of the paragraph contains the details.

Main Idea

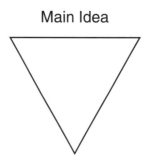

Read the following paragraph and write the number of the sentence that contains the main idea. Remember to check for all three characteristics of the main idea.

The Benefits of Walking

1. Walking is highly underrated as a pastime. 2. It gives us needed exercise. 3. It helps reduce stress. 4. Walking also allows us to view our surroundings "up close and personal"—not just in passing, from a distance, from behind the thick glass of a car window.

The main idea is _____.

Sentence #1, *Walking is highly underrated as a pastime,* is the main idea. All of the sentences in this paragraph tell why walking is a great activity. Only one sentence states the main idea.

Stated Main Idea at the End

The main idea or topic sentence can be located at the end of a paragraph. The upside-down equilateral triangle below illustrates how an author might use *inductive reasoning,* moving from specific details and concluding with a general statement. An author may choose this method in order to stress the main idea or topic sentence in the conclusion, just when the reader stops reading. Remember that,

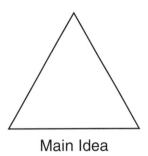

Main Idea

like the hub of a wheel, the paragraph has only one main idea. The rest of the paragraph contains the details.

Read the following paragraph and write the number of the sentence that contains the main idea. Remember to check for all three characteristics of the main idea.

The Importance of Literacy Volunteers

1. John Harris was illiterate until the age of 50. 2. The fact that Harris couldn't read made him feel inferior—even with his own children. 3. Finally, he reached out to literacy volunteers, and, slowly but surely, he learned to read. 4. It's impossible to underestimate the importance of literacy volunteers; with their help, people like John Harris can change their lives.

The main idea (topic sentence) is _____.

In this paragraph, the first three sentences provide background details. However, only the last sentence, *"It's impossible to underestimate the importance of literacy volunteers; with their help, people like John Harris can change their lives,"* states the main idea.

Stated Main Idea in the Middle

Sometimes the main idea or topic sentence is found in the middle of a paragraph. The diamond figure below illustrates the placement of the main idea or topic sentence in the middle of a paragraph. The author may want the main idea or topic sentence in the middle of the paragraph to introduce the general topic with an eye-catching introduction or provide some background details. Remember that, like the hub of a wheel, the paragraph has only one main idea. The rest of the paragraph contains the details.

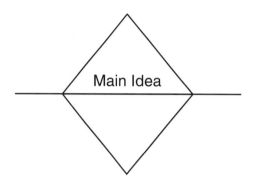

Main Idea

Read the following paragraph and write the number of the sentence that contains the main idea or topic sentence. Remember to check for all three characteristics of the main idea.

Names in the Backyard

1. How do we identify what's growing in our own backyards? 2. Some good ways to identify foliage are to consult books, call the local garden society, or simply ask a local gardener. 3. I used to call my arborvitae "that pretty green tree." 4. Now that I know its name, I actually take a greater interest in what's back there.

The main idea (topic sentence) is _____.

In this paragraph, the first sentence poses a question. A question is *not* the main idea. But, the answer to the question *is* the main idea. Therefore, the second sentence, *"Some good ways to identify foliage are to consult books, call the local garden society, or simply ask a local gardener,"* is the main idea because it states the topic (*identifying foliage*) and something about the topic (*ways to identify foliage*).

NOTE: This paragraph illustrates another important point about the main idea. While not always understanding the meaning of all of the words in this paragraph (e.g., "foliage" [greenery] or "arborvitae" [a type of shrub]) may be frustrating, it is NOT necessary to understand the meaning of every single word in order to identify the main idea. Remember that once you understand the main idea, you will have a basic understanding of just about *anything* you read!

Stated Main Idea at the Beginning and End

Sometimes an author repeats the main idea or topic sentence at the beginning and at the end of a paragraph. And in an essay, it is common for an author to state the main idea or topic sentence in the introduction and then repeat it using different wording in the conclusion. The chart above indicates this type of organization.

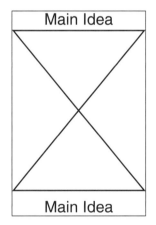

Read the following paragraph and write the number of the sentence that contains the main idea or topic sentence. Remember to check for all three characteristics of the main idea.

Reading to Children

1. The importance of reading to children cannot be over-rated. 2. Parents who read to their children are actually showing them an appreciation for the written word while introducing them to a world of fantasy and adventure. 3. Indirectly, these parents are also indicating that they themselves value the process of reading as an enjoyable and thought-provoking activity. 4. Often, reading tightens

the bonds between parent and child during this "special time" together. 5. Finally, this experience is a motivating factor for children to learn to read on their own. 6. By all accounts, reading to children certainly has benefits.

The main idea (topic sentence) is _____.

In this paragraph, the main idea or topic sentence is at the beginning. *"The importance of reading to children cannot be overrated"* states the topic (*reading to children*) and tells something about the topic (*reading to children cannot be overrated*). The last sentence, *"By all accounts, reading to children certainly has benefits,"* is also considered the main idea or topic sentence. The concluding sentence is a rewording of the first sentence, and expresses the same main idea or topic sentence. The other sentences in the paragraph function as details because they provide specific reasons for the importance of reading to children.

Exercise 7.4 Practice Locating the Main Idea in Textbooks

Directions: Now that you know where to find the main idea or topic sentence, try to identify its location in the following college textbook selections.

A. Public Speaking

1. While informative and persuasive speeches are the most frequent types, there are occasions when a speech must serve other purposes. 2. When you need to entertain an audience, as in an after-dinner talk, your remarks should be light and diverting; any elements of information or persuasion should be gracefully woven into the fabric of entertainment. 3. One device for an entertaining speech is to string together anecdotes, examples, or quotations on a single theme. 4. Extended narratives or descriptions also can be entertaining. (Gregory 408)

The main idea or topic sentence is __1_____.

B. Composition

1. Good descriptive writing also works this way. 2. The point is not to give an exhaustive list of details but to zero in with a discerning eye on the most telling features of a subject, what is most distinctive, most revealing, most pertinent to the purpose at hand. 3. This is much like sketching. 4. You draw just enough particulars to convey what's special about the subject and allow the reader to fill the rest. (Costanzo 136)

The main idea or topic sentence is __1 2_____.

C. Physics

1. Although w   have an intuitive feel for what hot and cold mean, putting that impr   n into words can be hard. 2. Try it before you read on. How would y   efine the term hot? 3. Even our senses can mislead us. 4. The pain that   feel when we touch something very hot can be hard to distinguish fr   e pain that we feel when we touch a very cold object. 5. A metal bloc   ls colder to the touch than a wooden block, even though the two bloc   ay have the same temperature. 6. In the end, temperature measure   t is a comparison, and the comparative terms hotter and colder have   e meaning than hot or cold themselves. *(Griffith 188-89)*

The main ide   topic sentence is __4 6_____.

D. Econom

1. In the sh   un, outsourcing clearly worsens the U.S. employment outlook. 2. But   e's a lot more to the story. 3. To begin with, the total number of outsour   obs averages less than 300,000 per year. 4. That amounts to only .002   U.S. jobs, and only 3-5 percent of total U.S. unemployment. 5. So ever   e worst case, outsourcing can't be a major explanation for U.S. unem   nent. *(Schiller 128)*

The main i   or topic sentence is ___5_____.

E. Theate

1. In the   d States, several people who were performers or directors with the Gro   eater in the 1930s went on to become important teachers of acting.   se included Sanford Meisner, Stella Adler, Robert Lewis, Lee Strasbe   d Uta Hagen. 3. Strasberg for many years headed the Actors Studio i   York, where a number of prominent film and stage stars studied, inc   Marlon Brando, James Dean, Paul Newman, Marilyn Monroe, and Al   o. 4. Uta Hagen, a well-known actress as well as a teacher, has wri   wo books, Respect for Acting and A Challenge for the Actor, which   quired reading in many actor training programs. *(Wilson 133)*

The mai   a or topic sentence is ___1_____.

F. Hea

1. Ob   ve sleep apnea is a potentially dangerous condition; occasionally, i   en fatal. 2. It is frequently seen in association with high blood press   nd it can increase the risk of heart disease and stroke. 3. Oxygen satur   of the blood decreases and levels of carbon dioxide rise when a perso   os breathing, increasing the likelihood that heart and blood vessel c   nalities may occur. 4. If sufficient oxygen is not delivered to the brai   th may occur during sleep. *(Teague et al. 142)*

The m   dea or topic sentence is ___1_____.

Another Note about Main Idea

Now that you understand that the main idea may be located anywhere in a paragraph, see if you can find the main idea in the following group of sentences.

1. World peace is an important issue. 2. It might rain today. 3. Sarah's mother has Alzheimer's. 4. I have gum on the bottom of my shoe.

You probably realize that finding the main idea or topic sentence here is impossible. The topic sentence is neither stated nor implied. The series of sentences bear no discernible relationship to one another, so this is *not* a paragraph, and finding the main idea is impossible. This might work in poetry, but in ordinary prose, you must establish a clear connection between the sentences in your paragraphs. However, *every well-constructed paragraph includes a main idea or topic sentence.* If you can identify the main idea, then you can comprehend the meaning of *any* paragraph.

Identifying the Thesis Statement

You have learned that each paragraph contains a main idea or topic sentence. In longer passages, composed of more than one paragraph, the main idea or topic sentence is identified as the **thesis statement.** It may be located in the same way you find the topic sentence, by identifying the three characteristics we have reviewed. Thesis statements may be found in research papers, newspaper articles, essays, and textbook selections.

> The **thesis statement,** found in selections of more than one paragraph, is the main idea or topic sentence the author conveys about a topic. It is the sentence that states the topic and says something about the topic. It contains all three characteristics of the main idea.

The following excerpt was written by the columnist Anna Quindlen, and first appeared in the *New York Times* in July 2000. Which sentence do you think is the thesis statement?

Introduction to "Aha! Caught You Reading"

1. The next time someone talks about the narrow interests of kids today, how they attend only to the raucous cry of the computer calling across a stretch of cable to its mate the Internet, remember this week. 2. Remember how the boys and girls of America went gaga over a book, a real old-fashioned black-letters-on-white-paper book, how they waited in line for it at the mall, cradled it to their bony little chests and carried it into their bedrooms, slipped into its imaginary world with big eyes and open minds as children have done almost since Gutenberg put the pedal to the metal of the printing press.

3. There's nothing so wonderful in America that someone can't create a kind of Calvary out of it, and so it is with the publication of the fourth Harry Potter book. 4. It is called Harry Potter and the Goblet of Fire, *but it could just as well have been called* Harry Potter and the Lingerie Sale at Saks *for*

all the difference a title would have made in its reception. 5. Bookstores stayed open after midnight on opening day to accommodate the publisher's embargo; children dressed up like Harry and the rest of the gang at the Hogwarts School. 6. And this was characterized as the triumph of hype, and the legerdemain of marketing. 7. But hype and marketing go only so far when a twelve-year-old settles down on the sofa for the long haul with a book longer than Crime and Punishment. 8. What remains is wonderfully retro: the beauty of reading for pleasure, and its enduring role in the life of the mind. (Quindlen, Loud and Clear 239–40)

© Peter Hansen, 2010. Used under license from Shutterstock, Inc.

The thesis statement is sentence _____.

Sentences #1 and #2 in the first paragraph set the introduction to the selection, defying the notion that children aren't readers by their enthusiastic response to the new Harry Potter book. In the next paragraph, in sentences #3 through #5, the author provides further details of how bookstores and children welcomed the new book. Sentence #6 is a detail that functions as a transition and focuses on the individual child's reaction to reading a good book. The last sentence, *What remains is wonderfully retro: the beauty of reading for pleasure, and its enduring role in the life of the mind*, is the thesis statement because the author conveys the idea that children have, and still have, a love for reading. The thesis statement is the sentence that is the writer's main idea or topic sentence. Therefore, it states the topic (*reading*), and it says something about the topic (*What remains is wonderfully retro: the beauty of reading for pleasure, and its enduring role in the life of the mind*). You may also write the thesis statement in your own words. It might read, Children will always love to read a good book.

Practice Locating the Thesis Statement in Textbooks

7.5 *Exercise*

Directions: Read the following psychology textbook selection on "Emotional Development," identify the thesis statement, and write it in your own words.

EMOTIONAL DEVELOPMENT

Emotional development in infancy is not an easy area to research. Since infants cannot verbalize how they feel, psychologists investigate emotional development on the basis of facial expressions, physiological responses, or the sounds infants make in response to some stimulus.

What Emotions Do Infants Show?

Many parents argue that their very young infants show identifiable and definite emotions almost from birth. They are correct. Young infants possess a limited number of discrete emotions (Izard, 1993; Malatesta et al., 1989). These specific emotions are innate, and include interest, disgust, physical distress, and a precursor of surprise, called a startle (see Table 7.1). Each of these emotions can be elicited at will. Novelty and human faces trigger interest, and bad-tasting foods result in disgust. The social smile is elicited at three weeks by a high-pitched human voice and at six weeks by the human face. Anger, surprise, and joy emerge in the next four months or so; sadness about the same time; and fear between five and seven months (Izard & Malatesta, 1987). The early distress emotion differentiates into a number of other emotions including sadness, fear, and anger, by 6 months or so. Anger has been observed as early as 3 to 4 months of age (Lemerese & Dodge, 2000), sadness by as early as 2½ months (Izard et al., 1995), and joy by 2½ months when infants are playing with their mothers (Izard et al., 1995). These emotions are referred to as **primary emotions** because they appear early in life, can be easily recognized from facial expressions, and are found in infants all around the world.

primary emotions
emotions that appear early in infancy, are innately determined, can be recognized through facial expressions, and reflect a subjective experience.

Adults agree on the emotional expressions infants show (Emde et al., 1985). Both trained and untrained college students have no difficulty identifying infant emotional responses to a variety of events, ranging from happiness during playful interactions to the pain from inoculations, to the expressions of surprise and sadness (Izard et al., 1980). These emotions result from biological programming (Izard, 1994).

Pleasure/Joy

Newborns show expressions that look like smiles, but these expressions occur during sleep or when infants are drowsy, and they are probably involuntary reactions (Lamb, 1988). By 3 to 6 weeks, however, infants show voluntary smiling in the waking state. This smile is shown not only to social stimuli, such as voices, but also to nonsocial stimuli, such as bells or a bull's-eye. Gradually, smiles become more limited to social stimuli. Infants also smile when they have mastered an action, reflecting pleasure or satisfaction.

At 3 months or so, infants smile at familiar events and faces they recognize and there is no doubt the smile is a sign of pleasure (Lewis, 1993). After four or five months, the frequency of smiling becomes dependent on the infant's family environment. Infant smiling that is reinforced with attention will increase in frequency (Etzel & Gewirtz, 1967). The social nature of the smile continues to develop in infancy. Older infants smile more when they are smiling at someone who is attentive

table 7.1 Infant Emotions: Age Range of Development	
Emotion	**Age (Months)**
Distress/Discomfort/Pain	Birth
Interest/Excitement	Birth
Disgust	Birth–3
Sadness	Birth–3
Pleasure/Delight/Joy	2–7
Surprise	3–6
Anger	4–7
Wariness/Fear	4–9
Rage	7–18
Affection/Love	18–36
Empathy/Sympathy	18–36
Embarrassment	24–36
Guilt	24–36
Pride	24–36
Shame	24–36

SOURCES: Izard & Malatesta, 1987; Lewis, 1993; Sroufe, 1996

than when the other person is not looking at them (Jones & Raag, 1989).

Infants living in every culture smile. In fact, a smile is interpreted as a positive expression all around the world, and the development of the smile is basically the same in every society. Blind infants smile in response to social stimuli at about the same time as sighted children, even though they have not seen a smile (Kaplan, 1996).

The smile, then, begins as an inborn response, but it soon evolves from an undifferentiated response to internal stimuli, to a response that is attached to social stimuli. Its frequency can be increased through reinforcement. If infants are rewarded for smiling by being picked up, talked to, and handled, the frequency of their smiling increases. The smile contributes to the establishment and maintenance of the infant-caregiver relationship, as most parents take pleasure in interpreting their child's smile as a positive response to their own activity, and the parent's actions are thus reinforced by the child (Rochat, Querido, & Striano, 1999).

The infant's smile is a powerful communicator of emotion. Image © Johanna Goodyear. 2008. Used under license from Shutterstock, Inc.

Anger

Anger develops between about 3 to 4 months to 7 months, and becomes more common in the later half of the first year (Snow & McGaha, 2003). Infants show their anger through crying and facial expression, as well as intense and increased motor activity. In the toddler stage, anger is expressed by kicking and throwing things, and after age 2 or so, hitting and pushing. Angry verbalizations clearly reflect the child's anger. Some anger may be a response to frustration. **Frustration** is experienced when a person's goal-directed activity is blocked. Frustration leads to anger. As the child develops, anger becomes more directed at a source, rather than being just a general reaction to a situation.

An early cause of anger is physical restraint that inhibits an infant's movements. Infants may also experience frustration when not being able to reach a goal, such as a toy. Later, anger is shown in more complex situations, such as being told to go to bed when the child does not want to, or being told that he can't have a particular toy to play with now (Sternberg & Camps, 1990).

frustration
an experience in which a person's goal is blocked by an obstacle. Frustration leads to anger.

Stranger Anxiety

Some time in the second half of the first year, parents are surprised by the way their infants react to kindly strangers. In the past, the baby showed curiosity, but now the child may show fear, manifested by crying and agitation. This is called **stranger anxiety**. Until about 4 months of age, infants smile even at strangers, but after that they do so less and less (Bronson, 1968). Most children go through a period in which they react with fear to strangers and even to relatives they do not see regularly. The stage usually comes between about 7 and 10 months, and may last through a good portion of the second year (Lewis & Rosenblum, 1975).

Some studies question whether this fear of strangers is inevitable. When an adult female was allowed to interact with infants and their mothers for ten minutes before making any attempt to pick up the babies, and the mothers acted in a friendly manner toward the other woman, the infants were neither fearful nor upset, and responded positively to the stranger (Rheingold & Eckerman, 1973). Infant response to strangers depends on the stranger and the context (Durkin, 1995). Infants show less or no fear of other children, perhaps because of the similarity in size (Lewis & Brooks-Gunn, 1972). Female strangers produce less fear than male strangers (Skarin, 1977). If the mother is present and the stranger appears in a familiar place, such as the child's home, less anxiety is generated than when the setting is unfamiliar. In addition, when infants are allowed to investigate the situation on their own, they do not always show stranger anxiety. It is wrong, then, to conclude that stranger anxiety is inevitable or that the appearance or lack of stranger anxiety indicates any problem. Rather, we can say that whether a child shows stranger anxiety depends upon the situation and a number of factors.

stranger anxiety
the anxiety generated when a stranger approaches a young child. Stranger anxiety arises in the later half of the first year and lasts through a good part of the second year.

Separation Anxiety

Separation anxiety begins at about 8 or 9 months and peaks at between 12 and 16 months (Metcalf, 1979). It can be found throughout the preschool period in some children, although its intensity

separation anxiety
fear of being separated from caregivers beginning at 8 or 9 months and peaking at between 12 and 16 months.

lessens with age. Some separations are predictable, as in the case of the mother who every weekday morning takes her child to the day care center. When the child can anticipate predictable separations and knows that mother will return, is familiar with the environment, and is well acquainted with the substitute caregivers, the child will not show much, if any, separation anxiety when the mother leaves (Maccoby, 1980). Unpredictable separations, such as when a child must enter the hospital, are different. The child is now presented with a novel situation in an unfamiliar environment and with strange people.

A child's reaction to any separation depends on the child's age, the familiarity of the situation, and the child's previous experiences. If the child has familiar toys or a companion (such as a sibling), or is left with a substitute caregiver for whom he or she feels an attachment, separation anxiety will be reduced.

Even the possibility that the mother will leave can be enough to cause some problems, especially in the unpredictable situation. For example, when the mother begins to pack for a trip, the child, in anticipating the loss, may start to cry and cling to her. Any increase in the risk of a separation can trigger some anxiety (Bowlby, 1982).

Separation anxiety may also be a function of temperament. The brain wave patterns of ten-month-old infants who cried both before and after separation from their mothers were different from the brain wave patterns of infants who did not cry (Davidson & Fox, 1989). These differences may demonstrate that reactions to separation are at least partly based on variations in temperament.

Both separation anxiety and stranger anxiety may have survival value, in that they keep the child closer to parents. It is possible to take an evolutionary approach to understanding why they occur. Obviously, perceptual abilities and cognitive growth are also involved, as children begin to differentiate between those people they know and those they do not, and to prefer the company of caregivers and familiar people.

Empathy

Hearing someone cry often has an emotional impact on us. This is true for infants as well. When newborns are exposed to tape-recorded cries of other neonates, the infants respond by crying (Simper, 1971). They are more sensitive to the cries of a 5-day-old neonate than to either a cry engineered through a computer or the cry of a 5.5-month-old infant. When one group of newborns listened to their own cries and another group heard the cries of another newborn, only the group of newborns exposed to the cries of another newborn decreased their sucking on a pacifier and showed facial expressions of distress (Dondi, Simion, & Caltran, 1999).

Could such **empathy** be innate? It is a possibility. When neonates who were either crying or calm listened to their own cries or those of other neonates, they demonstrated a remarkable degree of empathy (Martin & Clark, 1982). Infants who were originally calm cried when they heard the sounds of another neonate crying. Crying infants continued to cry when exposed to the cries of other infants, but stopped when they heard recordings of their own cry. Calm infants, hearing their own cries, did not begin to cry. When newborns were presented with tapes of a crying chimpanzee, an 11-month-old child, and another newborn, those exposed to the cry of another newborn cried, but the newborns did not cry when exposed to the cry of an 11-month-old or the chimpanzee. The researchers conclude that neonates as young as 18 hours can distinguish among their own cries, the cry of another infant or an older child, and that of a chimpanzee, and they will respond differently to these cries. Neonates seem to have an empathy that is astounding for their age.

Such reactions are an early and rudimentary form of empathy, but the further development of empathy requires cognitive advancements (see Chapter 9). Before about 1 year, infants are empathically aroused without the cognitive abilities that will later be important in experiencing empathy. They do not see themselves as distinct from others.

As children mature and become aware of themselves as distinct from others, they know when another person is in distress, and may become very distressed. They may feel compassion, with a desire to help (Azar, 1997; Hoffman, 1984). However, they assume that the other person is feeling the same way as they are. For example, an 18-month-old will get his mother to comfort his friend who is crying, although the other child's mother is available. Since the first child is accustomed to being comforted by his own mother, he assumes that his friend would also be comforted by the first child's mother and doesn't try to get the other child's mother to comfort him. Empathy continues to develop as the ability to take another person's point of view increases throughout childhood.

empathy
an emotional response resulting from understanding another person's state or condition

Write the thesis statement in your own words: 霸

Infants are unable to ~~speak~~ speak words, so they use facial and body language to get attention.

Locating the Thesis Statement in Textbooks 7.6 *Exercise*

Directions: The next excerpt is from a college history textbook. When you finish reading, write the thesis statement in your own words.

9

The Impending Crisis and the Challenge to Slavery (1850–1860)

With the continued agitation over slavery, the nation began to realize political and judicial remedies were only temporary solutions to a highly volatile issue. Moreover, individual acts of protest and violence escalated fears over the future of slavery in the states most dependent upon the institution. Northern white abolitionists viewed slavery as a moral wrong that, if not abolished, would stain the reputation of the democracy, retard cultural and technological development, or bring about a divine wrath for the continued immoral practice. Black abolitionists, on the other hand, began to increasingly call for militant action with regard to aiding fugitives and fostering resistance. Indeed, both white and black abolitionists had become more violent in their language and actions. The violent clashes between anti-slavery and pro-slavery factions in the 1850s only served to confirm their fears that there was a wide-spread northern conspiracy to abolish slavery. Despite this assumption, a considerable number of people in the North and Northwest regarded the slavery issue with passing interest. Indeed, many were adverse to the possibility of newly freed migrants moving into their states. Nonetheless, the issue over the expansion and preservation of slavery grew more heated. It was the growing agitation and anxiety that eventually lead to disunion and war. With the election of Abraham Lincoln, an anti-slavery Republican, states in the deep South seceded, and America spiraled along the path to civil war.

The coming of the Civil War was not a surprise to most. Growing sectional tensions and openly violent contests informed the people of the possibility of disunion and war. In document one, Henry Stanton writes a letter that accurately predicts the outcome of Abraham Lincoln's election and the actions that slaves would take as a result of the disruption of war. Document two highlights the legal punishments meted out to those who interfered, by aiding fugitive slaves, with the property rights of slaveholders. It provides an insight into the sacrifices that abolitionists were willing to make for their cause. Document three provides some insight into how slaveholders were willing to justify slavery. In fact, the document, which is an excerpt from a newspaper article, encourages the kidnapping of free blacks as a means of sustaining the "Peculiar Institution." Document four and document five provide examples of the violent clashes that occurred when kidnappers, federal marshals, or slaveholders attempted to recover fugitive slaves. In document four, a Maryland slaveholder is killed while attempting, with the help of federal marshals, to recover fugitives slaves hiding in Christiana, Pennsylvania. In document five, Frederick Douglass compares the killing of a bounty hunter with the patriots' fight for freedom during the Revolutionary War. In essence, he states that abolitionists and fugitive slaves are justified in killing those who attempt to return fugitive slaves to bondage. The scholarly essay, "In the Shadow of Old John Brown: Insurrection Anxiety and Confederate Mobilization, 1861–1863," highlights the growing fear of slave revolts and northern conspiracies. Furthermore, the essay shows that the South became more militaristic as a direct result of fear and paranoia. Ironically, however, it was the mobilization of non-slaveholding whites for the protection of slavery and the exemption from military duty of overseers and wealthy slaveholders that greatly hurt the Confederacy's war efforts.

Write the thesis statement in your own words: _____.

Details

Every paragraph contains the three elements of topic, main idea or topic sentence, and details. While the topic is the general subject, often located in the title, the main idea or topic sentence is the sentence that states the topic and says something about the topic, and the **details** are what make up the rest of the paragraph. In the wheel analogy, the details may be considered the "spokes" of the wheel. The spokes take up most of the wheel. Similarly, the details in a paragraph are sentences that take up most of the paragraph and help support the main idea.

> The **details** provide support for the main idea through explanation or examples.

In order to locate the details, you must return to the reporter's questions: *who, what, why, when, where,* and *how.* While the main idea will usually provide a basic answer to some of these questions, the details add more information about them.

There are two types of details, **major** and **minor**, and they play different roles in the paragraph.

Major details provide direct support, or explanation, for the main idea. **Minor details** provide support for major details, or add interest. Just as the main idea is **more general** than the major details, major details are **more general** than minor details.

Major and minor details can be found in different forms, or *rhetorical modes.* You will learn more about these forms in the next chapter.

Read the "Getting Rid of Clutter" paragraph. Then locate the major and minor details.

© sharpen, 2010. Used under license from Shutterstock, Inc.

Getting Rid of Clutter

1. Getting rid of clutter does not have to be an overwhelming task if you follow the right method. 2. First, organize objects. 3. Take a close look at your garage, for instance, and place items into three piles. 4. These piles would include (1) items you currently use; (2) items that have some value, but which you no longer use; 3) items you can throw away. 5. Hold onto and neatly stack those items that you still use. 6. The second pile may be saved for a garage sale. 7. Items you currently use might include tires and bicycles. 8. The items that have value for others might be old volley balls or tennis rackets. 9. Items like old basketballs, broken air pumps, or boxes of rusty nails could be thrown out. 10. With a neat, well-organized home, you will feel calm and happy.

Circle the topic.

Underline the main idea or topic sentence.

The major details are sentences _____.

The minor details are sentences _____.

Locating Topic, Main Idea, and Details   7.9 *Exercise*

Directions: Read the following paragraphs. Write the topic in your own words, underline the main idea or topic sentence, and list each detail next to a number.

A.

1. <u>People often learn from their mistakes.</u> 2. When a child burns his finger, the youngster learns not to get too close to a fire. 3. Similarly, when a teenager fails to study for an exam and does poorly, he or she will be sure to study for the next test. 4. An adult who makes poor investment choices causing income to deplete learns to be more astute with financial decisions in the future. 6. Such debacles <u>may be devastating, but often serve as lessons for success.</u>

Topic __Mistakes__

1. _____
2. _____
3. _____

B.

1. Sierra Leone, a West African country, is a part of CEDAE (Convention on the Elimination of all Forms of Discrimination against Women), and it is thus bound to the provisions of this convention regarding women's rights and discrimination and violence against girls and women. 2. <u>Yet, women are routinely hit and beaten at home.</u> 3. In this country, as in many others, this type of violence is often culturally accepted and not criminalized, and women and men come to believe that the women deserve to be hit. 4. Police authorities have a lax attitude toward this type of routine violence. 5. <u>Depending on the context and the severity of injuries, a beating can be recognized as a crime, but even then, the accused may never be punished.</u> (Shaw 47)

Topic __Beating woman__

1. _____
2. _____
3. _____

C.

1. <u>Relationships among boys are quite different than those among girls.</u> 2. Boys tend to open up to one another only when participating in an activity, like playing ball or a board game. 3. On the other hand, girls may get together and openly discuss their feelings without having to participate in any sort of activity. 4. In effect, girls are more language-centered than boys.

Topic __Relationships with boys and girls__

1. _____
2. _____

D.

1. The German shepherd's brown eyes rolled toward us, as if imploring. 2. I placed my cheek against her coarse gray hair, and felt my tears drop heavily against the animal. 3. I couldn't bear to leave her one last time, nor could I stay and watch the needle pierce through the rubbery pink skin beneath. Still, I heard her yelp, a mixture of fear and surprise, one last time, as I closed the door without looking back.

Topic ~~Puting your German shephard~~ to sleep.

1. _____

2. _____

E.

1. Michael Jackson was an icon who is best known for his incredible talent. 2. He possessed a unique melodic voice and an ingrained ability to dance, even as a young boy. 3. Yet his personal life was tortured, for his father was a stern taskmaster. 4. His appearance evolved drastically, and the "man with the glove" soon became instantly recognizable. 5. His relationships were rocked by scandal, and so was his tragic death from an accidental drug overdose. 6. Above all, Michael Jackson was a man who was misunderstood.

Topic _Understanding Michael Jackson_

1. _____

2. _____

F.

1. The evidence, at this point, demonstrates that concern for video game violence is reasonable and that it may have different effects, depending upon the background and personality of those who play them. 2. Violent video games, like violent television programs, can increase aggression (Anderson, 2004). 3. Special concern is raised for those who play video games for a great deal of time, as well as young players who may be impressionable. 4. There is also room for concern for heavy players where game-playing may substitute for exercise or family interaction. (Kaplan 455)

Topic _Video game vidance_

1. _____

2. _____

3. _____

4. _____

5. _____

6. _____

G.

> 1. Water from the soil enters a plant through its root hairs, which reach down into the particles of the soil. 2. A thin layer of water surrounds most particles of soil. 3. This water supply is called capillary water and provides water to the roots of the plant during a dry season.

Topic _____ Capilary water _____

1. _____

2. _____

H.

> 1. People are generally classified into two categories of effectiveness. 2. "Morning" people are usually most alert during the early hours of the day, while "night" people tend to be at their best when the sun is down. 3. "Morning" people living with "night" people may result in situations that lead to conflict. 4. Those in this predicament will certainly have to learn the art of compromise!

Topic _____ Two types of people _____

1. _____

2. _____

3. _____

Writing the Topic, Main Idea, and Details   7.10   *Exercise*

Directions: Read the following paragraphs. Write the topic and the main idea or topic sentence *in your own words.*

> 1. Psychologists have determined that color can influence our emotional state. Blue is often placed in bedrooms because of its tranquil, calming effect. On the other hand, a red environment stimulates anxiety or anger. Yellow puts people in a happy frame of mind. In general, it is a good idea to paint a baby's room in bright, primary colors since they stimulate brain activity.

Topic: _____ Colors affect our mood _____

Main Idea: _____ Depending on the certain color in your room, can depend on what mood your in.

2. *For various reasons, many couples are choosing to marry later in life. Some simply do not have the financial resources to sustain a marriage. Others believe that they need more time to mature and "find themselves" before committing to another individual. Still other singles would like to enjoy themselves by "playing the field" before they settle down.*

Topic: _Marry later on in life_

Main Idea: _People have decided to marry later in life for various reasons._

3. *Faking. There's the rub. Tugging at the fringes of my consciousness always is the terror that people are kind to me only because I'm a cripple. My mother almost shattered me once, with that instinct mothers have— blind, I think, in this case, but unerring nonetheless—for striking blows along the fault-lines of their children's hearts, by telling me, in an attack on my selfishness. "We all have to make allowances for you, of course, because of the way you are." . . . I could bear being called selfish: I am. But I couldn't bear the corroboration that those around me were doing in fact what I'd always suspected them of doing, professing fondness while silently putting up with me because of the way I am. A cripple. I've been a little cracked ever since. (Mairs)*

Topic: _Being cripple_

Main Idea: _Having a problem with fake people_

4. *Certain people become the center of attention not only because they have a particular talent that sets them apart, but also because they have a flamboyant style. Some athletes, for example, shatter records but shy away from the public eye, while others boast of their prowess but fail to accomplish their goals. The select few who possess extraordinary talent and a personality to match are those who attain worldwide fame. Muhammad Ali was such an athlete.*

Topic: _Attitude of ^Athletes to the public_

Main Idea: _Talent and personality help worldwide fame_

5. *For better or worse, the spouse of a candidate can influence the way someone votes. In the 2004 presidential election, Teresa Heinz, the wife of candidate John Kerry, displayed a style that the public often viewed as abrasive and bold, while First Lady Laura Bush was seen as both demure and supportive. Whether this difference was responsible for Kerry's loss, though, is highly unlikely.*

Topic: _Influences of Candidate spouses ~~Spouses the candidates~~_

Main Idea: _Spouses of Candidates_

Can

6. Writer's block is a frustrating phenomenon. The writer may have a productive period of a few weeks or even several months, where words seem to flow like water. But then, for no apparent reason, something mysterious happens. No matter what, the words and ideas refuse to emerge, and no matter how much pacing or pondering is done, nothing happens. The writer begins to wonder if he or she will ever be able to write another word again. And, sadly, some never do.

Topic: _____

Main Idea: _____

7. In search of a refuge, we may perhaps turn to hero-worship. But here we shall get no help, in my opinion. Hero-worship is a dangerous vice, and one of the minor merits of a democracy is that it does not encourage it, or produce that unmanageable type of citizen known as the Great Man. It produces instead different kinds of small men—a much finer achievement. But people who cannot get interested in the variety of life, and cannot make up their own minds, get discontented over this, and they long for a hero to bow down before and to follow blindly. (Forster)

Topic: _____

Main Idea: _____

8. In the distance, the sky sloped down to a dreamy blackness. The gray clouds parted over the face of the moon, which emerged full and golden like a new coin. If one listened carefully, the soft chirps of cicada and tree frogs could be heard complaining in the distance. We children leaned against a calm boulder and listened to the sweet promise of the evening that would soon turn into still another hot summer day. We knew that we would never forget this evening.

Topic: _____

Main Idea: _____

Exercise **7.11** **Locating the Topic Sentence in an Essay**

Olympic champ Muhammad Ali was a fighter in more ways than one. Strong in the ring, he fought his way out of the ghetto by using his unique talent. In the following selection, Elizabeth Wong details her desire to escape her Asian background by immersing herself into American culture. Unlike Ali, though, her escape was something she would later regret.

Directions: The following reading selection has been divided into paragraphs. In your own words, write the main idea or topic sentence for each paragraph. When you finish reading the entire selection, write the thesis in your own words.

The Struggle to Be an All-American Girl

1. It's still there, the Chinese school on Yale Street where my brother and I used to go. Despite the new coat of paint and the high wire fence, the school I knew 10 years ago remains remarkably, stoically the same.

Main Idea: _____

2. Every day at 5 P.M., instead of playing with our fourth- and fifth-grade friends or sneaking out to the empty lot to hunt ghosts and animal bones, my brother and I had to go to Chinese school. No amount of kicking, screaming, or pleading could dissuade my mother, who was solidly determined to have us learn the language of our heritage.

Main Idea: _____

© JupiterImages Corporation

© JupiterImages Corporation

From Los Angeles Times, September 7, 1980 by Elizabeth Wong. Copyright © 1980 by Elizabeth Wong. Reprinted by permission of the Author.

3. Forcibly, she walked us the seven long, hilly blocks from our home to school, depositing our defiant tearful faces before the stern principal. My only memory of him is that he swayed on his heels like a palm tree, and he always clasped his impatient twitching hands behind his back. I recognized him as a repressed maniacal child killer, and knew that if we ever saw his hands we'd be in big trouble.

Main Idea: _____

4. We all sat in little chairs in an empty auditorium. The room smelled like Chinese medicine, an imported faraway mustiness. Like ancient mothballs or dirty closets. I hated that smell. I favored crisp new scents. Like the soft French perfume that my American teacher wore in public school. There was a stage far to the right, flanked by an American flag and the flag of the Nationalist Republic of China, which was also red, white and blue but not as pretty.

Main Idea: _____

5. Although the emphasis at the school was mainly language—speaking, reading, writing—the lessons always began with an exercise in politeness. With the entrance of the teacher, the best student would tap a bell and everyone would get up, kowtow, and chant, "Sing san ho," the phonetic for "How are you, teacher?"

Main Idea: _____

6. Being ten years old, I had better things to learn than ideographs copied painstakingly in lines that ran right to left from the tip of a moc but, a real ink pen that had to be held in an awkward way if blotches were to be avoided. After all, I could do the multiplication tables, name the satellites of Mars, and write reports on "Little Women" and "Black Beauty." Nancy Drew, my favorite book heroine, never spoke Chinese.

Main Idea: _____

7. The language was a source of embarrassment. More times than not, I had tried to disassociate myself from the nagging loud voice that followed me wherever I wandered in the nearby American supermarket outside Chinatown. The voice belonged to my grandmother, a fragile woman in her seventies who could outshout the best of the street vendors. Her humor was raunchy, her Chinese rhythmless, patternless. It was quick, it was loud, it was unbeautiful. It was not like the quiet, lilting romance of French or the gentle refinement of the American South. Chinese sounded pedestrian. Public.

Main Idea: _____

8. My brother was even more fanatical than I about speaking English. He was especially hard on my mother, criticizing her, often cruelly, for her pidgin speech—smatterings of Chinese scattered like chop suey in her conversation. "It's not 'What it is,' Mom," he'd say in exasperation. "It's 'What is it, what is it, what is it!" Sometimes Mom might leave out an occasional "the" or "a," or perhaps a verb of being. He would stop her in mid-sentence: "Say it again, Mom. Say it right." When he tripped over his own tongue, he'd blame it on her: "See, Mom, it's all your fault. You set a bad example."

Main Idea: _____

9. What infuriated my mother most was when my brother cornered her on her consonants, especially "r." My father had played a cruel joke on Mom by assigning her an American name that her tongue wouldn't allow her to say. No matter how hard she tried, "Ruth" always ended up "Luth" or "Roof."

Main Idea: _____

10. After two years of writing with a moc but and reciting words with multiples of meanings, I finally was granted a cultural divorce. I was permitted to stop Chinese school. I thought of myself as multicultural. I preferred tacos to egg rolls; I enjoyed Cinco de Mayo more than Chinese New Year. At last, I was one of you; I wasn't one of them. Sadly, I still am. (Wong)

Main Idea: _____

Thesis Statement: _____

Creating Your SQ3R Cards

SQ3R cards are a study system to help you successfully comprehend what you are reading. As you read the longer reading selection, you will actively interact with the text before you read, while you read, and after you read.

"S": Survey the Reading Selection

- What is the topic?

_____

_____

_____

- What do I already know?

_____

_____

_____

- What is my purpose for reading?

_____

_____

_____

"Q": Turn a Section Title into a Question
Don't forget to turn key statements into questions as you read.

_____

_____

_____

_____

1st "R": Read

- Make predictions.

_____

_____

- Retrieve prior knowledge.

_____

_____

- State confusing ideas.

_____

_____

2nd "R": Recite

- Write the main point of this selection.
- Don't forget to annotate and take notes in the margin.

_____

_____

3rd "R": Review

- Recall what you have learned.
- React to what you have read.

_____

_____

_____

_____

_____

Comprehending Longer Selections   7.13

More Practice Understanding Main Idea

Step One: Before Reading

Vocabulary in Context Practice

Directions: Choose one of the following words to complete each of the sentences below. Use each word only once. Be sure to pay attention to the context clues provided.

g—enthusiastic, excited
ed—suspected, supposed
dote—a tale, short story
—excessive pride, arrogance
ash, shine
ly—without a doubt
m—suspension, pause
offe—offered for acceptance
oflig—wasteful
erat—it up with, endure

The a_____ _____ reapplies her makeup before going on stage for each p___mance.

was _____ _____ when my favorite actor appeared on stage.

I was _____ _____ a role in the sitcom I would be elated.

e _____ animal activist was seen wearing a fur coat.

e advertising g____ Times Square demonstrates how _____ we e with electrica___ er.

anging people's ior can occur when _____ is eliminated.

7. library placed a _____ _____ on the number of times we can take the same book.

8. en I looked down, I imr____ tely saw the _____ of the knife on able.

9. Jan could no longer _____ the neighbor's loud music, so she called the police.

10. Billy told such a funny _____ that it kept us laughing for hours.

Freewrite
In your journal, write about a time when the lights went out and how you reacted.

Step Two: Read the Selection
Note: As you read the following selection, concentrate and practice the steps of SQ3R. Remove the SQ3R card from the book and complete it as you read.

Moral conviction accounts for Muhammad Ali's decision to be a pacifist. The following article discusses another issue relating to ethics—preserving our environment.

A Shock to the System
By Anna Quindlen

© JupiterImages Corporation

1. Whenever you run into a bear out here in the country, someone will invariably ask if it was big. I never really know how to answer. All bears appear large to me, even the cubs. Something about the slope of the forehead, the glint of the eyes, the teeth and the claws. I don't take the time to assess relative size because I am so agog at the sheer bearness of the thing. Unlike Harrison Ford, a bear is not a creature you peer at in passing, thinking, "is that really . . . ?" It has a certain unmistakability.

2. The bears have become yet another species on the list of inconvenient animals in this part of America, right up there with the trash-picker possums and, of course, those loathsome shrubbery eaters, the deer. My favorite bear anecdote was the animal accused of getting physical after a man had proffered a bagel to get the bear to stick around for a photograph. The bear wanted more. What I want is an answer to this question: who gives a 250-pound wild animal baked goods?

3. The way in which modern people interact with their animal counterparts is one of those things that make us look as though our evolution took place on a bell curve and it's currently on the downside. Most of us now act toward native creatures the way our ancestors once acted toward Native Americans: we know that they were here first so we're willing

to tolerate them as long as they don't demand to share when we build unattractive structures atop their former homes.

4. If they don't cooperate, we slaughter them.

5. Ultimately the deer abattoirs along the highway, or the pest-control experts pulling bats out of attics, are, as one town official in New Jersey said of the bears not long ago, signs of a "people problem." Beneath it all is a cosmic question: how do Americans plan to live over the long haul? This was reinforced last week when, all over the Northeast, the power went out and millions found themselves suddenly humbled by their sheer reliance on electricity. What was remarkable was that the reaction was much the same as it is, on a smaller scale, to the animals. No talk of changing behavior, of finding a balance. Once the biggest power outage in history had begun, the only concern was for getting the juice back as quickly as possible. There was a faint undercurrent of revoked privilege. Where was the air conditioning, the pizza delivery, the ballgame on TV, all the things once seen as gifts and now assumed as birthrights?

6. What you saw time and time again was hubris brought low, people accustomed to instant communication without phone service, people accustomed to flying anywhere and at any time grounded at the airport. It was also hubris writ large. Office buildings, designed with windows that will not open, turning into saunas in the August sun. Office systems utterly dependent on computers turning into ghost towns in ghost cities.

7. Americans have been careless and casual with our natural resources for a long time. Can an accounting be long delayed? You could look at middle-class travelers sleeping like the homeless on the steps of public buildings during the blackout and see a vision of future unnatural disasters. The delivery grid is poorly conceived. The fail-safe systems must be improved. But not a word about a world so profligate with its power that it uses as much to fuel the advertising glitz of Times Square as it once used to sustain an entire town.

8. Watch great cities fade to black, look at the unchecked and unsightly overdevelopment all around them, and it is hard to imagine that will be a livable country a hundred years from now. The battle between human and animal is merely a reflection of that. Public officials are notoriously leery of the long view, but ordinary people are no better. The great contradiction: all those alleged nature lovers who fall for a forested range, then bring in the bulldozers. According to the National Association of Home Builders, the average American home has doubled in size in the past century. (Its report calls this a Century of Progress. Guess it depends on your definition.) This is not because families are larger. Quite the contrary. The three-car-garage-and-great-room trend—a great room being a living room on steroids—reflects family life that has devolved into individual isolation, everyone with his own TV and computer, centrally cooled to a frosty edge or heedlessly heated.

9. Irony of ironies, New York City may soon have a greater unbroken stretch of green (Happy 150th birthday, Central Park!) than the suburbs that once lured its people with the promises of grass and trees. The animals thus become more and more of a nuisance: get out of our way! Occasionally, we are forcibly reminded that human beings have created an environment in which, in some ways, we have less control than ever before; after all, the lack of power is, by definition, powerlessness. Meanwhile New Jersey, the most densely populated state (in case you hadn't noticed), wants very much to allow the hunting of bears. No one seems to have considered the obvious alternative: instead of issuing hunting permits, call a moratorium on building permits. Permanently. (Quindlen, Newsweek)

Step Three: Follow-Up Activities

Objective Test on "A Shock to the System"
Directions: Choose the best answer based on the reading.

1. The topic of this selection is:
   a. preserving the environment.
   b. bears.
   c. New York City.
   d. electricity.

2. The main idea (thesis statement) of Quindlen's essay is:
   a. The Northeast Blackout was a shock to the human system.
   b. The Northeast Blackout was a shock to the human system, creating a sense of powerlessness.
   c. The shock of the Northeast Blackout was a warning to humans to conserve natural resources.
   d. We need to be more aware of solar energy.

3. In paragraph #7, the main idea (topic sentence) is found in:
   a. the beginning.
   b. the middle.
   c. the end.
   d. there is no main idea.

4. In paragraph #8, the main idea (topic sentence) is found in:
   a. the beginning.
   b. the middle.
   c. the end.
   d. there is no main idea.

5. In paragraph #9, the sentence "The animals thus become more and more of a nuisance: get out of our way!" is considered the:
   a. topic.
   b. main idea.
   c. introduction.
   d. detail.

6. The first sentence of this selection, "Whenever you run into a bear out here in the country, someone will invariably ask if it was big," is considered the:
   a. topic.
   b. main idea.
   c. detail.
   d. question.

7. Anna Quindlen argues that we are:
   a. careless with our natural resources.
   b. concerned about our natural resources.
   c. unsure about our natural resources.
   d. destroying the entire world

8. True or False: Anna Quindlen thinks people take natural resources for granted.

9. Anna Quindlen compares Americans to:
   a. their animal counterparts.
   b. people in other countries.
   c. most politicians.
   d. executives in industry.

10. Which two details support the main idea or thesis of Quindlen's essay?
    A. ". . . a world so profligate with its power that it uses as much to fuel the advertising glitz of Times Square as it once used to sustain an entire town."
    B. ". . . the only concern was for getting the juice back as quickly as possible."
    C. "All bears appear large to me, even the cubs."
       a. A and B
       b. A and C
       c. B and C
       d. none of the above

Vocabulary Test on "A Shock to the System"
Directions: Choose one of the meanings to identify the highlighted word as it appears in the selection.

1. Something about the slope of the forehead, the **glint** of the eyes, the teeth and the claws.
   a. rudeness
   b. shine
   c. anger
   d. savagery

2. No one seems to have considered the obvious alternative: instead of issuing hunting permits, call a **moratorium** on building permits.
   a. suspension
   b. renewal
   c. cancellation
   d. review

3. The great contradiction: all those **alleged** nature lovers who fall for a forested range, then bring in the bulldozers.
   a. angered
   b. enthusiastic
   c. phony
   d. supposed

4. But not a word about a world so **profligate** with its power that it uses as much to fuel the advertising glitz of Times Square as it once used to sustain an entire town.
   a. elated
   b. wasteful
   c. powerful
   d. resourceful

5. My favorite bear **anecdote** was the animal accused of getting physical after a man had proffered a bagel to get the bear to stick around for a photograph.
   a. antidote
   b. staging
   c. story
   d. theory

6. My favorite bear anecdote was the animal accused of getting physical after a man had **proffered** a bagel to get the bear to stick around for a photograph.
   a. offered
   b. taken away
   c. teased with
   d. wasted

7. I don't take the time to assess relative size because I am so **agog** at the sheer bearness of the thing.
   a. saddened
   b. angered
   c. conflicted
   d. excited

8. What you saw time and time again was **hubris** brought low, people accustomed to instant communication without phone service, people accustomed to flying anywhere and at any time grounded at the airport.
   a. anticipation
   b. energy
   c. excessive pride
   d. insecurity

9. Whenever you run into a bear out here in the country, someone will **invariably** ask if it was big.
   a. secretly
   b. surprisingly
   c. without a doubt
   d. stupidly

10. Most of us now act toward native creatures the way our ancestors once acted toward Native Americans: we know that they were here first so we're willing to **tolerate** them as long as they don't demand to share when we build unattractive structures atop their former homes.
    a. honor
    b. anger
    c. justify
    d. put up with

Questions on "A Shock to the System"

1. What is the thesis of "A Shock to the System"?

   _____

   _____

   _____

2. What does Quindlen think about the public's use of energy?

   _____

   _____

   _____

3. How did most people react during the power blackout of the Northeast?

   _____

   _____

   _____

4. How has the average American home changed?

   _____

   _____

   _____

5. Why did people feel a sense of "powerlessness" during the blackout?

   _____

   _____

   _____

Journal Suggestions

1. List ways people are wasteful.
2. Write about your experience during an electrical blackout.

Collaborative Activities   ,

1. With your group, develop a plan to decrease one type of wastefulness in your home, community, or school/college. The plan must include a rationale, procedures, and an assessment tool. Include a visual aid.

2. Work with your group to create a poem or song about conserving resources, human wastefulness, or a futuristic prediction about the environment or natural resources.

Look It Up

Using the Internet, search for helpful tips in case of an electrical blackout.
   Prepare an attractive newsletter or pamphlet of helpful tips in preparation for an electrical blackout.

Getting the Picture

Muhammad Ali is a conscientious objector, someone who believes all wars are morally wrong, and so refuses to participate in them. Consider the sign and the main idea, or message, it implies. Do you believe that going to war is ever a reasonable or necessary thing to do? Do you believe that all war, essentially killing of other human beings, is ever justified? Explain your answer.

_____

_____

_____

© DphiMan, 2010. Used under license from Shutterstock, Inc.

_____

_____

_____

_____

_____

_____

_____

_____

_____

_____

_____

_____

_____

_____

_____

Chapter Highlights

What Have We Learned?

1. Every paragraph contains three basic elements: **topic, main idea** or **topic sentence,** and **details.**

2. The **topic** is the subject of the paragraph, article, essay, or short story. It is often found in the title, headline, or a label. The topic is not a sentence.

3. The **main idea** or **topic sentence** is the most important element of any paragraph or reading. If you understand the main idea, then you will have a basic comprehension of anything you read. There are three characteristics which help you locate the main idea. Remember that a main idea (1) states the general topic, (2) it says something about the topic, and (3) it is a complete sentence, which includes the general topic. The main idea may be found anywhere and is sometimes even indirectly stated, or implied. The main idea of a longer reading is called a *thesis or thesis statement.*

4. The **details** take up the biggest part of any paragraph or reading. Details support or develop the main idea. Major details provide direct support, while minor details comment or add interest. Moreover, the major details are more general than the minor details. Don't worry if you don't understand all the details, as long as you can identify the main idea.

Chapter 8

RHETORICAL MODES

In the last chapter, we learned that finding the main idea is the key to understanding anything we read. While this is true, locating the main idea is not the only way we can improve comprehension. The *details* are sentences that support the main idea by explaining *how* and *why;* also, they can provide examples to give us a broader understanding of the main idea. Because details take up most of whatever we read (remember that a main idea or thesis can be stated in only one sentence), learning the different *styles* in which details are written can improve our understanding of anything we read. Another name for these styles is **rhetorical modes.**

REMEMBER—**Rhetorical modes** *are ways in which writers develop a main idea. Identifying the styles writers use will help you better understand what you are reading.*

Signal words or phrases within the paragraph often provide clues to help us identify the rhetorical mode.

How Do Rhetorical Modes Support the Main Idea?

There are several types of rhetorical modes; here are six of the most basic methods used by writers:

Definition

A **definition** rhetorical mode develops an idea through the explanation, or definition, of a term. Signal words or phrases that provide clues include the following: *are, is, means, consists of, in other words, or,* and *defined as.* You can also recognize when a word is being defined if the word appears in boldface or italics.

Here is an example of the definition mode:

> A **paragraph** is a distinct portion of written matter. It consists of sentences that include a topic sentence, or main idea. Other sentences are details that develop the main idea. A paragraph is often a part of a longer piece of written work.

After determining that the first sentence is the main idea (a complete sentence that conveys the message and says something about the topic), we can focus on the details. In this paragraph, the function of the details is to more specifically define or explain just what a paragraph is. The **signal words** that provide a clue to the **definition** rhetorical mode are *is, are,* and *consists of.*

Illustration/Example

An **illustration/example** mode provides specific examples or types that support the main idea. **Signal words** include *for example, for instance, like,* and *character-*

istic of. This paragraph shows how a main idea can be supported by **illustration/ example:**

> Houses have different types of structures. For example, a colonial home has two levels. A center-hall colonial has a hallway that usually separates the living and dining rooms. Another example is the ranch home, where all the rooms are on one level. A split style has a short stairway that separates rooms.

In this paragraph, the first sentence is the main idea stating that there are different types of houses. The rest of the paragraph provides various examples of these structures, such as the center-hall colonial, split, and the ranch. Were you able to identify the **signal words** that provided clues for the **illustration/ example** mode? You should have spotted them easily. Of course, they included *for example* and *another example.*

Comparison/Contrast

The **comparison/contrast** mode develops the main idea with sentences that show how things or actions are alike and/or different. **Signal words** that show how things are *alike* (comparison) include *and, too, similar, in comparison, also, both, same, analogous to,* and *like.* **Signal words** that show how things are *different* (contrast) include *yet, though, in contrast, on the other hand, however, but, less, more, opposite,* and *even though.*

The following paragraph shows how the **comparison/contrast** mode is used:

> The American Revolution and the Civil War were similar, but also had differences. Both wars were fought on American soil, but were almost a century apart. While revolutionaries fought England, a power outside our territory, the Civil War often pitted brother against brother. Both wars were similar in the sense of patriotic zeal demonstrated by the soldiers. However, the Revolutionary War was fought for the cause of freedom, while the Civil War concerned the problem of slavery.

First, can you recognize the main idea? Again, the first sentence points are that the American Revolution and the Civil War had some similarities and differences. The rest of the paragraph points out how the wars were both alike and different in many respects. Did you also spot the **signal words** that indicate the **comparison/contrast** rhetorical mode? Words indicating similarities were *both* and *similar;* words indicating contrasts included *but, while,* and *however.*

Sequence of Events

To recognize the sequence of events mode, look for details of events placed in the order in which they occur. *First, second, third, then, later,* and *finally* are signal words that sometimes indicate the **sequence of events** mode. It is important to remember that these words do not always suggest a sequence of events; for example:

> Ruth's new dress is quite attractive. First, it is a stunning shade of pink; second, it is made of the finest silk fabric. Finally, the skirt is fitted and has lace flower appliqués.

The paragraph above is *not* in the sequence of events mode because the signal words are not used to indicate chronology, or time order. It is, in fact, a description, which will be discussed later in this chapter. The following paragraph, however, is written in the sequence of events style:

> First, separate the colored articles from the whites. Second, place the colored clothing in the washing machine. Then, add warm water and the appropriate amount of detergent. Finally, place the clothes in the dryer and start it. Do the same for the whites, except use hot water and bleach in the wash. As you can see, doing the laundry is really quite simple.

Here, the last sentence is the main idea that is the key to the meaning. Unlike the paragraph we just read, the signal words here, *first, second, then,* and *finally,* actually do indicate chronological order and, therefore, a **sequence of events** mode.

Cause and Effect

Another rhetorical mode is cause and effect, where the details show how something causes something else to happen. For example, this mode might explain how steam is the effect of boiling water or how driving recklessly may have bad consequences. Signal words that might indicate this mode are *cause, effect, because, due to, consequently, as a result,* and *therefore.* See how this paragraph illustrates the **cause and effect** mode:

> Men and women tend to spend longer and longer hours in the workplace. There is also the daily pressure of raising families, paying the mortgage, planning vacations, and organizing social events. Sometimes, unexpected situations like disease, accidents, or loss of a job can cause increased anxiety. These problems cause a sense of frustration, and a feeling of inability to cope. Stress is a major side effect of the harried lives people lead. As a result, people may feel depressed, experience high blood pressure, loss of appetite—all signals of stress.

In this paragraph, the main idea can be found in the middle. Can you spot it? If you chose "stress is a major side effect of the harried lives people lead," then you are correct. The first few sentences portray the causes of stress while the last sentence states the effects of stress in our lives. Signal words here are *cause, effect,* and *as a result.*

Description

Finally, the rhetorical mode of **description** is both the easiest and most difficult to spot. The details of this mode use several adjectives in order to create a sensory experience; that is, they appeal to all or some of our senses of sight, hearing, touch, smell, and taste. In this mode there are no signal words, but look for **describing words** or words that **relate to the senses** instead. At first, you might have difficulty identifying this mode because the main idea may not be directly stated. In fact, in a **description,** the **main idea (topic sentence) is usually (but not always)** *implied.* Take a look at this paragraph to understand this concept:

> The pathway to my home is dotted with soft zinnias and bunches of dew-covered pink tulips. An old oak casts a soft shadow over the emerald green

blades of grass that blanket the area. If you listen carefully, you can hear the breeze humming through the branches, and if you take a deep breath, you will inhale the perfumed fragrance of roses in bloom.

Notice the descriptive images that appeal to the senses in this paragraph. For example, the "zinnias," "pink tulips," "oak," "emerald green blades of grass" create a visual image. The phrase *hear the breeze humming* appeals to the sense of hearing, *perfumed fragrance* indicates smell, while the words *dew-covered, soft, breeze,* and *breath* suggest the sense of touch. All these details combine to imply the main idea, which might be stated as "The pathway to my home is beautiful in every way."

Exercise   **8.1   Your Turn—What Did You Learn?**

1. Rhetorical modes are made up of the _____ within a paragraph or essay.

2. The six basic rhetorical modes are _____, _____, _____, _____, _____, and _____.

3. Signal words help to _____.

4. The words *first, then,* and *finally* may indicate the _____ rhetorical mode.

5. The _____ rhetorical mode usually does not have a main idea that is directly stated.

Exercise   **8.2   Identifying Rhetorical Modes**

Directions: Underline the main idea in each paragraph. If the main idea (topic sentence) is implied, write what you think it might be in the line provided. Locate and note signal words before identifying the type of rhetorical mode in each paragraph.

© JupiterImages Corporation

5. No **sentimental** salvaging of birthday cards or the last letter a dying relative ever wrote.
   a. valuing a memory   c. storing
   b. fussy   d. happy

6. But while these ambitious plans take clearer and clearer shape in their heads, the books spill from the shelves onto the floor, the clothes pile up in the hamper and closet, the family mementos **accumulate** in every drawer, the surface of the desk is buried under mounds of paper and their unread magazines threaten to reach the ceiling.
   a. become messy   c. tear
   b. pile up   d. crowd

7. Neat people cut a clean swath through the **organic** as well as the inorganic world.
   a. organized   c. living
   b. neat   d. non-living

8. Neat people are bums and **clods** at heart.
   a. geniuses   c. wanderers
   b. freaks   d. dull, stupid people

9. Four hours or two weeks into the **excavation,** the desk looks exactly the same, primarily because the sloppy person is meticulously creating new piles of papers with new headings and scrupulously stopping to read all the old book catalogs before he throws them away.
   a. project   c. laziness
   b. digging   d. adventure

10. Four hours or two weeks into the excavation, the desk looks exactly the same, primarily because the sloppy person is **meticulously** creating new piles of papers with new headings and scrupulously stopping to read all the old book catalogs before he throws them away.
    a. carefully, showing attention to detail   c. without a care
    b. creatively   d. joyously

Questions on "Neat People vs. Sloppy People"

1. What is the thesis of "Neat People vs. Sloppy People"?

   _____

   _____

   _____

2. What is the major rhetorical mode used in this essay? Explain.

   _____

   _____

   _____

3. Why does Britt say that sloppy people are generally better than neat people?

   _____

   _____

   _____

4. Is this essay meant to be taken seriously? Why or why not?

_____

_____

_____

5. Do you think it is better to be neat or sloppy? Explain your answer.

_____

_____

_____

Journal Suggestion

Write an essay comparing and contrasting other characteristics of yourself and a member of your family. For example, choose introverted vs. extroverted, athlete vs. movie buff, or dominant vs. passive. Discuss your conclusions.

Collaborative Activity

Everyone knows people who are either sloppy or neat. Choose two people you know and write a short essay comparing their habits. Do their sloppy or neat habits really reflect their personality? Discuss your conclusions with others.

Look It Up

1. Using the Internet, look up the nature vs. nurture theory of psychology. How much are we influenced by our heredity and by our environment? Which factor do you believe exerts more influence on the people we ultimately become? Form two groups, each taking a side, and debate this issue.

2. Home organizing has become big business these days. Research the topic of home organization and take the role of a company representative persuading a homeowner to use your services. Why do you think so many people currently have a need to become organized? *Hoarding, curing individuals*

Comprehending Longer Selections   8.6

More Practice Identifying Rhetorical Modes

Apply what you have learned in this chapter to longer reading selections.

Step One: Before Reading
Vocabulary in Context Practice
Directions: Choose one of the following words to complete each of the sentences below. Use each word only once. Be sure to pay attention to the context clues provided.

acquaintance—person one knows
classic—typical
conceivably—possibly
coronary—related to the heart
discreetly—secretly
extracurricular—supplementary to one's work
marketable—capable of being used in the workplace
obituary—notice of death
precisely—exactly
thrombosis—development of a blood clot

1. John admitted that losing his family was _____ the worst thing that had happened to him.

2. My alarm rings at _____ 6 A.M. each morning.

3. I _____ told the speaker that her slip was showing.

4. Upon the mayor's death, we all read his _____ in the newspapers.

5. Joe is a(n) _____ of mine since I don't know him very well.

6. Having majored in art, Jill's skills weren't very _____ on Wall Street.

7. The man suffered a _____, but the heart attack was not fatal.

8. I love to ski when I am not working; it is a great _____ activity.

9. Marie found out she has a _____ problem, a rapid heartbeat.

10. Stress is a _____ symptom of working too hard.

Freewrite

Write about how much time you believe people should devote to their jobs Once you begin reading, use the margin for notes.

Step Two: Read the Selection

Note: As you read the following selection, concentrate and practice the steps of SQ3R. Remove the SQ3R card from the book and complete it as you read.

Every action in life has consequences. Muhammad Ali fought his way up the ranks to become a world champion boxer. However, his years of battering in the ring had profound harmful effects. In later years, Ali developed brain damage and Parkinson's disease, an ailment that now impairs his movement and speech. In "The Company Man" by Ellen Goodman we see the dangerous consequences of one man's decisions.

The Company Man
By Ellen Goodman

1. He worked himself to death, finally and precisely, at 3:00 A.M. Sunday morning.

2. The obituary didn't say that, of course. It said that he died of a coronary thrombosis—I think that was it—but everyone among his friends and acquaintances knew it instantly. He was a perfect Type A, a workaholic, a classic, they said to each other and shook their heads—and thought for five or ten minutes about the way they lived.

3. This man who worked himself to death finally and precisely at 3:00 A.M. Sunday morning—on his day off—was fifty-one years old and a vice-president. He was, however, one of six vice-presidents, and one of three who might conceivably—if the president died or retired soon enough—have moved to the top spot. Phil knew that.

4. He worked six days a week, five of them until eight or nine at night, during a time when his own company had begun the four-day week for everyone but the executives. He worked like the Important People. He had no outside "extra-curricular interests," unless, of course, you think about a monthly golf game that way. To Phil, it was work. He always ate egg salad sandwiches at his desk. He was, of course, overweight, by 20 or 25 pounds. He thought it was okay, though, because he didn't smoke.

5. On Saturdays, Phil wore a sports jacket to the office instead of a suit, because it was the weekend.

6. He had a lot of people working for him, maybe sixty, and most of them liked him most of the time. Three of them will be seriously considered for his job. The obituary didn't mention that.

7. But it did list his "survivors" quite accurately. He is survived by his wife, Helen, forty-eight years old, a good woman of no particular marketable skills, who worked in an office before marrying and mothering. She had, according to her daughter, given up trying to compete with his work years ago, when the children were small. A company friend said, "I know how much you will miss him." And she answered, "I already have."

8. "Missing him all these years," she must have given up part of herself which had cared too much for the man. She would be "well taken care of."

9. His "dearly beloved" eldest of the "dearly beloved" children is a hard-working executive in a manufacturing firm down South. In the day and a half before the funeral, he went around the neighborhood researching his father, asking the neighbors what he was like. They were embarrassed.

10. His second child is a girl, who is twenty-four and newly married. She lives near her mother and they are close, but whenever she was alone with her father, in a car driving somewhere, they had nothing to say to each other.

11. The youngest is twenty, a boy, a high-school graduate who has spent the last couple of years, like a lot of his friends, doing enough odd jobs to stay in grass and food. He was the one who tried to grab at his father, and tried to mean enough to him to keep the man at home. He was his father's favorite. Over the last two years, Phil stayed up nights worrying about the boy.

12. The boy once said, "My father and I only board here."

13. At the funeral, the sixty-year-old company president told the forty-eight-year-old widow that the fifty-one-year-old deceased had meant much to the company and would be missed and would be hard to replace. The widow didn't look him in the eye. She was afraid he would read her bitterness and, after all, she would need him to straighten out the finances—stock options and all that.

14. Phil was overweight and nervous and worked too hard. If he wasn't at the office, he was worried about it. Phil was a Type A, a heart-attack natural. You could have picked him out in a minute from a lineup.

15. So when he finally worked himself to death, at precisely 3:00 A.M. Sunday morning, no one was really surprised.

16. By 5:00 P.M. the afternoon of the funeral, the company president had begun, discreetly of course, with care and taste, to make inquiries about his replacement. One of three men. He asked around: "Who's been working the hardest?" (Goodman 317)

Step Three: Follow-Up Activities

Objective Test on "The Company Man"
Directions: Choose the best answer based on the reading.

1. True or False: The thesis of this selection is Phil wasted his life by concentrating too much on work and not enough on family.

2. The rhetorical mode of the selection is:
   a. comparison/contrast.
   b. definition.
   c. description.
   d. sequence of events.

3. Phil's children:
    a. thought about him a lot.   c. wanted to help him.
    b. hated him.   d. didn't know him very well.

4. Phil's wife probably:
    a. resented his boss.   c. would marry his boss.
    b. was grateful to his boss.   d. would work for his boss.

5. When Phil's youngest child said, "My father and I only board here," he meant:
    a. they were like strangers.
    b. they both had to pay to be there.
    c. no one was ever at home.
    d. they both cared more about work.

6. The term "company man" means someone who:
    a. works for one company and no others.
    b. will someday advance to president.
    c. places the company before anything else.
    d. has few friends, but many visitors.

7. The author states that Phil's youngest son was his favorite to make the point that Phil:
    a. spent the most time with him.
    b. worried about him, but didn't help him.
    c. was resented by his other children.
    d. became sick because of his son.

8. True or False: The selection implies that everyone needs to take more vacations.

9. True or False or Can't Tell: Phil's family will no longer have much money.

10. True or False or Can't Tell: Phil's family will be happier.

Vocabulary Test on "The Company Man"

Directions: Choose one of the meanings to identify the highlighted word as it appears in the selection.

1. He had no outside "**extracurricular** interests," unless, of course, you think about a monthly golf game that way.
    a. exciting   c. supplementary to one's work
    b. interesting   d. outside

2. So when he finally worked himself to death, at **precisely** 3:00 A.M. Sunday morning, no one was really surprised.
    a. preciously   c. approximately
    b. exactly   d. correctly

3. The **obituary** didn't say that, of course.
    a. officer   c. public comment
    b. notice of death   d. workplace

4. He was, however, one of six vice-presidents, and one of three who might **conceivably**—if the president died or retired soon enough—have moved to the top spot. Phil knew that.
    a. possibly   c. fortunately
    b. excellently   d. undeniably

HOW CAN I READ BETWEEN THE LINES?

CHAPTER 9   Fact vs. Opinion
CHAPTER 10 Intent, Attitude, and Tone

You now understand the importance of the main idea. You have learned ways of finding the main idea and types of details. However, sometimes you need to "read between the lines" to gain a clearer understanding. This is called "critical reading." Let's start with understanding the difference between fact and opinion.

Spotlight on

Fantasia (1984–)

Fantasia Barrino, known as Fantasia, is an African-American singer famous for being the 2004 *American Idol* winner. America's fondness for her was a turning point in her life, especially since she grew up in impoverished High Point, North Carolina where she dropped out of school in ninth grade, was raped at fifteen, and became pregnant at sixteen. In her memoir, *Life is Not a Fairy Tale*, she confesses to being functionally illiterate. So how did she win on *American Idol* when she could barely read? When she didn't know the words to a song, she would just listen to the vocal coach sing it. If she could change the past, Fantasia would not have dropped out of school. "Getting by in life" was not good enough; therefore, she went back to school and got a diploma. Fantasia's debut album, *Free Yourself*, has sold more than 1.5 million

© Fred Prouser/Reuters/Corbis

copies. This young woman who became successful at twenty-one, describes her style as "the punk-rock look." In August, 2006, on the women's cable channel, Fantasia played herself in a lifetime movie that showed how she overcame her personal crises of poverty, sexual abuse, and illiteracy in order to win the "American Idol" talent show. In 2008, her next album, *Fantasia*, earned three Grammy nominations. Fantasia entered a new phase of her career when she played the role of Celie in the Broadway musical, *The Color Purple*. In 2010, she debuted in her own reality show, "Fantasia For Real." Her single, "Bittersweet," won her a Grammy for Best Female R&B Vocal Performance.

Chapter 9

FACT VS. OPINION

Fantasia Barrino has a positive attitude about becoming a better reader. But Fantasia knows that learning to be a better reader means not only comprehending at the **literal level** or most basic level, but also at the **critical level**, so she can interpret what she reads. To comprehend critically, she must distinguish fact from opinion. A **fact** is anything that can be proven. For example, a statement such as "this room measures 20 by 30 feet" may be proven true simply by measuring the room. If the room measurement does not agree with the statement, then the statement is incorrect. An **opinion** is a statement that can be disputed. For example, the sentence "This is a comfortable chair" would be considered an opinion because the statement is an observation that can be disputed.

To help separate a fact from an opinion, you must know that **facts** are generally **objective** and **opinions** are usually **subjective.** People determine something as a fact after years of observation, experimentation, and research. But to reach an opinion about something or someone, people rely on a belief, feeling, or judgment. Words that might signal an opinion include adjectives such as *good, effective, interesting,* and adverbs such as *apparently* and *should.* Separating facts from opinions is not easy for three reasons. First, **facts change.** Second, **opinions can sound factual.** Third, **bias or prejudice can influence our acceptance of facts.** Because much of what we read is **a combination of facts and opinions,** it is important to distinguish between the two to comprehend at the critical level.

Exercise **9.1 Your Turn—What Did You Learn?**

1. Distinguishing between facts and opinions means understanding at a _____ level.

2. _____ are subjective and _____ are objective.

3. Words like *good, interesting, effective, perhaps, apparently,* and *should* help you identify _____.

4. Much of what we read is a combination of _____ and _____.

Exercise **9.2 Facts vs. Opinion**

Directions: Next to each statement, write an "F" for fact (something that can be proven or disproven), or an "O" for opinion (something that can be disputed).

1. _____ The world is round, not flat like some people once believed.

2. _____ Barack Obama is the 44th President of the United States.

3. _____ The election of Barack Obama was a joyful occasion.

4. _____ William Shakespeare was one of the greatest writers on the planet.

5. _____ Students receive an associate's degree upon graduation from a community college.

6. _____ Students receive a master's degree upon graduation from a community college.

7. _____ The community college is a good place to get a degree.

8. _____ Staying out too long in the sun can cause cancer.

9. _____ You should wear a hat whenever you are exposed to sunlight.

10. _____ Doctors advise using sunscreen during prolonged exposure to sunlight.

Identifying Facts

Directions: Carefully read the paragraphs. Then **underline the factual statements.** Hint: Facts are statements that can be supported with objective evidence.

1. Over 30,000 members of public worker unions and progressive groups rallied on May 22 at the Statehouse in Trenton to protest Governor Chris Christie's extensive budget cuts. They chanted, "We are not the problem!" stepping up the rhetoric between Christie and the unions, an animosity which has been brewing for the last few months. In fact, Christie should review these devastating cuts which have done the greatest harm to those who have worked diligently in schools, fire departments, and various social service agencies. The governor himself was not present at the rally. However, New Jersey Education Association president Barbara Keshishian warned that if legislators remain silent about this problem, "They are his accomplices." This is a warning which they should heed if they want to be re-elected.

© JupiterImages Corporation

2. In the U.S., one in six couples has difficulty conceiving or bearing a child. About 27 percent of women between ages 15 and 44 can't have children because of physical problems. The sperm count of U.S. males has fallen more than 30 percent in fifty years. Some 25 percent of men are considered functionally sterile. Experts suspect that environmental pollution is a cause. (Wellborn 22)

3. The purpose of education is to teach students to think, not to instill dogma or to train them to respond in predictable ways. Far from being banned, controversial material should be welcomed in schools. Students should be taught the critical ability to evaluate different ideas and to come to their own conclusions. It is a disservice to them and to society to restrict instructional material to a single viewpoint. (Los Angeles Times 23)

Exercise **9.4** **Identifying Facts in a Memoir**

Directions: A memoir is an account of aspects of someone's life experience which includes opinion based on some factual evidence. In her memoir, *Life is Not a Fairytale*, Fantasia Barrino relates how illiteracy held her back. Mary Turner had the same problem. The excerpts from Mary Turner's memoir, *Making the Most of Myself*, state her opinions and some facts which may be supported with objective evidence. See if you can find the factual statements and then place an "F" next to each.

1. My name is Mary Turner and I am thirty years old. _____ I am an elementary school teacher and the mother of four children. _____ I believe that I am intelligent and motivated. _____ But I wasn't always this way. _____ When I was twelve years old, my parents could no longer care for me and I was sent to live in a series of foster homes. _____ I resented my birth parents as well as my foster parents. _____ I became rebellious and succumbed to a world of drugs. _____ School? I cut more classes than I attended. _____ I later realized that was the worst thing I could do since a lack of education would eventually become an obstacle to my future. _____ When I was eighteen, I was arrested for using drugs and alcohol. _____ This turned out to be the best thing that ever happened to me. _____

2. Handcuffed, my body began to shake and I felt faint on the long ride to the police station. _____ Then when I saw my foster parents' distraught faces, I knew they wanted me, a recalcitrant teenager, out of their house. _____ I started feeling nauseous, knowing that my future was bleak. _____ Clearly, the thought of going to court and possibly jail was too much to accept. _____ Perhaps it was time to permanently exit life as I knew it. _____

3. Since my bail couldn't be posted, I had to sit in jail until my court date. _____ During my time in jail, I met some interesting individuals, some who were downright nasty, and others who were apathetic and had given up on life just as I had. _____ However, one person I met proved different from all the rest. _____ Her name was Isabel Vega, and she was twice my age. _____ She was not a prisoner, but one of the prison guards who later would tell me that she liked me because I reminded her of how she used to be when she was younger. _____ She already had two young children then and was living on the streets. _____ Isabel and I kept in touch after I was released from jail. _____ I was embarrassed when I saw the look on her face after I told her that I couldn't even read the directions for heating

up a frozen pizza in the microwave. _____ Isabel took my hand and I could see all the honesty and warmth that were in her eyes. _____ It was Isabel who sat with me for many months teaching me how to read. _____ After six months, I could read as well as any fifth grader. _____ But I had a long way to go. _____

4. Soon after my tutoring sessions with Isabel, I decided to pursue my G.E.D. (General Education Degree) _____ It would mean a lot of personal sacrifice. _____ No longer in foster care, I had my own apartment, which meant working full-time cleaning houses to pay the rent and my living expenses. _____ Now that getting a high school diploma was a goal, I had little time for personal pleasures. _____ Watching TV and going out with friends was not possible if I wanted good grades. _____ I had to constantly remind myself that if I persevered, I would succeed. _____

5. After receiving my G.E.D, I decided to go to college. _____ Years earlier, I would have never considered this, but Isabel had inspired me to think that anything was possible. _____ I married, had two children, divorced, and continued to support myself with a variety of jobs while going to school at night. _____ I decided to become a teacher to motivate young children to live up to their potential. _____ Today, instead of being a disappointment to my family, friends, and myself, I am a role model. _____ I am proud of myself for what I have accomplished, especially when it comes to my education. _____ In fact, one of my favorite places to spend time now is at the public library. _____ And yes, Isabel is still in my life. _____ She is the godmother to my children. _____

Creating Your SQ3R Cards

SQ3R cards are a study system to help you successfully comprehend what you are reading. As you read the longer reading selection, you will actively interact with the text before you read, while you read, and after you read.

"S": Survey the Reading Selection

- What is the topic?

  The topic is about a different path.

- What do I already know?

  Different paths can take you down good or bad roads.

- What is my purpose for reading?

  My purpose is to find out what path was chosen and was that a good path to choose.

"Q": Turn a Selection Title into a Question

Don't forget to turn key statements into questions as you read.

What was her reason to take a year off from school?
What can she gain from taking a year off?

1st "R": Read

- Make predictions.

_____

_____

- Retrieve prior knowledge.

_____

_____

- State confusing ideas.

_____

_____

2nd "R": Recite

- Write the main point of this selection.

- Don't forget to annotate and take notes in the margin.

To show an example of what can happen
if you take a year off from school.

3rd "R": Review

- Recall what you have learned.

- React to what you have read.

This path she chose worked for
her, but taking off from college
isn't for anyone. Luckily
she devoted herself to making
herself a better person

Comprehending Longer Selections 9.5 *Exercise*

Fact vs. Opinion

Step One: Before Reading

Vocabulary in Context Practice

Directions: Choose one of the following words to complete each of the sentences below. Use each word only once. Be sure to pay attention to the context clues provided.

begrudgingly—resentfully
extracurricular—being outside the regular curriculum of a school
frugal—thrifty
infuriating—enraging
internships—supervised "learning on the job" experiences
investment—a plan for security
sabbatical –a leave of absence before returning to work or school
self-esteem—self-confidence
trudge—walk heavily
unyielding—inflexible

1. Professors at the college can take a ___Sabbatical___ every seven years with full pay.

2. Sometimes we have to make an ___investment___ of time to learn a chapter well.

3. Priscilla was quite ___frugal___, and as a result most of her clothes were hand-me-downs.

4. Bill was forced to ___unyielding___ to work, knowing it would be his last day at the firm.

5. Criticizing children's work each day can sometimes harm their ___self-esteem___

6. The moviegoer's behavior was ___trudge___ the theatre patrons directly behind him.

7. High school and college sports are not academic activities but ___extracurricular___ activities.

8. Jimmy ate his vegetables ___begrudgingly___ at his parents' urging.

9. An _infuriating_ attitude will affect one's ability to make and keep friends.

10. _internships_ _____ related to one's career are becoming a requirement for employment.

Freewrite
Write about the reasons why you would or would not take a year off before college, or write about how you think your life would be if you dropped out of school in ninth grade.

Step Two: Read the Selection

Note: As you read the following selection, concentrate and practice the steps of SQ3R. Remove the SQ3R card from the book and complete it as you read.

Fantasia Barrino dropped out of school in ninth grade and regretted this decision. The essay you are about to read also involves a girl making a decision; however, she decides to take a year off before college.

A Different Path
by Serena Weber

© Diego Cervo, 2010. Used under license from Shutterstock, Inc.

1. Okay, I'll admit it. As I stood in front of my home in Edison, New Jersey watching my friends pile duffel bags, flat screen TV's, and laptops into their parents' rented vans, I wondered if I had made the right decision. I had taken the bold step of deciding to take a sabbatical between high school graduation and college. Instead of months studying in a college library and networking with new friends as I joined a sorority and academic clubs, I decided to make a different kind of investment in my future. While my parents and even friends found my decision infuriating at first, thinking I would never become a college student, they finally relented to my unyielding determination. As time passed, and my self-esteem rose, they began to see the wisdom of my decision to take a year off. More importantly, so did I.

2. Why did I make this decision? I realized that there had to be other ways of learning. I had witnessed too many students who graduated before I did, trudge begrudgingly off to school, only to become immersed in extracurricular activities at the expense of their school work. Sometimes they even flunked out of college altogether. Sadly, some became so discouraged that they never returned. Others stay in school, graduate, get lifelong jobs from which they do not

retire until age 65 or older, marry, have children, and never get a chance to see the world.

　3. My path led me a different way, however.

　4. During my sabbatical year, I have traveled throughout the country, taking on several, mostly non-paying, internships. I lived at various camp-sites and the homes of friends. I learned that hard work and a frugal lifestyle can yield many benefits. I taught five-year-olds how to read in a trailer park in Detroit, installed windows on homes for the poor in North Carolina while working for Habitat for Humanity, and worked flipping pancakes as a short order cook in Los Angeles, California. I can honestly say that I devoted my-self to each of these tasks as much as I would have to any course I could have taken in college.

　5. When I returned home, my parents noted the change in me. I felt confident not only in my new abilities, but also in the knowledge that I could handle any challenge I would be confronted with the following year in college. Sometimes, wisdom does come when you take a different path.

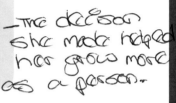
_seams she feels like she is making a difference.

_The decision she made helped her grow more as a person.

Step Three: Follow-Up Activities

Objective Test on "A Different Path"

Directions: Choose the best answer based on the reading.

1. The main point of this selection is:
   a. postponing college for a year can result in negative learning ex-periences.
   b. postponing college for a year can result in positive learning experi-ences.
   c. postponing college for a year is something most students would like to do.
   d. postponing college for a year is not for everyone.

2. <u>True</u> or False: The main point of this selection is stated.

3. <u>True</u> or False: "I realized that there had to be other ways of learning." This statement is a fact.

4. <u>True</u> or False: "During my sabbatical year, I have traveled throughout the country, taking on several, mostly non-paying, internships." This statement is a fact.

5. "Sometimes, wisdom does come when you take a different path."

   This statement is:
   a. an opinion.
   b. a metaphor (using a comparison to clarify meaning).
   c. a and b.
   d. a fact.

6. When the writer states that some students drop out of college, she is suggesting that:
   a. not everyone should go to college.
   b. taking time off before college may be a good idea.
   c. colleges are too hard for students.
   d. most students are too lazy.

7. The quote, "I learned that hard work and a frugal lifestyle can yield many benefits" suggests that the author:
   a. doesn't need to go to college.
   b. earned much money during the sabbatical.
   c. ~~suggests~~ believes internships are always better than college classes.
   d. believes taking time off can help one's character.

8. At first, the author's parents:
   a. were happy with her decision.
   b. were stubborn and angry about the decision.
   c. were angry and fearful about the decision
   d. were unsure about the decision.

9. After taking a year off between high school and college, the author is:
   a. smarter.   c. ready for college.
   b. more confident.   d. all the above.

10. True or False: This essay has more facts than opinions.

Vocabulary Test on "A Different Path"

Directions: Choose one of the meanings to identify the highlighted word as it appears in the selection.

1. I had witnessed too many students who graduated before they did **trudge** begrudgingly off to school, only to become immersed in extra-curricular activities at the expense of their school work.
   a. walk heavily   c. crawl
   b. skip   d. motivate

2. I had witnessed too many students who graduated before they did trudge **begrudgingly** off to school, only to become immersed in extra-curricular activities at the expense of their school work.
   a. happily   c. resentfully
   b. fearfully   d. boastfully

3. I had witnessed too many students who graduated before they did trudge begrudgingly off to school, only to become immersed in **extracurricular** activities at the expense of their school work.
   a. extra
   b. academic
   c. being outside the regular curriculum of a school
   d. athletic clubs

4. I learned that hard work and a **frugal** lifestyle can yield many benefits.
   a. thrifty   c. rich
   b. fine   d. smart

5. I had taken the bold step of deciding to take a **sabbatical** between high school graduation and college.
   a. a leave of absence before returning to work or school
   b. a special holiday
   c. vacation
   d. hospitalization

6. Instead of months studying in a college library and networking with new friends as I joined a sorority and academic clubs, I decided to make a different kind of **investment** in my future.
   a. money   c. a plan for security
   b. education   d. career

7. As time passed, and my **self-esteem** rose, they began to see the wisdom of my decision to take a year off.
   a. academic ventures   c. self-serving
   b. wisdom   d. self-confidence

8. During my sabbatical year, I have traveled throughout the country, taking on several, mostly non-paying, **internships.**
   a. supervised "learning on the job" experiences
   b. careers
   c. jobs
   d. hobbies

9. While my parents and even friends found my decision **infuriating** at first, thinking I would never become a college student, they finally relented to my unyielding determination.
   a. inaudible   c. confusing
   b. enraging   d. reasonable

10. While my parents and even friends found my decision infuriating at first, thinking I would never become a college student, they finally relented to my **unyielding** determination.
   a. confident   c. inflexible
   b. undeterminable   d. admirable

Questions on "A Different Path"

1. Why did Weber take a sabbatical?

_____

_____

_____

2. What did she do on her sabbatical?

_____

_____

_____

3. How did others react to Weber's decision? Explain.

_____

_____

_____

4. According to the author, why do some people flunk out of college?

_____

_____

_____

5. What lessons did Weber learn from her sabbatical?

_____

_____

_____

Journal Suggestions

1. Weber's intent is to persuade you to take a year off before college. List her reasons and argue for or against the idea of taking a year off before college.

2. Imagine taking a year off before college. Where would you go and what would you do? You must include a reasonable budget, such as living daily on $20 dollars. Consider expenses like lodging, food, travel, and entertainment.

Collaborative Activity

With a partner, debate two others in your group, one side explaining reasons one should take a year off before college, and the other side arguing against leaving school.

Look It Up

1. Using the Internet, find out if there are any other celebrities who are or were functionally illiterate. Write a report about your findings.

2. Research the statistics on illiteracy in the United States as well as the reasons for this problem.

Creating Your SQ3R Cards

SQ3R cards are a study system to help you successfully comprehend what you are reading. As you read the longer reading selection, you will actively interact with the text before you read, while you read, and after you read.

"S": Survey the Reading Selection

- What is the topic?

  _____

  _____

- What do I already know?

  _____

  _____

  _____

- What is my purpose for reading?

  _____

  _____

  _____

"Q": Turn a Selection Title into a Question

Don't forget to turn key statements into questions as you read.

_____

_____

_____

_____

1st "R": Read

- Make predictions.

_____

_____

- Retrieve prior knowledge.

_____

_____

- State confusing ideas.

_____

_____

2nd "R": Recite

- Write the main point of this selection.
- Don't forget to annotate and take notes in the margin.

_____

_____

3rd "R": Review

- Recall what you have learned.
- React to what you have read.

_____

_____

_____

_____

_____

Comprehending Longer Selections 9.6 *Exercise*

More Practice with Fact vs. Opinion

Step One: Before Reading

Vocabulary in Context Practice

Directions: Choose one of the following words to complete each of the sentences below. Use each word only once. Be sure to pay attention to the context clues provided.

abstract—not easily understood
alienation—separation
demise—termination
elaborate—detailed
highlight—emphasize
incompatible—incongruous, a poor good match
inexplicable—incapable of being explained or accounted for
pretentiously—showing off
subtle—hardly noticeable
trepidation—fear

1. The student revised her essay because her details were not _____ to support her thesis.

2. Her friend's _____ comments were meant to suggest that her promotion was not earned.

3. The _____ of the project was the result of mismanagement and worker indifference.

4. The couple broke off their engagement because they were too _____.

5. The _____ of their European vacation was skydiving in Interlaken, Switzerland.

6. The _____ accident resulted in high insurance premiums.

7. Jimmy had a feeling of _____ when diving into the pool for the first time.

8. The solution to the _____ problem would require a team of experts or pundits.

9. Feelings of _____ are common among foreign immigrants who enter another country that is unwilling to accept their cultural way of life.

10. Behaving _____, the young professional was ostracized by his co-workers.

Freewrite

Describe a dream you want to chase. If you are chasing your dream now, write about the progress you have made thus far.

Step Two: Read the Selection

Note: As you read the following selection, concentrate and practice the steps of SQ3R. Remove the SQ3R card from the book and complete it as you read.

Fantasia dropped out of school in ninth grade, but she returned to school and got a diploma. The essay you are about to read also involves a student returning to school. However, the author of this essay, John Gonzales, says, "My decision to chase a dream, return to college at age 24 and take the liberal arts courses that will help me become a journalist has forced me to become two people."

College Brings Alienation
by John Gonzales

1. My decision to chase a dream, return to college at age 24 and take the liberal arts courses that will help me become a journalist has forced me to be two people. One face is for family and longtime friends, another is for my classes and college friends.

2. My homeboys have not read Marx, Nietzsche or Freud. They do not care to probe the economics behind their being paid less, despite working more, than their fathers. They don't want to hear about the Oedipus complex or the nature of good and evil. For them, intellectual theories are elaborate, unnecessary attempts to explain the inexplicable. Ideas do not feed their families and only seem to highlight the fact that I have begun to change. "That's enough. Don't read any more. I don't understand a word you're saying," Fidel, my compadre, said after I responded to his request to read him a paragraph from one of my textbooks. He had telephoned while I was doing homework and jibed, "What the hell are you studying now?"

3. I also stumble to explain my studies to my parents. My father had a sixth-grade education. My mother earned her GED 15 years after leaving high school. I often reluctantly hand them my term papers they ask to see, knowing they won't truly comprehend them. After a careful reading, my mother's

usual response: "You write so beautifully, mijo, I didn't really understand all the words you used but we can just tell how educated you are."

4. A senior at the University of California, receiving a bachelor's degree in journalism and political science this May, I painfully realize the downside to education, a subtle alienation from friends and loved ones. I understand more clearly why Latinos approach higher learning with trepidation. For beyond the barriers of low income and racism lies another fight, the struggle to blend old and new identities.

5. It is not that education is discouraged; my family is proud of me and would be crushed if I were to quit. But disproportionately few Latinos acquire higher learning and those who do often must balance an incompatible past and future.

6. I envisioned my old friends and new friends at my graduation party: Would they eat, drink and laugh together or huddle in separate groups? Which group would I join? Who am I?

7. That is why many promising Latinos I know who attend college choose to major in business or other fields with more easily identifiable rewards for their parents and themselves. "I'm learning how to start and manage a restaurant," is certainly something my father, a part-time contractor, would grasp more clearly than the abstract knowledge I've obtained.

8. Noble careers that require no college sometimes seem even more attractive. My aunt, mother of an army sergeant, beams with pride at family gatherings when she recalls my cousin's boot-camp graduation. Yet my mother struggles to explain the value of my work as a journalist. Amid the music, food and drink of the get-together, a reporter is not a craftsman with words, not a guardian of democracy, not a voice against society's ills. Instead, journalists are perceived as the intrusive talking heads on the 11o'clock news, the Latino ones pretentiously pronouncing their surnames with forced accents.

9. For other Latinos I know studying philosophy, sociology, and literature, the struggle to retain identity is similar. In this political climate of Proposition 187, the demise of the Great Society and threats to affirmative action, analytical, creative Latino minds are needed more than ever. But the sacrifices are great indeed. (Gonzales)

Step Three: Follow-Up Activities

Objective Test on "College Brings Alienation"

Directions: Choose the best answer based on the reading.

1. The main idea of this selection is that:
   a. college brings alienation.
   b. latinos experience alienation between old and new friends as a result of education.
   c. immigrants experience alienation between old and new friends as a result of education.
   d. education makes uneducated people feel unsophisticated.

2. The author's audience is:
   a. Latinos.
   b. immigrants.
   c. college students.
   d. all of the above.

3. When the author's mother reads his papers, she:
   a. understands and likes them.
   b. doesn't understand but likes them.
   c. understands but does not like them.
   d. does not understand or like them.

4. True or False: The author suggests that uneducated Latinos do not value careers like journalism, philosophy, sociology and literature.

5. This essay:
   a. contains only facts.
   b. contains only opinions.
   c. contains opinions based on facts.
   d. has neither facts nor opinions.

6. True or False: The author suggests that his longtime friends would not feel comfortable socializing with his college friends.

7. The tone of this essay is
   a. complex.   c. nostalgic.
   b. somber.   d. enlightening.

8. True or False: The author says education has changed his identity.

9. True or False: Latinos no longer need to struggle to retain their identity.

10. True or False: The author says education is alienating him from his long-time friends and they no longer like him.

Vocabulary Test on "College Brings Alienation"
Directions: Choose one of the meanings to identify the highlighted word as it appears in the selection.

1. But disproportionately few Latinos acquire higher learning and those who do often must balance an **incompatible** past and future.
   a. harmonious   c. difficult
   b. incongruous, a poor match   d. confusing

2. Ideas do not feed their families and only seem to **highlight** the fact that I have begun to change.
   a. ignore   c. emphasize
   b. write   d. complain

3. I understand more clearly why Latinos approach higher learning with **trepidation.**
   a. fear   c. eagerness
   b. stubbornness   d. courageousness

4. For them, intellectual theories are **elaborate**, unnecessary attempts to explain the inexplicable.
   a. simple   c. detailed
   b. creative   d. confusing

5. A senior at the University of California, receiving a bachelor's degree in journalism and political science this May, I painfully realize the downside to education, a subtle **alienation** from friends and loved ones.
   a. friendliness   c. happiness
   b. depression   d. separation

6. For them, intellectual theories are elaborate, unnecessary attempts to explain the **inexplicable.**
   a. incapable of being explained or accounted for
   b. obvious
   c. opinionated
   d. factual

7. For "I'm learning how to start and manage a restaurant," is certainly something my father, a part-time contractor, would grasp more clearly than the **abstract** knowledge I've obtained.
   a. practical
   b. remote
   c. not easily understood
   d. concrete

8. Instead, journalists are perceived as the intrusive talking heads on the 11o'clock news, the Latino ones **pretentiously** pronouncing their surnames with forced accents.
   a. showing off
   b. rudely
   c. stupidly
   d. humorously

9. A senior at the University of California, receiving a bachelor's degree in journalism and political science this May, I painfully realize the downside to education, a **subtle** alienation from friends and loved ones.
   a. obvious
   b. hardly noticeable
   c. clear
   d. murky

10. In this political climate of Proposition 187, the **demise** of the Great Society and threats to affirmative action, analytical, creative Latino minds are needed more than ever.
    a. increase
    b. surrender
    c. termination
    d. discrimination

Questions about "College Brings Alienation"

1. What was Gonzales studying in college?

   _____

   _____

   _____

2. How does his family feel about his going to college?

   _____

   _____

   _____

3. How do his longtime friends feel about his going to college?

   _____

   _____

   _____

4. Compare how his family reacts to Gonzales and his cousin, who is in the military.

   _____

   _____

   _____

5. What is Gonzales afraid will happen at the graduation party?

   _____

   _____

   _____

Journal Suggestions

1. In a social setting, would your high school and college friends feel comfortable together? Explain why or why not.

2. Is it healthy to have two identities like the author, that is, one identity with longtime friends and family, and another identity with college friends?

Collaborative Activity

What are the advantages and disadvantages of having friends with and without a college degree? Debate this issue with others in your group.

Look It Up

1. Using the Internet, find out which celebrities do not have a college degree. Did they regret not having a college education? Explain.

2. Using the Internet, find out which celebrities have more than a college degree. How did advanced education affect their careers?

Getting the Picture

The photo is the book jacket of Fantasia Barrino's first book, a memoir. What do you think she means by the title, *Life is Not a Fairy Tale?* Using the bio you read earlier in the chapter, predict what kind of facts and opinions she probably included in her memoir.

FANTASIA

— THE —
NEW YORK TIMES
BESTSELLER

Life Is Not a Fairy Tale

Photo by Julie Brothers Photography. Cover design from the Fireside edition of Life is Not a Fairy Tale by Fantasia reproduced with permission of Simon & Schuster, Inc. Copyright © 2005 by Simon & Schuster, Inc. All rights reserved.

_____

_____

_____

_____

_____

_____

_____

_____

_____

_____

_____

_____

_____

_____

_____

_____

_____

_____

Chapter Highlights

What Have We Learned?

1. Understanding the difference between **fact and opinion** is a **critical reading skill**.

2. **Objective** details present the facts, while **subjective** details present a **point of view.**

3. **Bias** is a strong leaning in a **positive or negative** direction.

4. A **point of view** is an **opinion, attitude, or judgment.**

Chapter 10

INTENT, ATTITUDE, AND TONE

Comprehending critically means interpreting what is read. Fantasia Barrino will be a better reader if she can distinguish fact from opinion and identify a writer's **intent, attitude, and tone.** In fact, a well-crafted persuasive essay or news story uses intent, attitude, and tone to add **shades of meaning to the piece.** In this chapter, you will learn to identify a writer's intent, attitude, and tone as you analyze various readings and respond to questions.

What Is the Writer's Intent?

Intent is simply a writer's purpose for writing a piece of prose or poetry. The writer's intent answers the question "WHY?" To determine the intent, locate the main idea and examine how the details are developed. Understanding something about the author may also help. A writer's intent may be to inform or explain, to entertain, to analyze, to make someone laugh or cry, to satirize, or to persuade. The intent calls for a reaction on the part of the reader.

Exercise **10.1** **Determining the Writer's Intent**

Directions: Examine the following ideas and decide what the writer's intent, or purpose, is. Circle the correct response.

1. an editorial criticizing open space development
   a. inform   c. persuade
   b. entertain

2. a movie review of *The Twilight Saga: New Moon*
   a. inform   c. persuade
   b. entertain

3. the first chapter in *Harry Potter*
   a. inform   c. persuade
   b. entertain

4. a student essay on the importance of going green
   a. inform   c. persuade
   b. entertain

5. a newspaper article on global warming
   a. inform   c. persuade
   b. entertain

6. a government study on the hazards of eating trans-fats
   a. inform   c. persuade
   b. entertain

7. a description of the excitement in Time Square, New York City, on New Year's Eve
   a. inform   c. persuade
   b. entertain

8. an advice column on successful dating strategies
   a. inform   c. persuade
   b. entertain

9. a story about surviving a first skydiving experience
   a. inform   c. persuade
   b. entertain

10. a chapter on "The Reagan Years" in an American History textbook.
   a. inform   c. persuade
   b. entertain

What Is the Writer's Attitude?

Attitude is how the writer feels about the subject. While the writer does not necessarily state or explain how he or she feels about the subject, attitude may be determined by the message of the main idea as well as the type of details used to support it. Again, understanding other works by the author may provide a clue to attitude.

Determining the Writer's Attitude 10.2 *Exercise*

Directions: Examine the following topic sentences and determine the attitude, or how the writer feels about the subject. Is the attitude positive or negative? Circle the correct answer.

1. Home schooling has many advantages.
   a. positive
   b. negative

2. Euthanasia, or mercy killing, should be legalized for terminally ill patients.
   a. positive
   b. negative

3. Capital punishment is never justified.
   a. positive
   b. negative

4. Fad diets are temporary weight loss methods.
   a. positive
   b. negative

5. Taking a year off between high school and college may be worthwhile for some students.
   a. positive
   b. negative

6. The United States government should include women in the Selective Service.
   a. positive
   b. negative

7. *Pride and Prejudice* by Jane Austen is a classic worthy of multiple reads.
   a. positive
   b. negative

8. The artist's paintings were self-expressive and racist.
   a. positive
   b. negative

9. Budgeting money is necessary for financial independence.
   a. positive
   b. negative

10. Global warming poses an impending crisis for our planet.
    a. positive
    b. negative

What Is the Writer's Tone?

Tone is reflected in how the writer expresses himself or herself, and often it is what makes a piece memorable. The tone is the author's "voice" in the selection. The tone may be angry, persuasive, lighthearted, nostalgic, cynical, serious, or even condescending. When determining the writer's tone, you will answer the question "HOW?" How did the writer convey the message? You may have to read a selection more than once to determine the "feel" for the piece.

To better understand a writer's tone, let's examine **irony,** a popular device used in expressing tone. Irony is an outcome that is contrary, or opposite, of what is expected. For example, it is ironic when someone who always remembers an umbrella forgets it on the one day it rains. Another example of irony can be found in Jonathan Swift's, "A Modest Proposal." Jonathan Swift writes about the problem of starvation in Ireland and makes a proposal on how to solve it:

> I do therefore humbly offer it to public consideration that of the 120,000 children already computed, 20,000 may be reserved for breed, whereof only one-fourth part to be males; which is more than we allow to sheep, black cattle or swine; and my reason is, that these children are seldom the fruits of marriage, a circumstance not much regarded by our savages, therefore one male will be sufficient to serve four females. That the remaining 100,000 may at a year old, be offered in sale to the persons of quality and fortune through the kingdom; always advising the mother to let them suck plentifully in the last month, so as to render them plump and fat for a good table. A child will make two dishes at an entertainment for friends; and when the family dines alone, the fore or hind quarter will make a reasonable dish, and seasoned with a little pepper or salt will be very good boiled on the fourth day, especially in winter. (Swift)

If tone and intent are related, do you know Swift's purpose for writing "A Modest Proposal"? Hint: "A Modest Proposal" was written in 1792. Swift writes below the title these words: "For Preventing the Children of Poor People from Being a Burden to Their Parents or Country, and for Making Them Beneficial to the Public.

What was Swift's intent concerning the issue of starvation in Ireland?
Answer: Swift's intent, or purpose, was to make people aware of the seriousness of the problem.

What was Swift's attitude, or feeling, about this issue?
Answer: He condemned the situation in Ireland; he wanted it to stop.

What is the tone of Swift's "proposal"?
Answer: Swift's tone is ironic. In fact, it is his tone that makes this essay memorable. He suggests that the young children should be killed and eaten, thereby solving the problems of starvation and overpopulation. Clearly, Swift does not intend to be taken seriously, but by shocking the public through the use of irony (or satire, making fun of a serious issue to make a statement), he has gotten people to notice and act on a serious problem.

Determining the Writer's Tone

10.3 *Exercise*

Directions: Read the following statement(s) and decide the tone.

1. "Hey, it's not my problem. It's your problem. I'm going to do what I'm going to do. You don't like it, that's just tough."
   a. excited
   b. self-pitying
   c. contemptuous

2. "I can't decide if I should stay in school or drop out and get a job."
   a. peevish
   b. ambivalent
   c. playful

3. "Oh, thank you for the necklace. It's lovely. It's just what I've always wanted."
   a. informal
   b. appreciative
   c. objective

4. "Don't feel bad about forgetting my birthday, sweetie. I know you've been busy. It's really not that important."
   a. forgiving
   b. amused
   c. bitter

5. "You're late to pick me up again. This is the fifth time this week! Don't give me your excuses. I don't want to hear it."
   a. tragic
   b. surprised
   c. outraged

6. "Well of course you're right and I'm wrong. I keep forgetting that someone as brilliant as you say you are is never wrong.
   a. informal
   b. sarcastic
   c. humorous

7. "Of all the nerve. Can you believe some people? Hey, lady! I'm next in line. Wait your turn."
   a. angry
   b. befuddled
   c. sorrowful

8. "Mike, you're making far too many errors in your papers. I suggest you proof-read them more carefully."
   a. surprised
   b. witty
   c. critical

9. "He's had all kinds of problems and yet he just keeps on trying. I have nothing but respect for the guy."
   a. admiring
   b. solemn
   c. cheerful

10. "Tina was so sweet. She used to make little flowers and smiley faces for me when she was three. She was such a loving child."
    a. charming
    b. nostalgic
    c. amused

11. "Mommy, why does Ann always get to sit next to the window? I want to sit next to the window. You never let me sit there. It's not fair! And I'm hungry, too."
    a. optimistic
    b. formal
    c. whining

12. "I hate to loan you my car. Something bad always happens to it. I know it's not going to be any different this time either. Why should it be?"
    a. ironic
    b. nostalgic
    c. cynical

Exercise 10.4 Your Turn—What Did You Learn?

1. Another word for the author's purpose is _____.

2. How the author feels about a subject is the _____.

3. How an author expresses himself or herself is the _____.

4. When a writer states the opposite of what is really meant, this type of tone is called _____.

Exercise 10.5 Determining a Writer's Intent, Attitude, and Tone

Directions: As you read the following selection, look for the author's intent, attitude, and tone. Answer the questions after reading.

Big White
by Skip Rozin

A strange calm settled over me as I stood before the large white vending machine and dropped a quarter into the appropriate slot. I listened as the coin clunked into the register. Then I pressed the button marked "Hot Chocolate." From deep inside a paper cup slid down a chute, crackling into place on a small metal rack. Through an unseen tube poured coffee, black as night and smoking hot.

I even smiled as I moved to my customary place at the last table, sat down, and gazed across to the white machine, large and clean and defiant. Not since it had been moved in between the candy machine and the sandwich machine had I known peace. Every morning for two weeks I had selected a beverage, and each time the machine dispensed something different. When I pushed the button for hot chocolate, black coffee came out. When I pushed the button for tea with sugar, coffee with half and half came out. So the cup of coffee before me was no surprise. It was but one final test; my plan had already been laid.

Later in the day, after everyone else had left the building, I returned to the snack bar, a yellow legal pad in my hand and a fistful of change in my pocket. I approached the machine and, taking each button in order, began feeding in quarters. After the first quarter, I pressed the button labeled "Black Coffee." Tea with sugar came out, and I recorded that on the first line of my pad. I dropped in a second quarter and pressed the button for coffee with sugar. Plain tea came out, and I wrote that down.

I pressed all nine of the buttons, noting what came out. Then I placed each cup on the table behind me. When I had gone through them all, I repeated the process, and was delighted to find the machine dispensing the same drinks as before.

None was what I had ordered, but each error was consistent with my list.

I was thrilled. To celebrate, I decided to purchase a fresh cup of chocolate.

Dropping in two dimes and a nickel and consulting my pad, I pressed the "Coffee with Sugar and Half and Half" button. The machine clicked in response, and a little cup slid down the chute, bouncing as it hit bottom. But that was all. Nothing else happened. No hot chocolate poured into my cup. No black coffee came down. Nothing.

I was livid. I forced five nickels into the slot and punched the button for black coffee. A cup dropped into place, but nothing dropped down—empty. I dug into my pocket for more change, but found only three dimes. I forced them in, and got back a stream of hot water and a nickel change. I went berserk.

"White devil!" I screamed as I slammed my fists against the machine's clean enamel finish. "You white devil!"

I beat on the buttons and rammed the coin-return rod down. I wanted the machine to know what pain was. I slapped at its metal sides and kicked its base with such force that I could almost hear the bone in my foot crack, then wheeled in agony on my good foot, and with one frantic swing, sent the entire table of coffee-, tea-, and chocolate-filled cups sailing.

That was last night. They have cleaned up the snack bar since then, and I have had my foot X-rayed and wrapped in that brown elastic they use for sprains. I am now sitting with my back to the row of vending machines. I know by the steadiness of my hand as I pour homemade hot

© Arvind Balaraman, 2010. Used under license from Shutterstock, Inc.

> chocolate from my thermos that no one can sense what I have been through—except, of course, the great white machine over against the wall.
>   Even now, behind me, in the space just below the coin slot, a tiny sign blinks off and on:
>   "Make Another Selection," it taunts. "Make Another Selection." (Rozin)

Now answer the some questions about "Big White."

1. What is the author's general intent?
   a. to make us hate this vending machine
   b. to share an experience with us
   c. to provide a better understanding of vending machines
   d. to satirize the power of machines and human reactions

2. What is the author's attitude toward "Big White"?
   a. frustration   c. defeat
   b. hate   d. all of the above

3. What is the author's tone?
   a. entertaining   c. raucous
   b. nostalgic   d. serious

Determining a Poet's Intent, Attitude, and Tone

Exercise **10.6**

Directions: Read each short poem aloud several times. Mark any words you find significant by underlining or highlighting. Also, mark any words or lines you don't understand with a question mark. State the author's intent, attitude, and tone below each poem.

"To A Wasp"
by Janice Townley Moore (b. 1939)

> You must have chortled
> finding that tiny hole
> in the kitchen screen. Right
> into my cheese cake batter
> you dived,
> no chance to swim ashore,
> no saving spoon,
> the mixer whirring
> your legs, wings, stinger,
> churning you into such

© Kletr, 2010. Used under license from Shutterstock, Inc.

From Janice Townley Moore. Reprinted with permission.

delicious death.

Never mind the bright April day.

Did you not see

rising out of cumulus clouds

That fist aimed at both of us?

Intent:_____

Attitude: _____

Tone:_____

"Earth"
by John Hall Wheelock (b. 1886)

"A planet doesn't explode of itself," said dryly

The Martian astronomer, gazing off into the air-

"That they were able to do it is proof that highly

Intelligent beings must have been living there."

Intent:_____

Attitude: _____

Tone:_____

"A Man Said to the Universe"
by Stephen Crane (b. 1871)

A man said to the universe

"Sir, I exist!"

"However," replied the universe,

"The fact has not created in me

A sense of obligation."

Intent:_____

Attitude: _____

Tone:_____

"Pragmatist"
by Edmund Conti (b. 1929)

Apocalypse soon

Coming our way

Ground zero at noon

Halve a nice day

Copyright © 1985 by Edmund Conti. Reprinted by permission.

Intent:_____

Attitude: _____

Tone: _____

Creating Your SQ3R Cards

SQ3R cards are a study system to help you successfully comprehend what you are reading. As you read the longer reading selection, you will actively interact with the text before you read, while you read, and after you read.

"S": Survey the Reading Selection

- What is the topic?

  _____

  _____

  _____

- What do I already know?

  _____

  _____

  _____

- What is my purpose for reading?

  _____

  _____

  _____

  _____

"Q": Turn a Selection Title into a Question

Don't forget to turn key statements into questions as you read.

_____

_____

_____

_____

_____

1st "R": Read

- Make predictions.

_____

_____

- Retrieve prior knowledge.

_____

_____

- State confusing ideas.

_____

_____

2nd "R": Recite

- Write the main point of this selection.
- Don't forget to annotate and take notes in the margin.

_____

_____

3rd "R": Review

- Recall what you have learned.
- React to what you have read.

_____

_____

_____

_____

_____

Comprehending Longer Selections   10.7   *Exercise*

Intent, Attitude, and Tone

Step One: Before Reading

Vocabulary in Context Practice

Directions: Choose one of the following words to complete each of the sentences below. Use each word only once. Be sure to pay attention to the context clues provided.

dearth—scarcity
deterrence—something which discourages
evasion—avoidance
fervor—passion
forfeited—gave up something
intuitively—insightfully
macabre—gruesome
peripheral—not the main issue
pragmatic—practical
semantics—language

1. When responding to the prosecuting attorney's question, the defendant used _____, which was not acceptable to the judge.

2. The choir's _____ was contagious, resulting in an explosion of voices echoing throughout the church.

3. The twin sister knew _____ that her sister was injured in a car accident.

4. The corporation's board of trustees focused on the crucial issues facing the company and tabled the _____ issues for another meeting.

5. The children _____ the toys they had won and gave them to those who were needy.

6. After a natural disaster, there is a _____ of food and supplies.

7. The teenager's academic irresponsibility led to a _____ solution— two months of summer school.

8. The students could not understand the scientific study because of _____; the words were so confusing.

9. The _____ tales raised the hair on my skin.

10. _____ would be stronger if the first offense for drinking while intoxicated (DWI) was a jail sentence, license revoking, and a fine.

Freewrite

Capital punishment or the death penalty laws vary from state to state, but most states allow capital punishment. In your journal, state whether you think capital punishment is ever justified. If you feel capital punishment is permissible, should the guilty be gassed, electrocuted, hanged, or given lethal injections? Explain your answer.

Step Two: Read the Selection

Note: As you read the following selection, concentrate and practice the steps of SQ3R. Remove the SQ3R card from the book and complete it as you read.

In the previous chapter we learned that Fantasia Barrino knew she needed more than literal reading skills to overcome her illiteracy. Reading about controversial issues, such as the death penalty, requires a reader to recognize facts and opinions and an author's intent, attitude, and tone to comprehend the writer's viewpoint(s) on an issue. Therefore, becoming literate means comprehending at the critical level where you can interpret an author's viewpoint and formulate you own viewpoint regarding the issue from an author's presentation of facts and opinions, as well as purpose, attitude, and tone. In the following reading, see how one writer, Jacob Sullum, structures his argument.

Capital Punishment: Yes
By Jacob Sullum

1. Few questions of public policy stir the passions the way the death penalty does. The idea of deliberately taking a human life elicits strong visceral reactions. The vast majority of Americans tend to focus on the act of the murderer and therefore favor capital punishment. A sizable minority, however, concentrates on the act of the state, rejecting it with equal fervor.

2. Still, those who honestly reflect on the arguments of the other side cannot help but be disconcerted, if not swayed. Although they may return to their original position, they will do so better equipped to distinguish between the crucial and peripheral issues.

3. Prevention and deterrence, although frequently stressed in news coverage of the death-penalty, turn out to be of minor relevance. Capital punishment obviously has some impact on future murders, if only by stopping those who are executed from killing again. But that direct effect could in principle be achieved through lifetime imprisonment without parole.

Deterrence Debate

4. As for the death penalty's direct effect on crime, opponents note the dearth of evidence to support the intuitively appealing notion that the prospect of execution discourages potential murderers more than the possibility

of a life term would. Advocates respond that deterrence would be stronger if the death penalty were imposed more consistently and carried out more promptly. Since murderers are not very likely to face execution or life imprisonment, it is difficult to settle this debate.

5. Moreover, it's unnecessary. In the final analysis, the argument for capital punishment rests on the proposition that in cases of unprovoked, premeditated murder, justice requires it. This assertion is often supported, imprecisely but not inappropriately, through anecdotes intended to provoke moral outrage.

6. Consider the case of Robert Alton Harris, who was scheduled to be executed by the state of California until he was granted a stay. Harris was convicted in 1979 of kidnapping and murdering two teenagers whose car he stole to commit a bank robbery. The act was cold, callous, and calculated. He killed his victims after telling them they would not be harmed, shooting one as he walked away and the other as he begged for mercy. Afterward, Harris laughed about the murders and finished the boys' lunches.

© Linda Bucklin, 2010. Used under license from Shutterstock, Inc.

7. Does such a man deserve to live? Most people would say no, but they may still question whether the state may therefore take his life. They might ask how the state acquires such a right. They might also argue that even if the government may rightfully execute someone like Harris, it should refrain from doing so because such legally sanctioned killing demeans human life.

8. One way of responding to the first point is to ask what would happen in a state of nature following a murder. In the case of other crimes, the victim or the victim's agent would have the right to punish the aggressor. Could an offender avoid punishment by killing the victim? Surely not; the right of punishment would pass to relatives or friends of the person who was murdered. If so, they could legitimately transfer that right to an agency, such as the government, that assumes the function of punishing aggressors.

9. But should the punishment be death? Isn't this simply revenge? To respond, "No, it is retribution, and therefore just and proper," might seem to be semantic evasion. But what distinguishes revenge from retribution is the motive. The execution of a murderer makes a statement. It says that people like Robert Alton Harris have committed a crime so grave that they have forfeited their right to live; it elevates human life even as it ends the killer's.

Execution of the Innocent

10. Some people accept the view of the death penalty while retaining pragmatic objections to capital punishment. The most compelling is the fear that an innocent person might be executed. Of course, the possibility of unjust punishment exists with or without the death penalty, and while people who are wrongly imprisoned can be released, nothing can restore the years they have lost. Still, the finality of execution requires that accused murderers be given every reasonable opportunity to challenge their convictions. Stricter limits on appeals are nevertheless appropriate in cases, such as Harris's, where the facts of the crime are not in dispute.

11. Another practical issue is the inconsistent application of the death penalty. To pick just one notorious example, isn't it unjust to give Hillside Strangler Angelo Buono-who kidnapped, tortured, and murdered nine

women—a life sentence, while sending Harris to death row? Yes, but the injustice is not in executing Harris; it's in failing to execute Buono.

Upholding the Right to Life

12. It is fashionable in some circles to view capital punishment as a barbaric institution that is destined to fade away. Watching some of the macabre pro-death demonstrations attracted by pending executions, one is tempted to agree. But the true mark of civilization is the extent to which a society upholds the rights of its members, especially the right to life. There is only one appropriate penalty for the willful, unprovoked violation of that right. By imposing this penalty on those who dare to break the most basic rule of existence, we affirm the dignity of every other individual. (Sullum)

Step Three: Follow-Up Activities

Objective Test on "Capital Punishment: Yes"

Directions: Choose the best answer based on the reading.

1. Sullum's intent is to:
   a. persuade.
   b. entertain.
   c. inform.
   d. satirize.

2. Sullum's attitude is:
   a. for the death penalty.
   b. against the death penalty.
   c. for further study of the issue.
   d. against prisoners being set free.

3. Sullum's tone is:
   a. humorous.
   b. nostalgic.
   c. decisive.
   d. optimistic.

4. Sullum's thesis is stated in:
   a. paragraph #5.
   b. paragraph #6.
   c. paragraph #12.
   d. paragraphs #5 and #12.

5. True or False: Sullum believes the death penalty is a deterrent to others who may want to commit a murder.

6. True or False: Sullum feels the death penalty affirms and upholds the right to life.

7. True or False: Sullum supports his thesis with facts.

8. True or False: Sullum believes justice was not served in the case of Angelo Buono, for he should have been executed.

9. Fact or Opinion: In paragraph #6, Sullum says of the Robert Harris murders, "The act was cold, callous, and calculated."

10. Fact or Opinion: Hillside Strangler Angelo Buono kidnapped, tortured, and murdered nine women.

Vocabulary Test on "Capital Punishment: Yes"
Directions: Choose one of the meanings to identify the highlighted word as it appears in the selection.

1. As for the death penalty's direct effect on crime, opponents note the **dearth** of evidence to support the intuitively appealing notion that the prospect of execution discourages potential murderers more than the possibility of a life term would.
   a. famine
   b. scarcity
   c. surplus
   d. irrelevant

2. As for the death penalty's direct effect on crime, opponents note the dearth of evidence to support the **intuitively** appealing notion that the prospect of execution discourages potential murderers more than the possibility of a life term would.
   a. creatively
   b. insightfully
   c. skillfully
   d. charmingly

3. People like Robert Alton Harris have committed a crime so grave that they have **forfeited** their right to live."
   a. earned
   b. gave up
   c. financed
   d. killed

4. But should the punishment be death? Isn't this simply revenge? To respond, "No, it is retribution, and therefore just and proper," might seem to be **semantic** evasion.
   a. language
   b. word parts
   c. word spellings
   d. word

5. Some people accept the view of the death penalty while retaining **pragmatic** objections to capital punishment.
   a. meaningful
   b. constructive
   c. practical
   d. silly

6. Prevention and **deterrence**, although frequently stressed in news coverage of the death-penalty, turn out to be of minor relevance.
   a. instruction
   b. intimidation
   c. discouraged from doing something
   d. revenge

7. Watching some of the **macabre** pro-death demonstrations attracted by pending executions, one is tempted to agree.
   a. gruesome
   b. justified
   c. negative
   d. positive

8. Although they may return to their original position, they will do so better equipped to distinguish between the crucial and **peripheral** issues.
   a. not the main issue
   b. important
   c. insignificant
   d. unsavory

9. A sizable minority, however, concentrates on the act of the state, rejecting it with equal **fervor.**
   a. passion
   b. intensity
   c. motivation
   d. ambition

10. "No, it is retribution, and therefore just and proper," might seem to be semantic **evasion.**
    a. agreement
    b. contradiction
    c. avoidance
    d. wordiness

Questions about "Capital Punishment: Yes"

1. Is Sullum for or against capital punishment? Explain your answer.

   _____

   _____

   _____

2. According to Sullum, did Robert Alton Harris deserve the death penalty? Why or why not?

   _____

   _____

   _____

3. According to Sullum, did the Hillside Strangler Angelo Buono deserve the death penalty? Why or why not?

   _____

   _____

   _____

4. According to Sullum, is capital punishment a deterrent? Explain your answer.

   _____

   _____

   _____

5. How does Sullum respond to the idea that everyone has a right to life, and therefore we should outlaw the death penalty?

   _____

   _____

   _____

Journal Suggestions

1. Do you agree or disagree with Sullum's viewpoint? Why or why not?
2. What words or phrases develop Sullum's tone?

Collaborative Activities

1. Do you agree with Sullum when he says, "People like Robert Alton Harris have committed a crime so grave that they have forfeited their right to live." Why? Discuss your answers with your group.

2. Do you agree with Sullum when he says, "The injustice is not in executing Harris; it's in failing to execute Buono." Explain and discuss with your group.

3. Think of songs about crime. Make a list of as many songs you can think of. Then choose one song and write out the lyrics so you can explain the crime, resolution, and whatever else you deem important. Focus on the language of the lyrics to identify the author's intent, attitude, and tone. Discuss with your group.

Look It Up

1. Report on three more cases that support Sullum's viewpoint on the death penalty.

2. Come up with a short list of films, between five and ten, that consider the death penalty or life in prison. For each film, state the crime, sentence, and your reaction to the sentence.

3. Report on which actors or actresses have portrayed victims or offenders in more than one film. State the films, and their role in each film.

4. Prepare a reading list of books about crime. They can be contemporary or classical books. Designate if the book is contemporary or classical. Give a short blurb about each book as if you are marketing the books.

Creating Your SQ3R Cards

SQ3R cards are a study system to help you successfully comprehend what you are reading. As you read the longer reading selection, you will actively interact with the text before you read, while you read, and after you read.

"S": Survey the Reading Selection

- What is the topic?

  _____

  _____

  _____

- What do I already know?

  _____

  _____

  _____

- What is my purpose for reading?

  _____

  _____

  _____

"Q": Turn a Selection Title into a Question

Don't forget to turn key statements into questions as you read.

_____

_____

_____

_____

1st "R": Read

- Make predictions.

_____

_____

- Retrieve prior knowledge.

_____

_____

- State confusing ideas.

_____

_____

2nd "R": Recite

- Write the main point of this selection.
- Don't forget to annotate and take notes in the margin.

_____

_____

3rd "R": Review

- Recall what you have learned.
- React to what you have read.

_____

_____

_____

_____

_____

Comprehending Longer Selections   10.8   *Exercise*

More Practice

Step One: Before Reading
Vocabulary in Context Practices
Directions: Choose one of the following words to complete each of the sentences below. Use each word only once. Be sure to pay attention to the context clues provided.

cerebral—intellectual
gradations—stages
gurney—wheeled stretcher
hypocritical—insincere
inherently—innately
prime—most important
prone—lying face downward
recidivism—a tendency to return to criminal habits
retribution—punishment
imposed—forced

1. The nurses wheeled the patient on the _____ into the operating room.

2. The poetry reading was too _____ for the audience of young teens.

3. Those who smoke cigarettes and tell others not to do so are considered _____.

4. I believe exploiting human beings is _____ immoral.

5. Like dying, there are _____ of depression.

6. If a chronic shoplifter is finally caught, prosecuted, fined, and released, will _____ ever be eliminated?

7. When the police arrested the man, they placed handcuffs on him while he was in the _____ position.

8. The jurors _____ the death penalty.

9. Fantasia is a _____ example of someone who put effort into over-coming a serious problem.

10. If someone blatantly cheated from you and received a better final grade, would you seek _____?

Freewrite
In your journal, write whether you would defend an individual who you know is guilty based on the evidence.

Step Two: Read the Selection

Note: As you read the following selection, concentrate and practice the steps of SQ3R. Remove the SQ3R card from the book and complete it as you read.

You just read an essay concerning the legitimacy of the death penalty. In the essay you are about to read, Anna Quindlen assumes a different position on this subject. Use critical reading skills in order to determine the writer's intent, attitude, and tone.

Death Penalty's False Promise
By Anna Quindlen

1. Ted Bundy and I go back a long way, to a time when there was a series of unsolved murders in Washington State known only as the Ted murders. Like a lot of reporters, I'm something of a crime buff.

2. But the Washington Ted murders—and the ones that followed in Utah, Colorado and finally in Florida, where Ted Bundy was convicted and sentenced to die—fascinated me because I could see myself as one of the victims. I looked at the studio photographs of young women with long hair, pierced ears, easy smiles, and I read the descriptions: polite, friendly, quick to help, eager to please. I thought about being approached by a handsome young man asking for help, and I knew if I had been in the wrong place at the wrong time I would have been a goner.

3. By the time Ted finished up in Florida, law enforcement authorities suspected he had murdered dozens of young women. He and the death penalty seemed made for each other.

4. The death penalty and I, on the other hand, seem to have nothing in common. But Ted Bundy has made me think about it all over again, now that outlines of my '60s liberalism have been filled in with a decade as a reporter covering some of the worst back alleys in New York City and three years as a mother who, like most, would lay down her life for her kids.

5. Simply put, I am opposed to the death penalty. I would tell that to any judge or lawyer undertaking the voir dire of jury candidates in a state in which the death penalty can be imposed. That is why I would be excused from such a jury. In a rational completely cerebral way, I think the killing of one human being as punishment for the killing of another makes no sense and is inherently immoral.

© Olga Skalkina. 2010. Used under license from Shutterstock. Inc.

6. But whenever my response to an important subject is rational and completely cerebral, I know there is something wrong with it—and so it is here. I have always been governed by my gut, and my gut says I am hypocritical about the death penalty. That is, I do not in theory think that Ted Bundy, or others like him, should be put to death. But if my daughter had been the one clubbed to death as she slept in a Tallahassee sorority house, and if the bite mark left in her buttocks had been one of the prime pieces of evidence against the young man charged with her murder, I would with the greatest pleasure kill him myself.

7. The State of Florida will not permit the parents of Bundy's victims to do that, and, in a way, that is the problem with an emotional response to capital punishment. The only reason for a death penalty is to exact retribution. Is there anyone who really thinks that it is a deterrent, that there are considerable numbers of criminals out there who think twice about committing crimes because of the sentence involved? The ones I have met in the course of my professional duties have either sneered at the justice system, where they can exchange one charge for another with more ease than they could return a shirt to a clothing store, or they have simply believed that it is the other guy who will get caught, get convicted, get the stiffest sentence. Of course, the death penalty would act as a deterrent by eliminating recidivism, but then so would life without parole, albeit at greater taxpayer expense.

8. I don't believe deterrence is what most proponents seek from the death penalty anyhow. Our most profound emotional response is to want criminals to suffer as their victims did. When a man is accused of throwing a child from a high-rise terrace, my emotional—some might say hysterical—response is that he should be given an opportunity to see how endless the seconds are from the 31st story to the ground. In a civilized society that will never happen. And so what many people want from the death penalty, they will never get.

9. Death is death, you may say, and you would be right. But anyone who has seen someone die suddenly of a heart attack and someone else slip slowly into the clutches of cancer knows that there are gradations of dying.

10. I watched a television re-enactment one night of an execution by lethal injection. It was well done; it was horrible. The methodical approach, people standing around the gurney waiting, made it more awful. One moment there was a man in a prone position; the next moment that man was gone. On another night I watched a television movie about a little boy named Adam Walsh, who disappeared from a shopping center in Florida. There was a re-enactment of Adam's parents coming to New York, where they appeared on morning talk shows begging for their son's return, and in their hotel room, where they received a call from the police saying that Adam had been found: not all of Adam, actually, just his severed head, discovered in the waters of a Florida canal. There is nothing anyone could do that is bad enough for an adult who took a 6-year-old boy away from his parents, perhaps tortured, then murdered him and cut off his head. Nothing at all. Lethal injection? The electric chair? Bah.

11. And so I come back to the position that the death penalty is wrong, not only because it consists of stooping to the level of the killers, but also because it is not what it seems. Just before Ted Bundy's most recent execution date was postponed, pending further appeals, the father of his last known victim, a 12-year-old girl, said what almost every father in his situation must feel. "I wish they'd bring him back to Lake City," said Tom Leach of the town where Kimberly Leach lived and died, "and let us all have at him." But the death penalty does not let us all have at him in the way Mr. Leach seems to mean. What he wants is for something as horrifying as what happened to his child to happen to Ted Bundy. And that is impossible. (Quindlen)

Step Three: Follow-Up Activities

Objective Test on "Death Penalty's False Promise"

Directions: Choose the best answer based on the reading.

1. (True) or False: Quindlen says, "I think the killing of one human being as punishment for the killing of another makes no sense and is inherently immoral." This is Quindlen's thesis.

2. What does Quindlen claim is "the only argument" for the death penalty?
   - a. it is permitted in most states
   - (b.) retribution
   - c. rehabilitation is not effective
   - d. justice

3. Quindlen's tone is:
   - (a.) argumentative.
   - b. pessimistic.
   - c. optimistic.
   - d. instructive.

4. Fact or (Opinion): "And so I come back to the position that the death penalty is wrong, not only because it consists of stooping to the level of the killers, but also because it is not what it seems."

5. Fact or (Opinion): "'I wish they'd bring him [Bundy] back to Lake City,' said Tom Leah of the town where Kimberly Leach lived and died, 'and let us have at him.'"

6. Quindlen's viewpoint on the death penalty is supported with:
   - a. more facts.
   - (b.) more opinions.

7. (True) or False: Quindlen sees herself as a possible victim of Ted Bundy.

8. (True) or False: Quindlen uses personal observation to tell us about herself in order to support her argument for the death penalty.

9. Quindlen's attitude about the death penalty is:
   - a. scared.
   - b. in favor of it.
   - (c.) not in favor of it.
   - d. noncommittal.

10. Quindlen's intent is to
    - a. inform.
    - b. enlighten.
    - (c.) persuade.
    - d. instruct.

Vocabulary Test on "Death Penalty's False Promise"

Directions: Choose one of the meanings to identify the highlighted word as it appears in the selection.

1. The only reason for a death penalty is to exact **retribution**.
   - a. ridicule
   - b. criticism
   - (c.) punishment
   - d. murder

2. In a rational completely **cerebral** way, I think the killing of one human being as punishment for the killing of another makes no sense and is inherently immoral.
   - a. bodily
   - (b.) intellectual
   - c. social
   - d. emotional

3. But anyone who has seen someone die suddenly of a heart attack and someone else slip slowly into the clutches of cancer knows that there are **gradations** of dying.
   - (a.) stages
   - b. grades
   - c. grants
   - d. fears

4. The methodical approach, people standing around the **gurney** waiting, made it more awful.
   a. elevator
   b. wheelchair
   (c.) a wheeled stretcher
   d. escalator

5. One moment there was a man in a **prone** position; the next moment that man was gone.
   a. sitting
   b. crouching
   (c.) lying face downward
   d. lying face upward

6. In a rational completely cerebral way, I think the killing of one human being as punishment for the killing of another makes no sense and is **inherently** immoral.
   (a.) innately
   b. sinfully
   c. outrageous
   d. clearly

7. I have always been governed by my gut, and my gut says I am **hypocritical** about the death penalty.
   a. proud
   b. logical
   (c.) insincere
   d. honest

8. Of course, the death penalty would act as a deterrent by eliminating **recidivism**, but then so would life without parole, albeit at greater taxpayer expense.
   (a.) a tendency to return to criminal habits
   b. a tendency to behave insanely
   c. a tendency to lie
   d. a tendency to kill

9. But if my daughter had been the one clubbed to death as she slept in a Tallahassee sorority house, and if the bite mark left in her buttocks had been one of the **prime** pieces of evidence against the young man charged with her murder, I would with the greatest pleasure kill him myself.
   a. intellectual
   b. practical
   c. proven
   (d.) most important

10. I would tell that to any judge or lawyer undertaking the voir dire of jury candidates in a state in which the death penalty can be **imposed**.
    (a.) forced
    b. surrendered
    c. silenced
    d. removed

Questions about "Death Penalty's False Promise"

1. Why is Quindlen against the death penalty?

   _____

   _____

   _____

2. Why does Quindlen call herself a hypocrite?

   _____

   _____

   _____

3. What is Quindlen's response to the idea that the death penalty is a deterrent?

_____

_____

_____

4. According to Quindlen, do relatives of a victim have the right to seek retribution?

_____

_____

_____

5. Compare Quindlen's argument against the death penalty to Sullum's argument in favor of the death penalty.

_____

_____

_____

Journal Suggestions

1. Having read Quindlen's essay, write whether you agree or disagree with her viewpoint on the death penalty. Support you viewpoint with evidence from the essay.

2. Do you think the death penalty deters an individual from committing a heinous crime? Why or why not?

Collaborative Activities

1. Is Quindlen contradicting herself when she says she does not believe Ted Bundy should be put to death, yet if he killed her child, she would kill him herself "with the greatest pleasure"? Explain and discuss with your group.

2. When Quindlen says most proponents of the death penalty really want revenge, is she right? What evidence does she give to support this view? Discuss with your group.

Look It Up

1. Find at least two essays that support Quindlen's viewpoint on the death penalty. Compare Quindlen's style and structure with Sullum's. Keep in mind that a persuasive essay uses facts and opinions, and the author's intent, attitude, and tone are powerful persuasive devices. The essays do not have to be contemporary.

2. Report on a different society's/culture's handling of criminals committing heinous crimes. Discuss specific crimes and consequences. Be specific. Include as many details as you can. *Compare States*

Getting the Picture

Carefully examine the photo. Use your imagination to describe what these students are doing—be specific. What do you think their intent (purpose) is? How would you describe their attitude? Do you think both will be equally successful? There are no wrong answers!

© Anton Gvozdikov, 2010. Used under license from Shutterstock, Inc.

_____

_____

_____

_____

_____

_____

_____

_____

_____

_____

_____

_____

_____

_____

_____

_____

_____

_____

_____

_____

_____

Chapter Highlights

What Have We Learned?

1. **Comprehending critically** means interpreting what is read.

2. **Interpreting** what is read means being able to **distinguish facts from opinions,** and being able to identify the author's intent, attitude, and tone.

3. A well-crafted **persuasive** essay or news story uses **intent, attitude, and tone** to add shades of meaning to the piece.

4. **Intent** is simply a writer's **purpose** for writing a piece of prose or poetry.

5. **Attitude** is how the writer **feels** about the subject.

6. **Tone** is reflected in **how the writer expresses himself or herself,** and often it is what makes a piece memorable. In fact, think of tone as the author's "voice," which is often related to the author's purpose.

7. **Irony** is a popular device used in **expressing tone;** it is an outcome that is contrary, or opposite, of what is expected.

HOW CAN I EVALUATE WHAT I READ?

CHAPTER 11 Bias
CHAPTER 12 Propaganda

In Unit 5, you learned how to read between the lines to evaluate an author's viewpoint by focusing on facts, opinions, intent, attitude, and tone. In Unit 6, you will continue to develop your critical comprehension by learning how to evaluate what you read. Chapters 11 and 12 focus on recognizing bias and propaganda.

Spotlight on

Donald Trump (1946–)

Donald Trump is a famous entrepreneur known for his business savvy and outspoken personality. A native of New York City, he has established the "Trump" presence throughout the world. Donald Trump's mentor in real estate was his father, Fred Trump, a successful property developer. Trump graduated from the respected Wharton Business School, and later took over several large properties, brandishing them with his name. These include the Trump Casino, Trump International Hotel, Trump Marina Hotel and Casino, Trump Taj Mahal Casino Resort and Trump Tower. Trump also has holdings in Florida, Indiana, Illinois, and California. Besides resort hotels and casinos, he has acquired a river boat, a golf course, residential and business skyscrapers, and is part-owner of three beauty competitions, Miss Universe, Miss USA and Miss Teen USA. He is the owner of Mara-a-Lago, a private extravagant club in Palm Beach. In 2011, Trump flirted with the idea of a presidential candidacy but ultimately announced he would not run. His books, *The Art of the The Deal, Art of Survival and How to get Rich* have become best sellers. Trump, who has five children and has married three times, became a household name with his reality TV program, *The Apprentice,* as well as *Celebrity Apprentice,* and the catch phrase, "You're fired!"

© epa/Corbis

Chapter 11

BIAS

Would you like to be on *The Apprentice*? You might have a chance, but not if you were a friend or relative of Donald Trump or his staff. The show's winner needs to be chosen fairly, but having a relationship with anyone involved in judging might unfairly increase your chances of winning. This situation would create a **bias,** or a point of view favoring a particular candidate, which would not be fair to the other participants.

Bias is a prejudice, or showing a particular like or dislike of a person, thing, or idea.

Everyone has biases that come from personal experience or what we have learned. For example, John always looks for jobs that are outdoors because he always loved helping his father in a landscaping business. John has a *bias* for outdoor work.

© JupiterImages Corporation

Mary always leaves generous tips for waiters (even if the service is bad) because her best friend works hard as a waiter. She has a *bias* for giving good tips to waiters.

© JupiterImages Corporation

© Suzanne Tucker, 2010. Used under license from Shutterstock, Inc.

As someone who has been poor for most of her life, Lara believes that the government should offer more assistance to programs for the needy.

She has a *bias* toward government programs for the poor. Similarly, we all have *biases* against things (meat), people (strangers), and ideas (euthanasia).

We have learned that as critical readers, we need to examine a writer's *intent*, *attitude*, and *tone*. These ideas help us to understand a writer's *bias* so that we can judge its appropriateness and form our own reaction. In the same way, we should not let our own biases get in the way of objectively evaluating what a writer has to say.

Should all writing be free of bias? That depends. For example, newspaper editorials, political campaign literature, and writing that expresses a strong point of view concerning religion, economics, or international affairs are persuasive. Biases are permitted and fairly easy to identify in these types of writing. However, writing in which the intent is to present facts without taking sides should be free of overt bias. Newspaper articles and textbooks should present unbiased information. Writing that presents all sides fairly is called *objective*, while writing that stresses only one point of view is *subjective*, or *biased*.

Your Turn—What Did You Learn?

1. _____ is a prejudice toward a particular thing, person, or idea.

2. Writing that is not biased is said to be _____.

3. Writing that is biased is said to be _____.

4. One example of biased writing is _____.

5. One example of unbiased writing is _____.

Recognizing Bias

Recognizing biased material is important when forming our own opinions when we read. Can you recognize bias in reading material?

Directions: Write a "B" next to those sentences that are biased (subjective). Write a "U" next to those sentences that are unbiased (objective).

1. During the 1950s, most women did not work outside the home. _____

2. In spite of the fact that most women are more biologically equipped to stay home to raise children, increasingly, many are finding jobs outside the home. _____

3. Cigarette smoking can cause lung cancer. _____

4. When Hurricane Katrina struck New Orleans in 2005, many people believed that the response of the federal government was too slow. _____

5. The President of the United States must always make unilateral decisions during times of national crisis because he is the nation's most respected leader. _____

6. Circus animals are usually unhappy creatures. _____

7. Donald Trump's forceful personality is the reason for his success. _____

8. Donald Trump may not be the wealthiest business tycoon, but he is one of the most famous. _____

Exercise **11.3** **Bias in Writing**

In order to make careful judgments about what we read, we must first determine whether or not bias is appropriate for the material.

© JupiterImages Corporation

Directions: Decide if the following material should or should not include bias. If it should include bias, write a "B." If it should be unbiased, write "U." If there are cases when bias is sometimes allowed, write "S."

1. a student's book report about *Tom Sawyer* _____

2. a passage about the American Revolution in a history textbook _____

3. an editorial in the *New York Times* about raising teachers' salaries _____

4. a letter to a college president complaining about the food in the dining hall _____

5. a newspaper article about a bank robbery _____

6. a campaign pamphlet that advocates Mr. Jones for mayor _____

7. a movie review in the *New Yorker* magazine _____

8. a speech presented by a member of PETA _____

9. a police report _____

10. a student's report and evaluation of an art exhibit in a museum _____

Bias in Textbook Readings

11.4 *Exercise*

Directions: Read the following passages carefully to see if you can detect bias. Then answer the questions that follow the selections.

A

During the campaign, Clinton's proposed solution was to cut the deficit and stimulate the economy at the same time. Over and over, he spoke of the need to "grow the economy" to get the country moving again. All too soon, however, his economic stimulus package went down to defeat at the hands of Congress.

He was more successful with his first budget, but even this plan just barely squeaked by Congress. Budget cuts, along with tax increases, were necessary to reduce the deficit. Yet neither cuts nor taxes were popular with the public. The gas tax that was finally proposed—4.3 cents per gallon—was the result of a difficult compromise and continued to cause some complaints. New income taxes and taxes on social security benefits were met with similar discontent. The tax increases fell most heavily on the wealthiest Americans but still caused irritation among people who had to pay anything more. As they sought to gauge public opinion, legislators in both houses of Congress were reluctant to approve cuts that affected their own constituents. The final votes could not have been closer. (Cayton, Perry, and Winkler 963-64 from America: Pathways to the Present.)

© JupiterImages Corporation

B

Despite the warm reception for his State of the Union address, Clinton still had to wage a long and determined fight to complete his economic program. It took all-out arm twisting from the White House to get Congress to approve the final budget terms—$241 billion in new taxes and $255 billion in spending cuts, for a total reduction of $496 billion over four years. In late August, the House approved the budget by just two votes, and in the Senate, Vice President Gore cast his vote to break a 50 to 50 deadlock.

Despite the narrow margin, it was a major achievement. Clinton stood firm on deficit reduction, compromising on details but insisting on a program that promised to cut the deficit in half within four years. Moreover, he succeeded in winning approval for some of his education and job-training programs while increasing income tax rates on the wealthy from 33 to 39.6 percent. (Divine et al. 971)

Divine, Robert A.; Breen, T.H.H.; Fredrickson, George M.; Williams, R. Hal, America Past and Present, Single Volume Edition, 5th Edition, © 1999, Pgs. 963-964, 971, 1064–1065. Reprinted by permission of Pearson Education, Inc., Upper Saddle River, NJ.

Answer the following questions about the passages you just read:

1. What is the subject of both of these passages?

   _____

   _____

   _____

2. Which passage sounds more favorable to the Clinton economic plan? Why?

_____

_____

_____

3. In passages A and B, find the words that signal a bias for or against the plan. Write down the words you located.

A. _____

_____

B. _____

_____

4. What is the intent of Passage A and Passage B? (**HINT:** Check the source citations.)

_____

_____

_____

5. Is bias appropriate in these passages? Why or why not?

_____

_____

_____

Exercise 11.5   Bias in Political Cartoons

Directions: Political cartoons are intentionally biased to present a point of view that criticizes aspects of society. Review the following cartoons, both published on September 22, 2005, to determine the bias in each. Note: The U.S. space shuttle program officially came to an end on July 21, 2011.

A

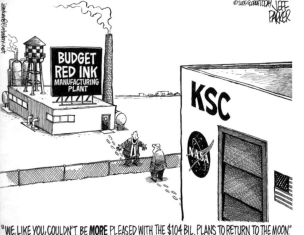

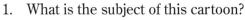

"WE, LIKE YOU, COULDN'T BE **MORE** PLEASED WITH THE $104 BIL. PLANS TO RETURN TO THE MOON."

From Detroit News, September 22, 2005 by Jeff Parker.
Copyright © 2005 by Jeff Parker, Cagle Cartoons. Reprinted by permission.

1. What is the subject of this cartoon?

_____

_____

2. What is the cartoonist's opinion of funding for space travel?

_____

_____

3. Explain why you agree or disagree with this opinion.

_____

_____

B

From San Diego Union-Tribune, September 22, 2005 by Steve Breen. Copyright © 2005 by San Diego Union-Tribune. Reprinted by permission.

1. What is the subject of this cartoon?

   _____

   _____

2. What is the cartoonist's message?

   _____

   _____

3. Explain why you agree or disagree with this opinion.

   _____

   _____

Collaborative Activities

1. Write a list of the advantages or the disadvantages of computer use. (Note: Since these articles were published, more advances such as Twitter have emerged.) Debate the issue with a partner who has taken the opposing side.

2. Discuss the meaning of bias with your group. Make a list of your personal biases (food, colors, animals, etc.) and share them with the others in your group. Write a journal entry explaining the reason for one of your personal biases.

Look It Up

1. Research the subject of bias and where it is appropriate. Use Internet and library sources for a report.

2. Use the Internet to locate articles that discuss the benefits and the setbacks of computer technology. (Note: Since these articles were published, more advances such as Twitter have emerged.) Write an objective report on your findings.

3. Research problems posed by computer technology, then write an essay suggesting how to solve at least one of them.

Getting the Picture

The photo depicts an employer who seems to be uttering Donald Trump's famous line, "You're fired!" Have you ever worked for someone who intimidated you? Do you think past job experiences make you biased against potential employers? Consider these questions and explain your answer.

_____

_____

_____

_____

_____

_____

_____

_____

_____

_____

_____

_____

_____

_____

_____

_____

_____

_____

_____

_____

_____

_____

Chapter Highlights

What Have We Learned?

1. **Bias** is a prejudice, or showing a particular like or dislike of a person, thing, or idea.

2. A one-sided presentation of a topic is considered **subjective.**

3. Material in which two sides are presented fairly is considered **objective.**

4. **Bias** is usually **not appropriate** in **textbooks** or **newspaper articles.**

Chapter 12

PROPAGANDA

In the last few chapters, we learned that reading critically is important to recognize a writer's intent, attitude, and tone. We can also detect bias in written work by critical reading, or looking for clues that help us to fully understand and form our own opinions about whatever we are reading. While bias is sometimes unintended, **propaganda** is *a particular kind of bias that is used deliberately to sway opinion.*

Sometimes governments use propaganda to sway public opinion. Political candidates may use propaganda to persuade citizens to vote for them. Organizations use propaganda to convince people to support a cause. In fact, propaganda is everywhere we go! Take a look around your classroom, look at the signs in the halls, listen to the car radio, and you will find examples of propaganda. Propaganda is even found on some of the clothes we wear.

Advertisements use forms of propaganda to sell products or services. Understanding the different techniques helps you become a more discerning reader and consumer.

Here is a list of some popular propaganda techniques:

Word Choice: Particular words are chosen that relate to the product or idea. These words are chosen to stick in the reader's mind. They may also produce an exaggerated image. Rhymes, alliteration, and superlatives are often used for this effect. For example, calling a candidate a "red, white, and blue citizen who serves the common man" is catchy and conveys a patriotic image. On the other hand, calling a candidate a "narrow-minded bureaucrat" suggests a negative image.

Testimonial: A famous person lends his or her name or photo to a product endorsement. For example, a beautiful actress might be used to sell cosmetics. Sometimes, the product or service being sold may be completely unrelated to the famous person's area of expertise. For example, a basketball player may be used to sell cereal. Because the famous person has a positive image, the consumer will relate it to the product.

Plain Folks: An "average" (non-celebrity) person or family is used in an ad so that people can relate to the images. For example, a woman in a busy household with children would be used to sell a household cleanser. A deodorant might be promoted by showing an active person throughout the day.

Bandwagon: Knowing that a great number of people are using a particular product or service may convince the consumer that getting on the "bandwagon" is a good idea. For example, if the ad shows a large group of teenagers wearing a particular type of jeans, the reader may wish to "join the bunch."

Card Stacking: When advertisers make comparisons between products by using statistics or other characteristics, an exaggerated impression is created. For example, stating that twice as many doctors recommend one cough medicine over another creates the impression that one medicine is superior. However, the impression may be a false one because variables, such as the number of doctors surveyed, may not be stated.

Transfer: This popular propaganda technique uses pictures or photographs to create a demand for the product or service. Sometimes, however, the product and picture may be completely unrelated. For example, a beautiful model may be used in a perfume ad to suggest that whoever uses the perfume will look like the model.

Exercise **12.1   Your Turn—What Did You Learn?**

1. _____ is a deliberate attempt to sway opinion.
2. Using a photo of a celebrity to sell a product is called _____.
3. Showing ordinary people to sell something is called _____.
4. Comparing prices or quality to sell something is called _____.
5. Using word alliteration or rhyme to sell a product or service is called _____.
6. _____ uses pictures to sell a product or service.
7. The idea of following the crowd is called _____.

Exercise **12.2   Identifying Propaganda Techniques**

Directions: Identify the propaganda technique used in each of the following:

1. Halle Berry uses Luscious Lipstick, and so should you!

   _____

2. Vote for I. M. DeBest because he has a proven record of service to the public and has a heart of gold where the public is concerned.

   _____

3. All of your friends now have the new Pop U Lar plasma TV. Don't be left out!

   _____

4. Mr. E. V. Reman finds that the R Car Mini-Van has enough room for the family, the dog, and his fishing equipment. Shouldn't this mini-van be a part of your life too?

   _____

5. Bet R. Realty Company has more realtors working to find you the right home and has sold 100 more homes than any other company has.

   _____

6. See those two sophisticated well-dressed women drinking Deelish Mocha Cappuccino in that café? They love it, and so will you!

   _____

7. You have to try these Grate Potato Chips. They are crispy, crunchy, and crackle with goodness!

_____

8. Brite White toothpaste is the reason Tom Cruise has such a terrific smile.

_____

9. Hurry in for Cheap Buys furniture Red Tag Sale before the big rush!

_____

10. Vote for Justin Case for mayor. He lives in your neighborhood and understands your problems.

_____

Exercise **12.3** **Propaganda in Advertisements**

Directions: Answer the questions concerning the following ads:

Selection 1

1. What is the product or service being marketed?

   _____

2. What is the prompt that attracts us to this ad?

   _____

3. What is the propaganda technique?

   _____

4. Is the ad successful? Why or why not?

   _____

   _____

Selection 2

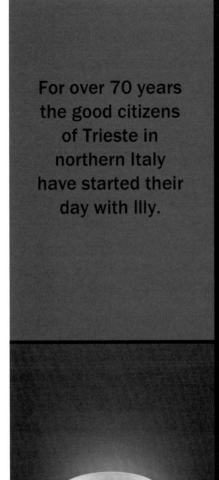

For over 70 years the good citizens of Trieste in northern Italy have started their day with Illy.

Now its *your* turn.
Illyusa.com

From Ad'Mat: Using the 25 Classic Advertising Formats by Michael Klassen et al. Copyright 2009. Reprinted by permission of Kendall Hunt Publishing Co.

5. What is the product or service being marketed?

_____

6. What is the prompt that attracts us to this ad?

_____

7. What is the propaganda technique?

_____

8. Is the ad successful? Why or why not?

_____

_____

Selection 3

From Ad'Mat: Using the 25 Classic Advertising Formats by Michael Klassen et al. Copyright 2009. Reprinted by permission of Kendall Hunt Publishing Co.

9. What is the product or service being marketed?

_____

10. What is the prompt that attracts us to this ad?

_____

11. What is the propaganda technique?

_____

12. Is the ad successful? Why or why not?

_____

_____

Selection 4

Your Dog.
Your Best Friend.
Your Favorite Bike.

Discover Arizona.
Rediscover your inner kid.

From Ad'Mat: Using the 25 Classic Advertising Formats by Michael Klassen et al. Copyright 2009. Reprinted by permission of Kendall Hunt Publishing Co.

13. What is the product or service being marketed?

_____

14. What is the prompt that attracts us to this ad?

_____

15. What is the propaganda technique?

_____

16. Is the ad successful? Why or why not?

_____

_____

Selection 5

This is either the most expensive economy car in the world,
or the least expensive Gran Turismo car in the world.
We'll sell you either one.

17. What is the product or service being marketed?

_____

18. What is the prompt that attracts us to this ad?

_____

19. What is the propaganda technique?

_____

20. Is the ad successful? Why or why not?

_____

_____

Creating Your SQ3R Cards

SQ3R cards are a study system to help you successfully comprehend what you are reading. As you read the longer reading selection, you will actively interact with the text before you read, while you read, and after you read.

"S": Survey the Reading Selection

- What is the topic?

  _____

  _____

  _____

- What do I already know?

  _____

  _____

  _____

- What is my purpose for reading?

  _____

  _____

  _____

"Q": Turn a Selection Title into a Question

Don't forget to turn key statements into questions as you read.

_____

_____

_____

_____

1st "R": Read

- Make predictions.

_____

_____

- Retrieve prior knowledge.

_____

_____

- State confusing ideas.

_____

_____

2nd "R": Recite

- Write the main point of this selection.
- Don't forget to annotate and take notes in the margin.

_____

_____

3rd "R": Review

- Recall what you have learned.
- React to what you have read.

_____

_____

_____

_____

_____

_____

3. No one seems to stop to think that—no matter what environments they come from—most kids don't put school first on their list unless they **perceive** something is at stake.
   a. intellectualize
   b. contemplate
   c. fear
   d. have a feeling

4. It would mean facing the tough reality that passing kids who haven't learned the material—while it might save them grief for the short term—dooms them to long-term **illiteracy.**
   a. incapable of being educated
   b. inability to read or write
   c. inability to find a job
   d. failure

5. I know one example doesn't make a case, but at night I see a parade of students who are angry and **resentful** for having been passed along until they could no longer even pretend to keep up.
   a. silent
   b. feeling offended
   c. harsh
   d. hopeful

6. Many students I see at night could give expert **testimony** on unemployment, chemical dependency, abusive relationships.
   a. denial
   b. partiality
   c. assertion
   d. wonder

7. I regained my **composure** and managed to say that I thought she was right.
   a. confidence, calmness
   b. understanding
   c. happiness
   d. harmony

8. I am your basic do-gooder, and prior to teaching this class I blamed the poor academic skills our kids have today on drugs, divorce and other **impediments** to concentration necessary for doing well in school.
   a. harbingers
   b. faults
   c. inspiration
   d. obstacles

9. Suddenly English became a **priority** in his life.
   a. sore spot
   b. what comes first
   c. easy to understand
   d. inspiration

10. It was a **radical** approach for these times, but well, why not?
    a. unusual
    b. plausible
    c. extreme
    d. futuristic

Questions about "In Praise of the F Word"

1. Mary Sherry states that students are being cheated by the educational system. What evidence does she give of this?

   _____

   _____

   _____

2. Why do teachers pass students who do not deserve to pass?

   _____

   _____

   _____

3. Why did Sherry change her opinion about passing students?

_____

_____

_____

4. How does passing students with poor grades cheat them and their employers?

_____

_____

_____

5. Why does Sherry call flunking students a "positive teaching tool"?

_____

_____

_____

Journal Suggestion

Mary Sherry discusses a situation in which she felt her son was treated unfairly, but she later changes her mind. Write about a time when you thought you were treated unfairly, how you reacted, and how the problem was ultimately resolved. Looking back, would you have handled the issue differently?

Collaborative Activity

There are several theories on how to motivate students to be successful. Do you agree that failure motivates students to try harder, or that factors besides academics (such as personal problems, etc.) should be taken into consideration when grading? Form groups, each group listing advantages for one side of the issue, then debate.

Look It Up

1. Use the Internet to research theories for motivating students to be successful. Write a short paper comparing three different ideas for this dilemma and discuss which theory you believe would be most effective.

2. Is success in school really something to be desired by everyone? Research the Internet for the meaning of success and write about your findings.

3. Research careers that require a college education and careers that require another type of training. Include your own career interests in your search. Document your results.

Getting the Picture

Donald Trump's popular reality show is called, "The Apprentice." An apprentice is someone who learns important skills on the job. This photo depicts young apprentices, or interns who often do not work for a salary, but for college credits. Have you ever worked as an intern? If so, discuss your experience. Do you think it is unfair not to pay interns for their work? Explain.

© Andresr, 2010. Used under license from Shutterstock, Inc.

Chapter Highlights

What Have We Learned?

1. **Propaganda** is a form of bias that is a deliberate attempt to sway opinion.

2. **Advertising** is a type of propaganda that is appropriate in certain circumstances.

3. Different forms of propaganda include **Word Choice, Testimonial, Plain Folks, Bandwagon, Card Stacking,** and **Transfer.**

HOW CAN I UNDERSTAND THE WORLD THROUGH NEWSPAPERS?

You now have an understanding of critical reading strategies. Let's apply these strategies in order to better understand our world through newspapers.

Spotlight on

Angelina Jolie (1975–)

The Oscar-winning Angelina Jolie has become famous for her numerous films as well as her political activism. This stunningly beautiful actress first gained popularity for her role as supermodel Gia Marie Cangi in the HBO movie *Gia* (1998). She then played the love interest in *Pushing Tin* (1999), a film about the life of air-traffic-controllers. Jolie was presented with an Oscar for best supporting actress for her depiction of a distraught mental patient in *Girl, Interrupted* (1999). Her other roles include the video game heroine Lara Croft in *Tomb Raider* (2001) and *Tomb Raider: Cradle of Life* (2003); Brad Pitt's counterpart in *Mr. & Mrs. Smith* (2005); a special appearance in the CGI fantasy *Beowulf* (2007); the voice of the tigress in *Kung Fu Panda* (2008); and an action hero in *Wanted* (2008). In 2009, Jolie was nominated for an Oscar for her performance as the mother of an abducted child in Clint Eastwood's *Changeling*. In 2010, she was featured in the film, *Salt*. Jolie, whose plush-lipped exotic looks and numerous tattoos often adorn the tabloids, was married to the actor Billy Bob Thornton from 2001–2003, and two years later met Brad Pitt on the set of *Mr. & Mrs. Smith*. The two live with their children, Maddox, adopted from Cambodia in 2002, Zahara from Ethiopia (in 2005), and Pax Thien from Vietnam (2007). The couple also have a daughter, Shiloh, born in 2006, and twins Knox and Vivienne, born in 2008. Jolie was named a goodwill ambassador for the United Nations High Commissioner on Refugees in 2001. She has regularly attended World Refuge Day in Washington, D.C., and she was an invited speaker at the World Economic Forum in Davos in 2005 and 2006.

© Edward Le Poulin/Corbis

Chapter 13

NEWSPAPER COMPREHENSION

Angelina Jolie is often in the news for being both a movie star and a humanitarian. Obviously, people like to read about celebrities and high-profile people. Did you know that news stories are classified or divided into **hard news, soft news (feature stories),** and **opinions?** Each of these different types of news stories appeals to a variety of readers, which explains why people read the news. In addition to different kinds of stories, there are different kinds of newspapers: **major newspapers** such as the *New York Times* and the *Chicago Tribune,* **local newspapers,** and **special interest newspapers/monitors/chronicles** with a specific orientation (e.g., religion, education, or politics). Many people are involved in newspaper production whether the paper is daily, weekly, bi-monthly, or monthly. Specifically, the two people the news depends on are the editor and the reporter. The **editor** assigns stories to reporters, decides where stories are placed in the paper, writes editorials, and edits material. The **reporter** writes the stories in the "five W's and H" format (discussed later in the chapter), without expressing any opinions. The editor expresses his opinion or the paper's opinion in an editorial. Now that you know the difference between the editor and the reporter, let's look more closely at the parts of the newspaper.

- **Hard news** is current breaking news. For example, the election of Barack Obama in 2008 would be *hard news.* A *sidebar* is an article related to a feature story. For example, a sidebar concerning the election of Barack Obama might contain the opinions of various voters.
- **Soft news** can be about any subject but is not news about fast-breaking events. For example, soft news stories may be about nutrition, celebrities, or any issue people may face.
- **Opinions** are found in soft news as well as in the editorial section of the newspaper. The newspaper's editor represents the voice of the newspaper establishment, which identifies the political slant of the newspaper and publisher as being conservative, liberal, left-wing, right-wing, Republican, Democratic, libertarian, or some other philosophy. Besides the *editorials,* opinions are found in *columns* and *reviews.* When you read advice columns; book, movie, theater, and restaurant reviews; and gardening, pet, car, and health tips; you are reading a combination of facts and opinions. *Reviews* are opinions written about movies, food, books, plays, etc.

Finally, have you wondered **what news makes the front page?** For example, would a story about the War in Vietnam make tomorrow's front page? Of course not; only **timely news** makes the front page. What about a story where a man wakes up in the middle of the night and breaks his toe on a piece of furniture? Of course not; only **stories with general public interest** make the front page.

Exercise 13.1 Your Turn—What Did You Learn?

1. News stories are classified into _____, _____, and _____.

2. Different kinds of newspapers include _____, _____, _____.

3. The _____ assigns stories to reporters, decides where stories are placed in the paper, writes editorials, and edits material.

4. The _____ writes the news stories.

5. Stories that are _____ and _____ make the front page of a newspaper.

6. _____, _____, and _____ represent opinions in the news.

Exercise 13.2 Practicing News Story Comprehension

Did you know that new stories are typically written in the "five W's and H" format? The lead—pronounced "leed"—or first paragraph of a story will answer the questions *who, what, where,* and *when.* The more difficult questions, the *how* and *why,* are not often in the lead, but in the body of the story, providing important information. Sometimes, though, the answers are implied. If a news story does not answer the *how* and *why* questions, it is likely that the writer does not know the answers either.

Directions: To practice finding the *how* and *why* questions in a news story, read the following lead from an article in the *New York Times* and tell "why" the helmets are being changed. Next, read another article to find out "how" the Red Wings defeated the Islanders.

A. Army Replacing Steel Helmets

WASHINGTON, Nov. 30 (AP)—After 40 years and three wars, the Army is trading in its metal helmet for a new, stronger, fiberglass model that looks like the headgear worn by the Germans in World War II.

© JupiterImages Corporation

Question: Why are the helmets being changed?

Answer: _____

_____

_____

B. Red Wings Defeat Islanders
By John Radosta

Special to The New York Times

DETROIT, Dec. 8—The Islanders, winners of the Stanley Cup the last three seasons, were beaten, 2-0, tonight by the Detroit Red Wings, the team with the worst record in the National Hockey League.

Although the Islanders still hold first place in the Patrick Division, they have a 5-10-5 record in their last 20 games. They have won only two of their last 10 games, and this was the third time in 15 games, since Nov. 11, that they were shut out.

Detroit, last in the Norris Division, won for only the fifth time this season.

The Islanders played tentatively and ineffectively. Although they surpassed the Red Wings in shots on goal, 24-22, they could not score against Corrado Micalef, a 21-year-old goaltender in his first full season in the N.H.L. Last season, Micalef played 18 games for the Red Wings and has a goals-against revenge of 4.67.

A measure of the Islanders' fortunes during the evening came from the goal scored by Stan Weir, a Detroit center. It was his first in 20 games, and it came off a rebound from an Islander skate. The Red Wings' other goal, also in the second period, was scored by Willie Huber.

For the first time since Dec. 14, 1980, the Islanders were awarded a penalty shot. Clark Gillies took the shot and was stopped by Micalef.

This was the second of three meetings between the teams this season. The first, on Nov. 3, ended in a 3-3 tie.

Until last Saturday, the Wings had gone 14 straight games without a victory. They have the lowest number of goals in the league, 75.

Four Islanders could not make this trip because of illnesses and injuries—Tomas Jonsson, Anders Kallur, Bob Bourne and Dave Langevin. On an emergency basis, the club has called up Darcy Regier, a defenseman, and Mats Hallin, a right wing, from the Indianapolis farm club. (Radosta)

Question: How did the Red Wings defeat the Islanders?

Answer: _____

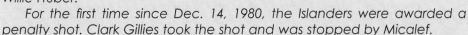

_____

Exercise **13.3**

Understanding the 5W's and H in the Newspaper Article

Directions: You will get to know more about Angelina Jolie by reading the following articles.

A. Angelina Jolie Appointed Goodwill Ambassador
By Harriet Simon

NEW YORK, August 27, 2001.—The United Nations has a new and very famous Goodwill Ambassador. The actress Angelina Jolie was appointed today by Rudd Lubbers, United Nations High Commissioner for Refugees (UNHCR).

Jolie explained why she wanted to become involved, stating, "Reading stories and statistics about refugee tragedies piqued my interest in the different organizations doing humanitarian work. However, it was UNHCR's startling statistics such as there are more than twenty million refugees, 1.1 billion people lack access to safe drinking water, one-third of the world has no electricity, more than 100 million children are out of school, and one in six children in Africa dies before the age of five, which triggered my involvement with UNHCR."

To better understand the issues facing refugees in Africa and elsewhere in the world, Jolie was compelled to work with the UNHCR staff to find solutions for the refugees in places like Africa, Cambodia, and Pakistan. Her book, Notes from My Travels, gives a first hand account of her field visits to refugee camps in Africa, Asia, and South America.

Directions: Why was Angelina Jolie appointed Goodwill Ambassador by Rudd Lubbers, United Nations High Commissioner for Refugees (UNHCR)? To answer this question, answer the reporter's questions:

Who? _____

What? _____

Why? _____

When? _____

Where? _____

How? _____

B. The Ugly Truth about Tattoos
By Georgia Littlejohn

A TEENAGER who paid £90 to have his arm tattooed with Chinese characters got a shock when he learned the message read: "At the end of the day, this is an ugly boy."

Hairdresser Lee Becks thought he had Mandarin for "Love, honour and obey" etched into his skin.

The 18-year-old found out that he had been tricked when he saw the effect it had on a woman serving at a Chinese take-away.

"At first, she said something about me making people laugh and talked about a crown," he said.

"But then I realised she was really saying clown, not crown. The young woman blushed and was very reluctant to translate for me. Then she admitted what it really said."

A "totally mortified" Mr Becks went back to the tattoo parlour in Southend, the next day—only to find it had closed.

He added: "I suspect the tattooist knew he was closing and just wanted to get his own back for some reason. I always wanted a tattoo and the design looked great. Now I am stuck with it but have to keep it covered up."

When he dared show off his arm at a nightclub, a group of Chinese girls came up—and burst out laughing. Even his friends have been finding it hard to keep straight faces.

His employer, Gary Doyle, said: "He's a bit sensitive about the tattoos— they look very trendy if you don't know what they really mean. I don't think Lee stands much of a chance with any attractive young Chinese lady he may meet."

Mr Becks plans to spend £600 to have the tattoo removed by laser.

From Metro, June 6, 2002 by Georgina Littlejohn. Copyright © 2002 by Solo Syndication. Reprinted by permission.

Directions: Angelina Jolie is known for her tattoos. Answer the reporter's questions to learn why you should be careful when choosing a tattoo.

Who? _____

What? _____

Why? _____

When? _____

Where? _____

How? _____

Creating Your SQ3R Cards

SQ3R cards are a study system to help you successfully comprehend what you are reading. As you read the longer reading selection, you will actively interact with the text before you read, while you read, and after you read.

"S": Survey the Reading Selection

- What is the topic?

  _____

  _____

  _____

- What do I already know?

  _____

  _____

  _____

- What is my purpose for reading?

  _____

  _____

  _____

"Q": Turn a Selection Title into a Question

Don't forget to turn key statements into questions as you read.

  _____

  _____

  _____

  _____

1st "R": Read

- Make predictions.

_____

_____

- Retrieve prior knowledge.

_____

_____

- State confusing ideas.

_____

_____

2nd "R": Recite

- Write the main point of this selection.
- Don't forget to annotate and take notes in the margin.

_____

_____

3rd "R": Review

- Recall what you have learned.
- React to what you have read.

_____

_____

_____

_____

Name _____   Section _____

Step One: Before Reading
Vocabulary in Context Practice
Directions: Choose one of the following words to complete each of the sentences below. Use each word only once. Be sure to pay attention to the context clues provided.

abduction—kidnapping
ad hoc—for a special purpose
clout—influence
constellation—a gathering of similar or related persons or things
gregarious—friendly
guile—cleverness
provinces—areas outside a capital or population center of a country
surveillance—observation
transients—people passing through from one place to another
throngs—crowds of people

1. The tours to the different historical sites were mainly in _____ outside the city limits.

2. The police were contacted immediately when the mother thought her child was the victim of a(n) _____ from the school grounds.

3. The teacher's _____ nature made her popular with her students.

4. Even though the car salesman used _____ and charm with his customers, he sold only three cars in a month.

5. Outside the celebrity's residence, _____ of fans waited patiently for her greeting and acknowledgement.

6. Working parents with a babysitter or a live-in nanny should consider purchasing a _____ camera to see how their nanny interacts with their child or children.

7. The _____ of factories was surrounded by makeshift housing for the transient employees.

8. A(n) _____ committee was formed to evaluate the employees' satisfaction with the working conditions in the factory.

9. People with political and financial _____ have power.

10. Migrant workers are _____ because they are always moving to wherever the next job takes them.

335

Freewrite

Choose one of the following topics and write about it in your journal.

1. Write about something you had that was lost or stolen. Give specific details with the outcome and how you felt.

2. Write about the passing of someone you know. Tell what you miss the most about this person, giving specific examples.

Step Two: Read the Selection—Computer Studies

Note: As you read the following selection, concentrate and practice the steps of SQ3R. Remove the SQ3R card from the book and complete it as you read.

Angelina Jolie stars in the film Changeling, *which is based on a true story of a single mother coming home from work to find that her son is missing. Her son's abduction is similar to the circumstances in this news article from the* New York Times *about China's problem with boys being kidnapped and the police's inability or unwillingness to stop this horrific crime.*

Chinese Hunger for Sons Fuels Boys' Abductions
By Andrew Jacobs and Jimmy Wong

Thousands of Chinese children have been kidnapped, transported to other provinces and sold for profit in a crime authorities seem unable or unwilling to stop, Andrew Jacobs and Jimmy Wang report.

1. SHENZHEN, China—The thieves often strike at dusk, when children are playing outside and their parents are distracted by exhaustion.

2. Deng Huidong lost her 9-month-old son in the blink of an eye as a man yanked him from the grip of his 7-year-old sister near the doorway of their home. The car did not even stop as a pair of arms reached out the window and grabbed the boy.

3. Sun Zuo, a gregarious 3½-year-old, was lured off by someone with a slice of mango and a toy car, an abduction that was captured by police surveillance cameras.

4. Peng Gaofeng was busy with customers when a man snatched his 4-year-old son from the plaza in front of his shop as throngs of factory workers enjoyed a spring evening. "I turned away for a minute, and when I called out for him he was gone," Mr. Peng said.

5. These and thousands of other children stolen from the teeming industrial hubs of China's Pearl River Delta have never been recovered by their parents or by the police. But anecdotal evidence suggests the

children do not travel far. Although some are sold to buyers in Singapore, Malaysia and Vietnam, most of the boys are purchased domestically by families desperate for a male heir, parents of abducted children and some law enforcement officials who have investigated the matter say.

6. The demand is especially strong in rural areas of south China, where a tradition of favoring boys over girls and the country's strict family planning policies have turned the sale of stolen children into a thriving business.

7. Su Qingcai, a tea farmer from the mountainous coast of Fujian Province, explained why he spent $3,500 last year on a 5-year-old boy. "A girl is just not as good as a son," said Mr. Su, 38, who has a 14-year-old daughter but whose biological son died at 3 months. "It doesn't matter how much money you have. If you don't have a son, you are not as good as other people who have one."

8. The centuries-old tradition of cherishing boys—and a custom that dictates that a married woman moves in with her husband's family—is reinforced by a modern reality: Without a real social safety net in China, many parents fear they will be left to fend for themselves in old age.

9. The extent of the problem is a matter of dispute. The Chinese government insists there are fewer than 2,500 cases of human trafficking each year, a figure that includes both women and children. But advocates for abducted children say there may be hundreds of thousands.

10. Sun Haiyang, whose son disappeared in 2007, has collected a list of 2,000 children in and around Shenzhen who have disappeared in the past two years. He said none of the children in his database had been recovered. "It's like fishing a needle out of the sea," he said.

11. Mr. Peng, who started an ad hoc group for parents of stolen children, said some of the girls were sold to orphanages. They are the lucky ones who often end up in the United States or Europe after adoptive parents pay fees to orphanages that average $5,000.

12. The unlucky ones, especially older children, who are not in demand by families, can end up as prostitutes or indentured laborers. Some of the children begging or hawking flowers in major Chinese cities are in the employ of criminal gangs that abducted them. "I don't even want to talk about what happens to these children," Mr. Peng said, choking up.

Police Indifference

13. Here in Shenzhen and the constellation of manufacturing towns packed with migrant workers, desperate families say they get almost no help from the local police. In case after case, they said, the police insisted on waiting 24 hours before taking action, and then claimed that too much time had passed to mount an effective investigation.

14. Several parents, through their own guile and persistence, have tracked down surveillance video images that clearly show the kidnappings in progress. Yet even that can fail to move the police, they say. "They told me a face isn't enough, that they need a name," said Cai Xinqian, who obtained tape from a store camera that showed a woman leading his 4-year-old away. "If I had a name, I could find him myself."

15. Chen Fengyi, whose 5-year-old son was snatched from outside her apartment building in Huizhou, said she called the police the moment she realized he was missing. "They told me they would come right over," she said. "I went outside to wait for them and they never came."

16. When she is not scouring the streets at night for her son, Ms. Chen and her husband go to the local police station and fall to their knees. "We cry and beg them to help," she said, "and every time they say, 'Why are you so hung up on this one thing?'"

17. *Many parents take matters into their own hands. They post fliers in places where children are often sold and travel the country to stand in front of kindergartens as they let out. A few who run shops have turned their storefronts into missing person displays. "We spend our life savings, we borrow money, we will do anything to find our children," said Mr. Peng, who owns a long-distance phone call business in Gongming, not far from Shenzhen. "There is a hole in our hearts that will never heal."*

18. *The reluctance of the police to investigate such cases has a variety of explanations. Kidnappers often single out the children of migrant workers because they are transients who may fear the local police and whose grievances are not treated as high priorities.*

19. *Moreover, the police in China's authoritarian bureaucracy are rarely rewarded for responding to crimes affecting people who do not have much political clout. Mr. Peng said the police preferred not to even open a missing person's inquiry because unsolved cases made them appear inefficient, reducing their annual bonuses.*

20. *There are exceptions. In a number of high-profile cases, the police have cracked down on trafficking rings and publicized the results. But such help remains rare, parents say.*

Turning to Beijing

21. *Mr. Peng says that boys' abductions are a growing problem that only the central government can address. He and others have been agitating for the establishment of a DNA database for children and stronger antitrafficking laws that would penalize people who buy stolen children. "If the government can launch satellites and catch spies, they can figure out how to find stolen children," said Mr. Peng, who helps run a Web site called Baby Come Home.*

22. *Chen Shiqu, the director of the Office of Combating Human Trafficking, a two-year-old government agency based in Beijing, said the problem of stolen children was exaggerated. He said that, contrary to parent advocates and some news reports, the number of cases was on the decline, although he was unable to provide figures to back up that assertion. "Just say they are dropping by 10 percent a year," he said. He added that if parents were unsatisfied with the police response, they should call 110, China's equivalent of 911.*

23. *Yang Jianchang, a legislator in Shenzhen, said he had been trying to get the central government's attention, with little success. Two years ago, he said, a group of local businessmen tried to start a foundation to track missing children. But the government, which requires that the establishment of private organizations be approved, has yet to grant them permission.*

24. *Last June, after he sent a report on the issue to the central government and got no response, Mr. Yang started sending the Ministry of Civil Affairs a copy every month or so. "I just don't understand why no one is paying attention to this problem," he said. "We need someone in the central government who will fight for the rights of the people, someone who has a conscience."*

25. *For the parents of missing children, the heartbreak and the frustration have turned into anger. Last September, about 40 families traveled to the capital to call attention to the plight of abducted children. They staged a brief protest at the headquarters of the national television broadcaster, but within minutes, dozens of police officers arrived to haul them away.*

26. *"They dragged us by our hair and said, 'How dare you question the government,'" said Peng Dongying, who lost her 4-year-old son. "I hate*

myself for my child's disappearance, but I hate society more for not caring. All of us have this pain in common, and we will do anything to get back our children."

Buyers' Remorse

27. In Anxi, a verdant county in Fujian where some of Shenzhen's stolen boys are thought to have been sold, people focus more on the pain of the families without sons.

28. Zhen Zibao, a shopkeeper in the Kuidou, said that buying a son was widely accepted and that stolen children could be found in most towns and villages. She and other residents noted that when a daughter married and moved to her husband's home, it often left her parents without a caretaker in old age. Then there is the dowry, a financial burden that falls to the family of a bride.

29. If you have only girls, you don't feel right inside," said Ms. Zhen, who has one child, an 11-year-old son. "You feel your status is lower than everyone else."

30. Although many Chinese still cherish male heirs, the Communist Party has largely succeeded in easing age-old attitudes about gender. In major cities, where one-child families have become the norm, many parents say they are happy to have a daughter and no son.

31. Still, in many rural areas, including Anxi County, a resident whose first child is a daughter is allowed to have a second. Having a third child, however, can mean steep fines as high as $5,800 and other penalties that include the loss of a breadwinner's job.

32. A boy, by contrast, can often be bought for half that amount, and authorities may turn a blind eye if the child does not need to be registered as a new birth in the locale. (Jacobs)

Step Three: Follow-Up Activities

Objective Test on "Chinese Hunger for Sons Fuels Boys' Abduction"
Directions: Choose the best answer based on the reading.

1. This news article is an example of a story based on:
   a. soft news.   c. hard news.
   b. an editorial.   d. a review.

2. The topic of this news article is:
   a. China's migrant workers.
   b. China's kidnapped children.
   c. China's tradition of cherishing boys.
   d. China's tradition of limiting births.

3. **Who** is doing the abductions?
   a. the Chinese government
   b. Chinese thieves
   c. families that do not have a daughter
   d. families that do not have a son

4. **When** have most of the abductions happened?
   a. in the daytime   c. in the evening
   b. in the night   d. in the morning

5. **Where** are most of the abductions taking place?
   a. China's cities   c. China's rural areas
   b. other countries   d. China's borders

6. **What** does the title of the news article "Chinese Hunger for Sons Fuels Boys' Abductions" mean?
   a. A girl is better than a son.
   b. Boys are a family's future heir.
   c. Sons are caretakers of their elderly parents.
   d. A son takes care of his wife.

7. Fact or Opinion: "Thieves strike at dusk when children are playing outside."

8. **Why** doesn't the government help the parents of missing children?
   a. There are not enough kidnapped children to make this problem a priority.
   b. The parents of the missing children do not have political clout or influence.
   c. Anti-trafficking laws are weak.
   d. The missing children are not native Chinese.

9. True or False: This news article suggests that Chinese society does not care about missing children.

10. **Why** does the Chinese Communist Party limit the number of children in a family to one? (However, if the first child is a daughter, a second child is allowed. Yet, a third child can mean steep fines and other penalties.)
    a. A male gives a family status.
    b. A female will leave her family and live with her husband's family.
    c. China is too populated.
    d. China does not want to support indigent families.

Vocabulary Test on "Chinese Hunger for Sons Fuels Boys' Abduction"
Directions: Choose one of the meanings to identify the highlighted word as it appears in the selection.

1. Thousands of Chinese children have been kidnapped, transported to other **provinces** and sold for profit in a crime authorities seem unable or unwilling to stop.
   a. cities
   b. countries
   c. areas outside a capital or population center
   d. neighborhoods in a capital or population center.

2. Mr. Peng says that boys' **abductions** are a growing problem that only the central government can address.
   a. dying   c. kidnappings
   b. births   d. gangs

3. Sun Zuo, a **gregarious** 3½-year-old, was lured off by someone with a slice of mango and a toy car, an abduction that was captured by police surveillance cameras.
   a. cranky   c. shy
   b. friendly   d. chubby

4. Sun Zuo, a gregarious 3½-year-old, was lured off by someone with a slice of mango and a toy car, an abduction that was captured by police **surveillance** cameras.
   a. picture   c. observation
   b. movie   d. digital

5. Moreover, the police in China's authoritarian bureaucracy are rarely rewarded for responding to crimes affecting people who do not have much political **clout.**
    a. knowledge
    b. influence
    c. money
    d. friends

6. Kidnappers often single out the children of migrant workers because they are **transients** who may fear the local police and whose grievances are not treated as high priorities.
    a. shopkeepers
    b. people passing through from one place to another
    c. farmers
    d. pilgrims

7. Peng Gaofeng was busy with customers when a man snatched his 4-year-old son from the plaza in front of his shop as **throngs** of factory workers enjoyed a spring evening.
    a. circle of people
    b. line of people
    c. crowds of people
    d. row of people

8. Several parents, through their own **guile** and persistence, have tracked down surveillance video images that clearly show the kidnappings in progress.
    a. ignorance
    b. friendliness
    c. cleverness
    d. happiness

9. Mr. Peng, who started an **ad hoc** group for parents of stolen children, said some of the girls were sold to orphanages.
    a. new
    b. for a special purpose
    c. political
    d. religious

10. Here in Shenzhen and the **constellation** of manufacturing towns packed with migrant workers, desperate families say they get almost no help from the local police.
    a. many
    b. few
    c. gathering
    d. isolation

Questions about "Chinese Hunger for Sons Fuels Boys' Abduction"

1. Who is abducting Chinese boys?

    _____

    _____

    _____

2. Why are the Chinese boys abducted?

    _____

    _____

    _____

3. How many Chinese boys have been abducted?

    _____

    _____

    _____

4. Do any birth parents see their abducted boys again? Explain.

_____

_____

_____

5. Do you feel the abduction of Chinese boys will be more vigorously addressed by the Chinese government? Why or why not?

_____

_____

_____

Journal Suggestion

Is this news article factual or opinionated? Explain.

_____

_____

_____

Collaborative Activity

Debate the advisability of government's limiting the number of births. Some members of your group will discuss the "pros" and others will respond with the "cons" of this dilemma.

Look It Up

1. Find an abduction news story that is historical. Read and summarize your findings.

2. Find a current abduction news story. Read and summarize your findings.

Creating Your SQ3R Cards

SQ3R cards are a study system to help you successfully comprehend what you are reading. As you read the longer reading selection, you will actively interact with the text before you read, while you read, and after you read.

"S": Survey the Reading Selection

- What is the topic?

  _____

  _____

  _____

- What do I already know?

  _____

  _____

  _____

- What is my purpose for reading?

  _____

  _____

  _____

"Q": Turn a Selection Title into a Question

Don't forget to turn key statements into questions as you read.

  _____

  _____

  _____

  _____

  _____

1st "R": Read

- Make predictions.

_____

_____

- Retrieve prior knowledge.

_____

_____

- State confusing ideas.

_____

_____

2nd "R": Recite

- Write the main point of this selection.
- Don't forget to annotate and take notes in the margin.

_____

_____

3rd "R": Review

- Recall what you have learned.
- React to what you have read.

_____

_____

_____

_____

_____

_____

Comprehending Longer Selections
13.5

More Practice
Step One: Before Reading
Vocabulary in Context Practice
Directions: Choose one of the following words to complete each of the sentences below. Use each word only once. Be sure to pay attention to the context clues provided.

arduous—difficult
bona-fide—authentic; genuine
contentious—quarrelsome
exhibits—displays
bickering—arguing
memorabilia—keepsakes; a reminder of the past
obsession—an intense or abnormal preoccupation
procuring—obtaining; acquiring
spectators—observers of an event
ultimate—greatest extreme

1. The antiques dealer purchased the painting, knowing the signature was _____.

2. The gallery _____ received kudos from the reception attendees.

3. If you cannot control your buying and spending, you probably have a shopping _____.

4. The lawyer's _____ nature helped him win the case.

5. She soon forgot the _____ work involved in preparing her marketing strategy for the client's new cosmetics line.

6. The office walls were covered with twentieth-century movie _____.

7. It took days to _____ a solution to the challenging problem.

8. "As the _____ arbiter of the Constitution, the Supreme Court occupies a central place in our scheme of government" (Richard A. Epstein).

9. The arena _____ cheered when the wrestling champion entered the ring.

10. John and Paul were _____ over who would bat first.

Freewrite

Write about a movie star whom you idolize. If you do not idolize a movie star, write about a movie star you would like to spend the day with. Use the reporter's "five W's and H" format in your description of a day with a movie star.

Step 2: Read the Selection

Entertainment

Note: As you read the following selection, concentrate and practice the steps of SQ3R. Remove the SQ3R card from the book and complete it as you read.

Angelina Jolie has many fans and probably some are obsessed with her like the Rod Stewart fan you will read about in the next selection, from the New Yorker magazine.

Stardust: The Talk of the Town
By Jake Halpern

1. In October, when Rod Stewart made an appearance on Hollywood Boulevard to unveil his star on the Walk of Fame, perhaps no one was prouder than Marcy Braunstein, a fifty-two-year-old woman from Pittsburg. Braunstein is the ultimate Rod Stewart fan. This becomes evident to anyone who visits her house and stumbles upon her Red Room—a cramped space that contains more memorabilia than one might find in a modest Presidential library. These mementos include a framed dress shirt that Rod once wore and a water glass that Rod sipped from on the set of "Oprah."

2. "I like to joke that if my husband and I ever had kids my Rod Room would be a nursery," Braunstein said recently. "But it's not. It's a Rod Room instead."

3. Braunstein is proud of her obsession. "I will chat online with other Rod fans, and we will often say that we are going through 'Rod withdrawal' or we need a 'Rod fix,'" she said. Braunstein typically satisfies this need by following Stewart on tour and dragging her husband, David Jones, along. Jones is not a Rod fan. "I'm going to be honest," he said. "There is no way I could put my foot down. If I tried, it would be, like, 'You can go, because Rod is staying.'"

4. Several years ago, on one of these road trips, Braunstein and Jones passed through Hollywood and discovered that Rod Stewart did not have a star on the Walk of Fame. Braunstein called the Hollywood Chamber of Commerce and demanded an explanation. The explanation was simple: no one had ever nominated Rod. So Braunstein filled out a nomination form and began raising money for the fifteen-thousand-dollar fee that would be required if and when Rod's star was approved.

5. Getting a star on the Walk of Fame is an arduous process that involves procuring approval from the (honorary) mayor of Hollywood, who is an eighty-two-year-old former talk-show host named Johnny Grant. According to Grant, he is constantly being buttonholed by would-be inductees. "I was at a funeral the other day and someone was pitching me to be on the Walk of Fame!" he said. Grant says that the process can be contentious with officials bickering over who is a bona-fide celebrity and who isn't: "We've got one guy on the Chamber committee who says for every nomination, 'Why would you want to give that asshole a star?'"

6. Rod Stewart's nomination sailed through without incident. And so, on October 11th, several hundred people, including Stewart, Grant, and Braunstein, gathered on Hollywood Boulevard. Grant sat in a folding chair, leaning forward on a cane and uttering pleasantries to passing young women: "Hey, looking good, baby. Are you on the menu?" He stood up to greet Braunstein, who told him all about the Rod Room. "That's nuts!" Grant said after she walked away. "Still, thank God for fans like that, who keeps the business going."

7. Several minutes later, Rod Stewart, who is sixty, showed up with four of his children and his fiancée, Penny Lancaster, who was pregnant (she delivered a boy, Alastair Wallace Stewart, a few weeks later). He wore white pants, a black blazer, and an orange tie. The crowd roared, and Marcy Braunstein's eyes misted with tears. "I can't believe this is finally happening," she whispered. Grant escorted Stewart and Braunstein onto a stage, where he tried to make a speech over the noise of the spectators, who were shouting, "Rod! Rod! Rod!" Finally, he said, "Enough! You just blew out my hearing aid."

8. Later, at her hotel, Braunstein said that she was enormously pleased with the day's events, except for one thing: she had failed to acquire any new exhibits for her Rod Room. So the following day she drove to Stewart's house, in the Hollywood Hills, to ask him to sign her copy of the original 45 of "Maggie May." When she arrived at the front gate, she spoke her name into a security intercom, and the gate swung open. She drove in slowly, clutching the steering wheel with one hand and snapping photographs with the other. At the top of the driveway, a personal assistant appeared and explained that Mr. Stewart was in the shower but that he would gladly sign the record and mail it back to her. "So it all worked out," she said. (Halpern)

Step Three: Follow-Up Activities

Objective Test on "Stardust: The Talk of the Town"
Directions: Choose the best answer based on the reading.

1. **Who** is the ultimate Rod Stewart fan?
   a. Johnny Grant   c. Marcy Braunstein
   b. David Jones   d. Allister Wallace

2. **Where** are the stars on the Walk of Fame?
   a. San Francisco   c. Sacramento
   b. Los Angeles   d. Hollywood

3. **What** does Braunstein want to do?
   a. get Carey Grant a star on the Walk of Fame
   b. get Jimmy Stewart a star on the Walk of Fame
   c. get Rod Stewart a star on the Walk of Fame
   d. get Tom Jones a star on the Walk of Fame

4. **How** does one get a star on the Walk of Fame?
   a. fill out a nomination form and raise the twenty-thousand-dollar fee if the star was approved
   b. convince the city's Chamber of Commerce that the celebrity deserves a star on the Walk of Fame
   c. fill out a nomination form and raise the fifteen-thousand-dollar fee if the star was approved
   d. raise the thirty-thousand-dollar fee if the star was approved

5. **Why** was Rod Stewart's star on the Walk of Fame approved?
   a. Chamber of Commerce officials said Stewart was a bona-fide celebrity.
   b. Chamber of Commerce officials were given a generous donation for city projects.
   c. Chamber of Commerce officials like his music.
   d. Chamber of Commerce officials were invited to Stewart's home.

6. **What** did Braunstein want from Rod Stewart?
   a. a dinner invitation to his home
   b. a photograph with Rod Stewart
   c. a song written in her honor
   d. his signature on her copy of the original 45 of "Maggie May"

7. Marcy Braunstein is the ultimate Rod Stewart fan because:
   a. she occasionally needs a "Rod Fix."
   b. she buys all his records.
   c. she follows Stewart on tour.
   d. she has a Rod Room in her house, which contains lots of memorabilia.

8. How old is the honorary mayor of Hollywood, Johnny Grant?
   a. 52   c. 95
   b. 82   d. 60

9. At the top of Stewart's driveway, who appeared and explained to Marcy Braunstein that Mr. Stewart was in the shower but that he would gladly sign the record and mail it back to her?
   a. his wife   c. his personal assistant
   b. his doorman   d. his agent

10. "So it all worked out," she (Braunstein) said.
    a. This quote refers to Stewart receiving a star on the Walk of Fame.
    b. This quote refers to Braunstein chatting online with Rod fans.
    c. This quote refers to Braunstein getting through his home security to speak with his personal assistant.
    d. This quote refers to Braunstein getting her original 45 of "Maggie May" signed by Stewart.

Vocabulary Test on "Stardust: The Talk of the Town"

Directions: Choose one of the meanings to identify the highlighted word as it appears in the selection.

1. Getting a star on the Walk of Fame is an **arduous** process that involves procuring approval from the (honorary) mayor of Hollywood, who is an eighty-two-year-old former talk-show host named Johnny Grant.
   a. long
   b. demanding great care, effort, or labor; difficult
   c. full of hardships
   d. hard to climb or surmount

2. Braunstein is the **ultimate** Rod Stewart fan.
   a. crazed
   b. greatest extreme
   c. necessary
   d. initial

3. Grant says that the process can be **contentious** with officials bickering over who is a bona-fide celebrity and who isn't.
   a. estranged
   b. strive against rivals
   c. persuasive
   d. quarrelsome

4. Grant says that the process can be contentious with officials bickering over who is a **bona-fide** celebrity and who isn't.
   a. sincere
   b. authentic; genuine
   c. trustworthy
   d. generous

5. Grant says that the process can be contentious with officials **bickering** over who is a bona-fide celebrity and who isn't.
   a. bouncing
   b. arguing
   c. remembering
   d. debating

6. Braunstein is proud of her **obsession.**
   a. intense or abnormal preoccupation
   b. hobby
   c. career
   d. commitment

7. Getting a star on the Walk of Fame is an arduous process that involves **procuring** approval from the (honorary) mayor of Hollywood, who is an eighty-two-year-old former talk-show host named Johnny Grant.
   a. creating
   b. obtaining; acquiring
   c. choosing
   d. losing

8. Later, at her hotel, Braunstein said that she was enormously pleased with the day's events, except for one thing: she had failed to acquire any new exhibits for her Rod Room—a cramped space that contains more **memorabilia** than one might find in a modest Presidential library.
   a. memories
   b. trinkets
   c. keepsakes; a reminder of the past
   d. items

9. Grant escorted Stewart and Braunstein onto a stage, where he tried to make a speech over the noise of the **spectators,** who were shouting, "Rod! Rod! Rod!"
   a. people
   b. crowds
   c. observers of an event
   d. public

10. Later, at her hotel, Braunstein said that she was enormously pleased with the day's events, except for one thing: she had failed to acquire any new **exhibits** for her Rod Room.
    a. demonstrations
    b. displays
    c. contests
    d. official introduction

Questions about "Stardust: The Talk of the Town"

1. Why is Marcy Braunstein the ultimate Rod Stewart Fan?

   _____

   _____

   _____

2. How does a celebrity receive a star on the Walk of Fame?

_____

_____

_____

3. When was Rod Stewart honored with a star on the Walk of Fame?

_____

_____

_____

4. Who was present when Rod Stewart was honored with a star on the Walk of Fame?

_____

_____

_____

5. Describe the honorary mayor of Hollywood, indicating how you feel about him being a part of the process selecting bona-fide celebrities for the Walk of Fame.

_____

_____

_____

Journal Suggestion

Choose a celebrity who is not on the Walk of Fame in Hollywood, California. Tell how you would raise money so this celebrity could become a "star" on the Walk of Fame.

Collaborative Activities

1. Create a visual presentation of five ordinary people who are "stars" by your standards. Give a detailed account of why these people are "stars." Then create a timeless memorial for them.

2. Write and share a creative poem, song, play, or short story about a celebrity.

3. Debate the idea of charging exorbitant fees for honors such as a star on the Hollywood Walk of Fame.

Look It Up

1. Make a list of specific fan clubs. Give a detailed background of at least one fan club.

2. Find out where one celebrity's star is located on the Walk of Fame in Hollywood. Report on the ceremony in which that celebrity's Walk of Fame star was "unveiled."

Getting the Picture

In this chapter, you learned the difference between hard news and soft news. Examine the photo and tell if it represents hard news or soft news. Then, like a reporter, answer the 5W's and H questions about the photo.

_____

_____

_____

_____

_____

_____

_____

_____

_____

_____

_____

_____

_____

_____

_____

_____

_____

_____

_____

_____

_____

Chapter Highlights

What Have We Learned?

1. Hard News is the **current breaking news.** This news is in the general public interest.

2. **Soft news** is a **human interest feature.** This news is not as dated as a hard news story.

3. There are different kinds of newspapers, such as **major, local,** and **special interest newspapers/monitors/chronicles.**

4. A reporter writes the stories in the **"Five W's and H" format,** without expressing any opinions.

5. **Timely news in the general public** interest makes the front page.

Chapter 14

OPINIONS IN THE NEWS

In Chapter 13, you learned that a news story (hard and soft news) should be objective. However, some articles in a newspaper or magazine do include the writer's opinion. **Editorials,** written by a newspaper editor, present the opinion of the newspaper. It is in the editorial that candidates are "endorsed," or supported, or opinions offered on topical issues. **Columns** are opinions given by experts in a particular field, such as sports, politics, or even dating. Sometimes these columns are *syndicated,* that is, they are written by one person and the article may appear in newspapers or magazines in several states. Finally, **reviews** provide information and opinions on books, plays, movies, restaurants, concerts, and special events. People often consult reviews when deciding if they should see a particular movie, show, etc. Remember that these types of articles are a combination of facts and opinions, and you will need to practice both literal and critical comprehension skills that you learned in previous chapters.

Exercise **14.1 Your Turn—What Did You Learn?**

1. Three types of news are _____, _____, and
   _____.

2. _____ present the opinion of the newspaper.

3. _____ are provided by experts in a particular field.

4. _____ give advice about books, plays, and movies.

5. When reading articles that present opinions, you must use _____
   and _____ reading skills.

Exercise **14.2 Freedom of Speech in the News**

Directions: The article you are about to read comments on the action taken by the federal appeals court concerning the number of billboards along New York City's roadways and parks.

NYC Billboard Rules Don't Violate First Amendment, 2nd Circuit Says
By The Associated Press

© ssguy, 2010. Used under license from Shutterstock, Inc.

NEW YORK—A federal appeals court ruled yesterday that the city did not violate the First Amendment by limiting the number of billboards along its roadways and parks.

The 2nd U.S. Circuit Court of Appeals in Manhattan said the city's goals of reducing visual clutter, improving the overall aesthetic appearance of the city and regulating traffic safety were reasonable.

"The fact that the city has chosen to value some types of commercial speech over others does not make the regulation irrational," the appeals court said. It concluded that it did not matter that the city had enforced its regulations sporadically since 1940.

A lower court judge reached the same conclusion in the case last year. That ruling was appealed by companies, including Clear Channel Outdoor Inc. and Metro Fuel LLC, that market hundreds of billboards.

They said the city infringed on commercial-speech rights by stiffening rules against big billboards and lighted signs near parks and highways while letting smaller signs flourish on lampposts, taxicabs and phone booths. A lawyer for the companies did not return a phone message for comment in time for this story.

The appeals court said the city may allow advertising on street furniture while also reducing clutter on city sidewalks.

"Allowing some signs does not constitutionally require a city to allow all similar signs," the three-judge panel said. "The city's interests in aesthetics, preservation of neighborhood character and traffic safety continue to be advanced, even though limited and controlled advertising is permitted on street furniture."

Since 1940, the city has banned commercial billboards that don't advertise on-premises businesses near major roads.

Clear Channel derives about $10 million annually from operating 236 sign faces in the city. The appeals court said about 85 of the signs face arterial highways, including more than 70 expressways, parkways, boulevards and toll crossings.

Metro Fuel operates about 440 internally illuminated panel signs, each about 23 square feet, in the city. The 2nd Circuit said the city regulations impact 324 of Metro Fuel's signs.

Edward Fortier, executive director of the Special Enforcement Unit at the Department of Buildings, said the ruling will let the department "more effectively enforce against these illegal signs and the companies behind them."

1. Besides the federal appeals court, which other court said New York City did not violate the First Amendment?

   _____

   _____

   _____

2. Since 1940, in which areas has there been some enforcement against signs?

   _____

   _____

   _____

3. Why has New York City chosen to regulate big billboards and lighted signs?

   _____

   _____

   _____

4. Name two companies that market hundreds of billboards.

   _____

   _____

   _____

5. How did the judges defend their decision?

   _____

   _____

   _____

6. Give specific locations where signs are allowed.

_____

_____

_____

7. Which New York City department is responsible for enforcing the rules against illegal signs and the companies behind the signs?

_____

_____

_____

Exercise **14.3**

Understanding Opinions in Newspaper Columns

Directions: The following advice column by Carolyn Hax appeared in the *Washington Post*. Read the column using both literal and critical comprehension skills, and answer the questions that follow.

Tell Me about It : Boyfriend Tricked Her, Fed Her Beef
By Carolyn Hax

Question: *I had an unusual experience last night. My boyfriend of eight months invited me over to his parents' house for dinner. The menu consisted of sloppy joes, with turkey joes to be provided for me. I haven't eaten beef in 16 years, for various reasons, and everyone who knows me knows this.*

Well, not one to refuse to eat food a host has graciously provided (I always communicate my restriction in advance, and these particular people were aware of it), I muddled through what I thought was a beefy-tasting turkey joe. Once I was finished, my boyfriend revealed that he added beef to the turkey to see if I could "tell the difference."

I've never been in this situation because I've never had anyone trick me like this. Is this relationship-ending stuff, or just a minor violation? It's really bothering me.

A: It should—the literal version of trusting your gut.

Granted, many don't know that eating beef can make a non-beef eater feel sick. But even that wouldn't clear him, at all, of the outrageous disrespect he showed for your dietary choices. Religious reasons, humane reasons, health reasons, taste reasons, capricious reasons, whatever. They're your reasons, to be honored as such.

Whether this is a minor violation or a relationship-ending beef is up to him. If he is able to listen to you, understand why his trick was outrageously disrespectful, and feel remorseful, then probably you can get past it.

But if he defends what he did or, worse, digs at you for overreacting, then it's a promise of more disrespect, and Turkey Joe's gotta go.

Q: My live-in boyfriend's mother came to stay with us for a "short" one-month period while she looked for work and a new living situation.

Well, three months later, his mother is still in our cramped two-bedroom condo with no job prospects in sight—let alone a new place to live. She spends her days surfing the Net, talking on the phone, and making negative comments about my relationship with her son.

It's obvious my boyfriend's mother is depressed, among other problems. I've asked, discussed, nagged, and cajoled him to speak with her. Nothing has happened. The cramped conditions, lack of privacy, and my boyfriend's inability to confront his family issues are taking a toll on our six-year relationship (that I expect will result in marriage).

What can I do to make my boyfriend realize I can't live with his mother indefinitely!

A: Your boyfriend doesn't realize this because you are, in fact, living with his mother indefinitely.

So the answer is to demonstrate, not say, that you won't live with her indefinitely. Sit down with him to establish a seven-day, 15-day, whatever-day plan to get her on her feet and out of your house. Demonstrate, don't say, that this is not negotiable, by making a Plan B to get out of the house if she doesn't.

It's not that he won't confront his mother. It's that he'd rather let things drag on than make an unpopular decision—since any decision he makes will upset one of you. And with someone who's not strong enough to make an unpopular decision, you can't really expect much of a happy result. (Hax)

© JupiterImages Corporation

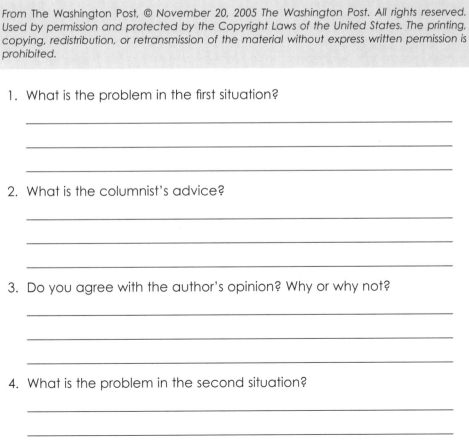

1. What is the problem in the first situation?

   _____

   _____

   _____

2. What is the columnist's advice?

   _____

   _____

   _____

3. Do you agree with the author's opinion? Why or why not?

   _____

   _____

   _____

4. What is the problem in the second situation?

   _____

   _____

   _____

5. What is the columnist's advice?

_____

_____

_____

6. Do you agree with the author's opinion? Why or why not?

_____

_____

_____

Exercise 14.4 Understanding Opinions in Newspaper Editorials

Directions: The following editorial on the legal controversy over "intelligent design" appeared in the *Washington Post* on December 22, 2005. After reading the editorial, answer the questions that follow by using literal and critical skills.

Religion, Science and Civility

© JupiterImages Corporation

Judge John Jones III issued a compelling decision Tuesday, ruling that "intelligent design" is religion, not science, and can't be taught in public school classrooms. In theory, the federal court ruling is binding only on the Dover Area School District in central Pennsylvania. But it is likely to have much wider influence. That's good because there's far more of value here than legal argument. There's wisdom.

In the decision, Jones cuts through much of the confusion swirling around intelligent design and evolution, providing Americans a sharply drawn primer in the difference between science and religion. Evolution, tested by a century and a half of research and observation, is science. Intelligent design, or ID, is religion because it suggests an unprovable supreme being as the "designer" of all life.

Note that the judge distinguished science from religion. He did not declare one superior or subordinate to the other. In explaining why, he not only solved a classroom crisis, but offered Americans a wise and intriguing way to think about the nexus of science and religion.

This part didn't make headlines. But deep in the opinion, here's what Jones wrote: ". . . [M]any of the leading proponents of ID make a bedrock assumption which is utterly false. Their presupposition is that evolutionary theory is antithetical to a belief in the existence of a supreme being and to religion in general." In the trial, the judge continued, the scientific experts who testified against ID said *"that the theory of evolution represents good science, is overwhelmingly accepted by the scientific community, and that it in no way conflicts with, nor does it deny, the existence of a divine creator."*

In other words, science and religion—evolution and intelligent design— can exist together; they are not mutually exclusive. That's an important message that has been trampled as many rush to the barricades, taking sides in what's been billed as another "culture war."

Because the battleground is the classroom—our kids—the vitriol has been thick. To be clear: The ruling doesn't mean it's taboo for individual teachers to mention "creationism" or "intelligent design" in the proper context. As Glenn Branch, deputy director of the National Center for Science Education, has said: "Religious advocacy is what's forbidden, but acknowledging that there are religious controversies and objections around evolution is another thing. It would be perfectly acceptable for there to be a discussion of the fact that there are religious objections to evolution."

What's not acceptable is to proselytize in the classroom, or to stray from real science.

The argument about evolution has provoked legal skirmishes for decades. It won't stop here.

On a larger scale, this debate is about the limits of science and the limitless depths of faith. There will always be room for different explanations and beliefs on the origins of life—and important constitutional limits on what can be said in the classroom.

By writing that science and religion need not be sworn enemies, however, Jones offers Americans something valuable: a way to think and talk, respectfully, about issues that divide us. (Chicago Tribune 22)

1. What is "intelligent design"?

   _____

   _____

2. What was Judge Jones's decision?

   _____

   _____

3. What was the reason for this decision?

   _____

   _____

4. What is the opinion of the newspaper concerning this decision?

   _____

   _____

5. Do you agree or disagree with the decision? Explain your answer.

   _____

   _____

Understanding Opinions in Newspaper Reviews

Exercise 14.5

Directions: Read the following movie review by Sabrina Warren about *Changeling*, staring Angelina Jolie. Then answer the questions which follow, using both literal and critical skills.

Staying Faithful
By Sabrina Warren
Published: October, 2008

There is no doubt that Clint Eastwood is an accomplished director and Angelina Jolie is an adept and beautiful actor. So, when Eastwood's latest venture, Changeling, hit the screens, we felt a reasonable amount of anticipation of another Oscar-worthy film. And yes, Eastwood's vision at the onset seemed outstanding, Jolie's nuances dramatic and riveting. And yet, Changeling, sad to say, falls somewhat short. All the right ingredients were there, so how did we come up with such a tasteless dish?

The screenplay stays faithful to the real story which screamed from the headlines that March of 1928. And perhaps that is the problem—perhaps if the screenplay had not stayed so faithful, the story could have been dramatized with more zeal, if not accuracy.

Jolie portrays Christine Collins, supervisor of a switchboard and single mother to Walter (Gattlin Griffith). One day, she comes home from work to find her young son missing. Her frustration builds as she encounters one obstacle after another in the form of the Los Angeles Police Department which refuses to take her plight seriously. She (and the audience) are appalled when police chief (Colm Feore) reunites her with a boy who claims to be her son, and is most definitely not her Walter. Jolie acts and reacts with understandable shock, indignation, and even hysterics. In response, she is locked in a mental institution. The audience rides this rollercoaster of drama along with Jolie, but then the film proceeds to take dips, curves and dives as we witness the unjust treatment of Collins, her relentless fight for the truth, with the help of a minister (John Malkovich) and an attorney (Geoff Pierson), and bittersweet vindication as the truth is finally realized.

Ah, but there is more to the story, much more. And we have all of it in this film—flashbacks, reunions, scenes of grisly violence featuring a demented serial killer (Jason Butler Harner), as well as a detailed resolution. At almost two and a half hours, the adherence to truth becomes, in fact, quite dizzying, and most viewers have long since gotten off the ride.

What Clint Eastwood has in Changeling is a fine drama, a superb actress, and a film which because of its length falls just a little short.

"Changeling" is rated R (Under 17 requires accompanying parent or adult guardian). It has scenes of violence and profanity.

1. Explain the plot of *Changeling*.

_____

_____

_____

2. What is Sabrina Warren's opinion of the film?

   _____

   _____

   _____

3. Based on this review, would you want to see this movie? Explain your answer.

   _____

   _____

   _____

Creating Your SQ3R Cards

SQ3R cards are a study system to help you successfully comprehend what you are reading. As you read the longer reading selection, you will actively interact with the text before you read, while you read, and after you read.

"S": Survey the Reading Selection

- What is the topic?

  _____

  _____

  _____

- What do I already know?

  _____

  _____

  _____

- What is my purpose for reading?

  _____

  _____

  _____

"Q": Turn a Selection Title into a Question

Don't forget to turn key statements into questions as you read.

_____

_____

_____

_____

1st "R": Read

- Make predictions.

_____

_____

- Retrieve prior knowledge.

_____

_____

- State confusing ideas.

_____

_____

2nd "R": Recite

- Write the main point of this selection.
- Don't forget to annotate and take notes in the margin.

_____

_____

3rd "R": Review

- Recall what you have learned.
- React to what you have read.

_____

_____

_____

_____

_____

Comprehending Longer Selections

Newspapers

Step One: Before Reading

Vocabulary in Context Practice

Directions: Choose one of the following words to complete each of the sentences below. Use each word only once. Be sure to pay attention to the context clues provided.

adopted—took possession of something or someone
blatantly—obviously
devastated—overcome by circumstances
interference—something which is a hindrance or obstacle
lure—to tempt or attract; entice
prior—preceding in time or order; before
prospective—expected
pulpit—a stand or elevated platform used in preaching or conducting a religious service
tactics—maneuvers for achieving a goal
unethical—not honorable

1. College students who work more than twenty hours a week may find their job is a(n) _____ to their academic responsibilities.

2. Everyone knew Mary Ellen had _____ told a lie since it was obvious she had had a facelift.

3. The doctor asked his patient to fast _____ to the blood test.

4. Buyers need to be savvy about advertisements that _____ them to purchase bait-and-switch merchandise.

5. The hurricane victims were _____ when they saw the condition of their homes and neighborhoods.

6. The preacher delivered his Sunday sermon from the _____.

7. The English department _____ a new handbook for the next semester.

8. Cutting and pasting research without citing the authors is plagiarism, which is _____.

9. The high school guidance counselors discussed the college admission process with _____ college students.

10. The salesman's selling _____ were unethical and unprofessional.

Freewrite

In your journal, respond to the following question: Do you think it is important for an adopted child to have continued contact with his or her birth parents? Explain.

Step 2: Read the Selection

Note: As you read the following selection, concentrate and practice the steps of SQ3R. Remove the SQ3R card from the book and complete it as you read.

Angelina Jolie's long-term commitment to humanitarianism is exhibited by her adoption of a Cambodian boy in 2001, an Ethiopian girl in 2005, and another boy from Vietnam in 2007. The selection you will read is about adoption.

"Fast Track Adoption" Ends in Suicide
By Laurie Frisch

1. (PRWEB) April 13, 2004—Susan Burns, Psy.D. is undoubtedly proud of her book "Fast Track Adoption" which provides prospective adopters some ideas on how to go about soothing a frightened young woman's fears and making her feel she is making a good decision for her child. But, there is one angle her book does not cover: How will your adopted child's natural mother feel when she finds out how proud you are of the methods you used to talk her out of her child? How will she feel when you break all the promises you made to her?

2. Burns writes: "Without an agency's interference, (the child's parents) and (the people considering adoption) have a greater voice in making key decisions, often resulting in a better "fit" for everyone involved." ". . . knowing about the (prospective) adopting family prior to the placement can assist a (natural) mother in her grieving process by reassuring her that she has made the right choice."

3. It seems unlikely to me that Burns is truly concerned about everyone involved or about the grieving process of a mother who has lost her child to adoption.

4. I got this email today (April 9, 2004) from a friend who is very involved with the open adoption community: "I'm grieving my good friend right now. Cindy was a member of my adoption group for a year and a half—we were supposed to meet next month. The (people who adopted) her daughter broke promises and Cindy never recovered. She took her life yesterday. Her daughter will be three on the 19th." "I'm trying to help the members of my group . . . and myself grieve. We were all SO close. She also left behind two teen boys. Please keep them in your prayers." "(The woman who adopted her daughter) wrote the sickening new adoption book "Fast Track Adoption" . . . and may even appear on 20/20 talking about how to get a baby quick. Cindy found out about this book by accident and was devastated by its contents and how she was left out and used."

5. Many people are unaware of this dark side of adoption. The adoption industry has found ways to thwart attempts by natural moms and adoptees to voice their concerns about unethical adoption practices. One of the most revolting of the tactics used to obtain babies is the prom-

ise of "open adoption," the promise of continued contact with their child, made only with the intent to lure in unsuspecting mothers who might have otherwise kept their child. Open adoption agreements are not legally binding as other child custody or visitation agreements are and this frequently has devastating consequences. Many a mother is grieving the loss of a child to adoption. This grieving is compounded when she has so obviously, blatantly been used as a baby-making machine and then tossed out like yesterday's garbage once her child is in possession of the adopters. In Cindy's case, not only she but her sons and probably other family members were expecting contact with their sister, granddaughter, niece as well.

6. This is for Cindy Jordan and for all other moms who have been so used. This is for Cindy's daughter, her sons, her mother and father, her whole family. I hope our churches will mention this from the pulpit and work to enact change. I hope our human rights organizations will take note and work to enact changes. I hope women's organizations will for once stand up for these women who have been so long marginalized in this way and work to prevent further abuse. Not everyone benefits from adoption and it's time people knew about it and did something. Those mothers and fathers who are making a decision whether to keep their child or surrender their child for adoption deserve legal protections which include real information about the emotional risks to themselves, their child and other family members. They deserve to be protected from slick advertising and sales pitches from those seeking to adopt independently, from the adoption industry and from adoption lawyers. They deserve to be protected from the pressure put on them to choose prospective adopters before their child is even born which makes it very hard for them to disappoint them later. They deserve to be treated with the respect due a human being, with the respect due a parent who is trying to make the best decision possible for their child and their families. (Frisch)

Natural mother commits suicide after "Fast Track Adoption" book reveals how she was used by the woman who adopted her daughter.

Step Three: Follow-Up Activities

Objective Test on "'Fast Track Adoption'" Ends in Suicide"
Directions: Choose the best answer based on the reading.

1. This article is probably a(n):
   a. front page article.　　　　c. book review.
   b. editorial.　　　　　　　　d. sidebar.

2. The author:
   a. is in favor of fast-track adoption.
   b. is opposed to fast-track adoption.
   c. is an adoptive parent.
   d. is impartial.

3. True or False: Cindy Jordan committed suicide because the woman who adopted her daughter broke promises.

4. True or False: "Open adoption" is legally binding.

5. "Open adoption" negatively affects:
   a. the birth mother.　　　　c. siblings.
   b. grandparents.　　　　　　d. all of the above.

6. True or False: The author of the book *Fast Track Adoption* is responsible for the death of the birth mother.

7. True or False: "Open adoption" is subject to slick advertising and sales pitches.

8. True or False: Jordan has two children.

9. True or False: This news article states the reporter's opinion regarding "open adoption."

10. True or False: The news in this article would be considered "fast breaking," or hard news.

Vocabulary Test on "'Fast Track Adoption' Ends in Suicide"

Directions: Choose one of the meanings to identify the highlighted word as it appears in the selection.

1. The people who **adopted** her daughter broke promises and Cindy never recovered.
   a. give birth to a child
   b. trade a child for someone else's child
   c. take possession of something or someone
   d. take a child to an orphanage

2. Cindy found out about this book [*Fast Track Adoption*] by accident and was **devastated** by its contents and how she was left out and used.
   a. ruined   c. overcome by circumstances
   b. hated   d. accused

3. This grieving is compounded when she [Cindy] has so obviously, **blatantly** been used as a baby-making machine and then tossed out like yesterday's garbage once her child is in possession of the adopters.
   a. obviously   c. unusually
   b. strangely   d. cruelly

4. One of the most revolting of the **tactics** used to obtain babies is the promise of "open adoption," the promise of continued contact with their child, made only with the intent to lure in unsuspecting mothers who might have otherwise kept their child.
   a. outcomes
   b. maneuvers for achieving a goal
   c. rewards
   d. penalties

5. One of the most revolting of the tactics used to obtain babies is the promise of "open adoption," the promise of continued contact with their child, made only with the intent to **lure** in unsuspecting mothers who might have otherwise kept their child.
   a. offer   c. to tempt, attract; entice
   b. send   d. harm

6. They [birth mothers] deserve to be protected from the pressure put on them to choose **prospective** adopters before their child is even born which makes it very hard to disappoint them later.
   a. expected   c. surprised
   b. deleted   d. paid

7. I hope our churches will mention this from the **pulpit** and work to enact change.
   a. elevated platform
   b. parish
   c. choir
   d. clergy

8. The adoption industry has found ways to thwart attempts by natural moms and adoptees to voice their concerns about **unethical** adoption practices.
   a. righteous
   b. benevolent
   c. moral
   d. not honorable

9. ". . . knowing about the prospective adopting family **prior** to the placement can assist a natural mother in her grieving process by reassuring her that she has made the right choice."
   a. after
   b. before
   c. later
   d. now

10. "Without an agency's **interference,** (the child's parents) and (the people considering adoption) have a greater voice in making key decisions, often resulting in a better "fit" for everyone involved."
    a. compliance
    b. hindrance, obstacle
    c. testimony
    d. intermission

Questions about "'Fast Track Adoption' Ends in Suicide"

1. What is the thesis of the book *Fast Track Adoption*?

   _____
   _____
   _____

2. Why did Cindy Jordan commit suicide?

   _____
   _____
   _____

3. What is the writer's opinion of "open adoption"?

   _____
   _____
   _____

4. How does adoption affect entire families?

   _____
   _____
   _____

5. What type of news is this—hard, soft, or opinion? Explain your answer.

   _____
   _____
   _____

Journal Suggestion

This news story discusses the concept of "open adoption." Write a journal entry explaining your opinion on this subject.

Collaborative Activities

1. The reading selection states that "open adoption agreements are not legally binding as other child custody or visitation agreements are." Do you think "open adoption" agreements should be legally binding? Conduct a debate on this issue with other group members.

2. As a group, compose a letter to a human rights organization asking them to take note of the "open adoption" agreement and to work to enact change.

Look It Up

1. Research and list the human rights organizations that will take note and work to enact "open adoption" changes. Write a report about your findings.

2. Find other articles on the subject of adoption and summarize points of view about this issue.

3. The television series *Find My Family* united adopted children with mothers, fathers, and siblings of their birth family. Research movies or television dramas that have dealt with the subject of adoption, and write a report about your findings.

Creating Your SQ3R Cards

SQ3R cards are a study system to help you successfully comprehend what you are reading. As you read the longer reading selection, you will actively interact with the text before you read, while you read, and after you read.

"S": Survey the Reading Selection

- What is the topic?

  _____

  _____

  _____

- What do I already know?

  _____

  _____

  _____

- What is my purpose for reading?

  _____

  _____

  _____

"Q": Turn a Selection Title into a Question

Don't forget to turn key statements into questions as you read.

_____

_____

_____

_____

_____

1st "R": Read

- Make predictions.

  _____

  _____

- Retrieve prior knowledge.

  _____

  _____

- State confusing ideas.

  _____

  _____

2nd "R": Recite

- Write the main point of this selection.
- Don't forget to annotate and take notes in the margin.

  _____

  _____

3rd "R": Review

- Recall what you have learned.
- React to what you have read.

  _____

  _____

  _____

  _____

  _____

Comprehending Longer Selections 14.7 *Exercise*

More Practice with Newspapers
Step One: Before Reading
Vocabulary in Context Practice
Directions: Choose one of the following words to complete each of the sentences below. Use each word only once. Be sure to pay attention to the context clues provided.

candid—honest; impartial
chronic—prolonged; lingering
homilies—sermons
inextricable—impossible to escape or get free of
odyssey—an extended adventurous wandering; journey
parlance—manner of speaking
progressive—advancing; moving forward
resonates—has an emotional impact
spectrum—range
terminal—fatal

1. She learned to live with diabetes, for it is a _____ disease.

2. The congregation had a difficult time concentrating on the tedious moralizing _____.

3. Not everyone uses politically correct _____.

4. The new employment bill _____ with those who have lost their jobs.

5. I gave him my _____ opinion about his poor decorating.

6. His involvement in the _____ tangle of protective lies was obvious.

7. The colon cancer was _____ or fatal, for it was diagnosed too late.

8. The _____ reading approach, which slowly built on skills, was adopted unanimously by the faculty.

9. The whole _____ of twentieth-century thought was discussed in the book.

10. The pilgrimage was a(n) _____ of spiritual discovery.

Freewrite

Do you think that there are ever cases where adoptions should be denied? Why or why not?

Step Two: Read the Selection

Note: As you read the following selection, concentrate and practice the steps of SQ3R. Remove the SQ3R card from the book and complete it as you read.

The selection you will read, from the Philadelphia Inquirer, *expands on the adoption issue.*

Adoptive Parents Tell It Like It Is—and with Love
By Jeff Gammage

1. One of the things that's changed about adoption is that it has developed its own affirming, positive vocabulary.

2. No longer are children to be described as given up, surrendered or placed. The new, progressive parlance is to say that the people who gave birth to them "made an adoption plan."

3. But that language hardly applies to children like mine, who were born in China.

4. My eldest, now 5, was found alone in an alley when she was three days old. My youngest was discovered outside the door of a health clinic. To say that their Chinese parents "made an adoption plan" is to obscure the enormity of the act.

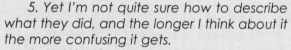

5. Yet I'm not quite sure how to describe what they did, and the longer I think about it the more confusing it gets.

6. Judging from a new book, A Love Like No Other (Riverhead Books), a lot of other parents are in the same boat.

7. A collection of essays by adoptive mothers and fathers, A Love Like No Other goes straight at the hard issues—abandonment, race and divorce, illnesses chronic and terminal, birth parents absent and present. The book shows that a one-size-fits-all approach, in experience or the terms used to define it, doesn't work in 2005, when Americans are raising 2.1 million adopted children.

© JupiterImages Corporation

8. Today the word adoption has become a lot like the word rainbow, a single term employed to describe what is actually a spectrum of color, light and view. A Love Like No Other tries to examine all the shades that are visible, and a few that aren't.

9. "We wanted to kind of shake it up a little bit," says co-editor Pamela Kruger, a contributing editor at Child magazine. "We're not giving answers

here. We just want people to think about this stuff, and hopefully provoke conversation."

10. Kruger and co-editor Jill Smolowe believed the adoption oeuvre had grown thick with procedural guides but thin on how to actually raise children. So they asked 20 writers, some well-known, some not, to present frank and honest accounts.

11. And boy, do they ever:

12. Melissa Fay Greene writes of how love-at-first-sight homilies held no meaning for her; she was certain she would never love her Bulgarian-born son, adopted when he was 4. "He was like the sleepover friend who overstays his welcome. 'When is that family going to pick this child up?'"

13. Greene, author of the acclaimed Praying for Sheetrock, learns that post-adoption depression can be as soul-sapping as post-partum depression. And that it's common among mothers of older adopted children. Medicine and friends help pull her out. She learns that her body is willing, even eager, to mother her child, and her heart and mind soon follow.

14. Bonnie Miller Rubin finds her Gerber-perfect baby in a shanty near Santiago, Chile, but as her daughter grows she develops disabling anger and learning problems, initiating a decade-long odyssey of psychiatric care. Some parents yearn for their teenagers to attend Ivy League colleges. Rubin hopes hers will someday be able to make change from a five-dollar bill.

15. "Do all adoptions turn out this way? Obviously not," says Kruger, the mother of two daughters, one of them adopted from Kazakstan. But "part of having a candid discussion is having a story like that."

16. A Love Like No Other suffers from having a title better suited to a porn flick, and a cover with all the sparkle and charm of a dental-school textbook. And that's too bad. Because the stories, told by single mothers and fathers, by couples gay and straight, by parents who were themselves adopted, are never less than interesting—and often compelling.

17. In "She Is Among Us," Christina Frank walks the streets of Hanoi, where she adopted her daughter, Lucy, searching the faces of passersby. She wonders if this one or that one is the woman who gave birth to her child.

18. Her story will resonate with many parents, particularly those with children from China, where coercive government birth quotas and a societal preference for sons result in the routine abandonment of baby girls.

19. "Lucy will always have two mothers," Frank writes, "and I am inextricably linked to the other one whether or not we ever meet. I needed her to create Lucy. She needed me to raise her."

20. Her musing is poetic—and a world away from the birth-mother reality endured by newspaper columnist Dan Savage and his young son, DJ.

21. "Instead of being a mystery," Savage writes, "DJ's mother was a mass of sometimes very distressing specifics."

22. The highlights: drinking, drug use and a defiant homelessness, what Savage sees as a slow-motion suicide.

23. He knows that DJ's mom so loved her child that she was willing to let him go, to spare him the chaos of her life. "I wonder if this answer will be good enough for DJ when he asks us why his mother couldn't hold it together just enough to stay in the world for him. I kind of doubt it."

24. Most adoption stories, though, have happier endings, families more likely to face challenges of ignorance than indigence.

25. Jacquelyn Mitchard, the best-selling author of The Deep End of the Ocean, describes her dragon-fire response to a reporter who insists on knowing, "Which ones are yours?" Mitchard refuses to offer the obvious answer: All of them.

26. When friends ask whether her daughter may want to see her "real mother," Mitchard responds that she already does, "everyday when I roll her out of bed before school." She teaches her family to understand that her children were adopted, not that they are adopted, a one-time event, not an ongoing condition.

27. She is frustrated that it matters so much to others, this question of who is adopted and who is not. Adoptive families "are still a curiosity—still regarded as a little on the shady side of regular," she writes. "We most often are not aware of it, and that's because we're used to being odd."

28. Odd? Maybe. But definitely more common. And never more visible. (Gammage)

Step Three: Follow-Up Activities

Objective Test on "Adoptive Parents Tell It Like It Is—and with Love"
Directions: Choose the best answer based on the reading.

1. True or False: This news article is about a collection of essays by adoptive mothers and fathers.

2. According to the author, most adoptions are:
   a. positive.   c. confusing.
   b. negative.   d. illegal.

3. True or False: The essays in the book cover issues like race, divorce, illnesses, abandonment, and birth parents.

4. The author does not like:
   a. the book.   c. the book's title and cover.
   b. inconsistencies in the book.   d. the book's point of view.

5. True or False: According to the editors of *A Love Like No Other*, the collection of essays was written to make readers think about the "hard issues" presented by adoptive mothers and fathers.

6. True or False: In 2005, Americans were raising almost a million adopted children.

7. True or False: The reporter, Jeff Gammage, includes his opinion about this collection of essays.

8. True or False: In *A Love Like No Other*, Melissa Fay Green notes how her adopted child changed her life in a positive way.

9. True or False: Bonnie Miller Rubin's experience with her adopted child was disappointing.

10. According to Mitchard, an adoptive parent:
    a. needs to meet the real parent.   c. is not unusual.
    b. is the real parent.   d. has problems.

Vocabulary Test on "Adoptive Parents Tell It Like It Is—and with Love"
Directions: Choose one of the meanings to identify the highlighted word as it appears in the selection

1. The new **progressive** parlance is to say that the people who gave birth to them "made an adoption plan."
   a. stagnant   c. advancing
   b. aggressive   d. backward

2. The new progressive **parlance** is to say that the people who gave birth to them "made an adoption plan."
   a. tasks   c. lists
   b. manner of speaking   d. argument

3. A collection of essays by adoptive mothers and fathers, *A Love Like No Other* goes straight at the hard issues—abandonment, race and divorce, illnesses **chronic** and terminal, birth parents absent and present.
   a. prolonged   c. minor
   b. fatal   d. resistant

4. A collection of essays by adoptive mothers and fathers, *A Love Like No Other* goes straight at the hard issues—abandonment, race and divorce, illnesses chronic and **terminal,** birth parents absent and present.
   a. temporary   c. fatal
   b. mild   d. cancerous

5. Today the word *adoption* has become a lot like the word *rainbow*, a single term employed to describe what is actually a **spectrum** of color, light and view.
   a. line   c. scattering
   b. range   d. cluster

6. Bonnie Miller Robin finds her Gerber-perfect baby in a shanty near Santiago, Chile, but as her daughter grows she develops disabling anger and learning problems, initiating a decade-long **odyssey** of psychiatric care.
   a. trip   c. journey
   b. destination   d. treatment

7. But "part of having a **candid** discussion is having a story like that."
   a. subjective   c. biased
   b. honest   d. opinionated

8. Her story **resonates** with many parents, particularly those with children from China, where coercive government birth quotas and a societal preference for sons result in the routine abandonment of baby girls.
   a. brings joy to   c. has an emotional impact
   b. confuses   d. silences

9. "Lucy will always have two mothers," Frank writes, "and I am **inextricably** linked to the other one whether or not we ever meet.
   a. impossible to achieve   c. impossible to escape
   b. impossible to understand   d. impossible to meet

10. Melissa Fay Greene writes of how love-at-first-sight **homilies** held no meaning for her; she was certain she would never love her Bulgarian-born son, adopted when he was 4.
    a. plays   c. poems
    b. stories   d. sermons

Questions about "Adoptive Parents Tell It Like It Is—and with Love"

1. What is included in the book, *A Love Like No Other*?

   _____

   _____

   _____

2. Provide three examples from the article of adoptions that didn't turn out as expected.

_____

_____

_____

3. What is the writer's opinion of *A Love Like No Other*?

_____

_____

_____

4. Why is Jacquelyn Mitchard unwilling to identify her adopted children?

_____

_____

_____

5. What type of news is this—hard, soft, or opinion? Explain your answer.

_____

_____

_____

Journal Suggestions

1. Is this newspaper article considered an editorial, column, or review? Explain.

2. The book *A Love Like No Other* presents a different side to adoption. Explain what is meant by this statement.

Collaborative Activity

Divide your group into two sides and debate the advantages and disadvantages of adoption.

Look It Up

1. Research and report on five adoption stories. The stories you select can be told by single mothers and fathers, by couples gay and straight, or by parents who were themselves adopted.

2. Research and report on China where a preference for sons results in the routine abandonment of baby girls.

3. Research and report the similarities and differences of post-adoption depression and post-partum depression.

Getting the Picture

In this chapter, you learned to distinguish facts from opinions in news stories. For this photo, list facts (things you can see in the picture) and opinions (things you are guessing about). For example, a *fact* would be that there are several people who seem to be at work. An *opinion* is that the man standing is the boss.

© Marcin Balcerzak, 2010. Used under license from Shutterstock, Inc.

Chapter Highlights

What Have We Learned?

1. **Editorials, columns**, and **reviews** have **facts and opinions**.

2. An **editorial** is the opinion of the newspaper.

3. A **column** is written by an expert in a certain field.

4. A **review** is someone's advice about a movie, restaurant, play, book, concert, or special event.

DOES THAT STORY MAKE SENSE?

CHAPTER 15 Narratives
CHAPTER 16 Narrative Strategies

In Unit 7 you learned how to comprehend newspapers and evaluate opinions in the news. In Unit 8 you will learn how to appreciate the wonderful world of books.

Spotlight on

J. K. Rowling (1965–)

J.K. (Joanne Kathleen) Rowling is best known as the author of the *Harry Potter* book series for children. Born in Chipping Sodbury near Bristol, England, Rowling went on to graduate from Exeter University and later worked as a secretary and a teacher. Rowling later became unemployed; divorced and living with her young daughter, she found it difficult to make ends meet. While riding on a train in 1990, she came up with the idea of Harry, a young wizard who attended Hogwarts School of Witchcraft and Wizardry. After several unsuccessful attempts to have her book published, Rowling found Bloomsbury Publishing. In 1997, *Harry Potter and the Philosopher's Stone* was published in England, and the book was an instant success. By

© Rune Hellestad/Corbis

the end of 1999 the top three slots on the *New York Times* list of bestsellers were taken by the first three books in the *Harry Potter* series. By the 2000 release of the fourth book in the series, *Harry Potter and the Goblet of Fire*, *Harry Potter* had become one of the most popular series of books for children. Rowling herself had become one of the world's best-known and best-paid authors. After the 2003 release of the fifth *Harry Potter* book, *The Order of the Phoenix*, the BBC reported that Rowling's books had been translated into 60 languages (including ancient Greek) and had sold over 250 million copies worldwide. The sequels to the original book are: *Harry Potter and the Chamber of Secrets* (1999), *Harry Potter and the Prisoner of Azkaban* (1999), *Harry Potter and the Goblet of Fire* (2000), *Harry Potter and the Order of the Phoenix* (2003), *Harry Potter and the Half-Blood Prince* (2005), and *Harry Potter and the Deathly Hallows* (2007). In 2008 she published *The Tales of Beedle the Bard*, a collection of fairy tales that was mentioned in the book *Harry Potter and the Deathly Hallows*. Her books have spawned six films, making a star of the actor Daniel Radcliffe, who played Harry Potter. Rowling is a noted philanthropist, supporting such charities as Comic Relief and the Multiple Sclerosis Society of Great Britain.

Chapter 15

NARRATIVES

J. K. Rowling gained fame because of her best-selling Harry Potter series, and because people love a good story.

Do you know someone who loves to read? Have you ever thought about why they love it so much? Most of us who like reading enjoy it because we love a good story. Stories can be found everywhere: in novels, plays, anthologies, even in movies and on the stage. A good story can make us laugh, cry, become afraid, angry, feel inspired, and move us in numerous ways as we immerse ourselves in its magical world. Some stories are about real life adventures while others lead us to a fantastical universe where anything is possible. Stories deal with family, science fiction, romance, mystery, and almost anyplace occupied by reality and the imagination. Yes, this is why people love to read! Everyone loves a good story.

Another name for a story is a **narrative.** A narrative is a story that contains action, a sense of movement, and change from beginning to end. It differs from a **description,** which is static, or just describes a scene (a backyard view, for example) with no change from beginning to end. Where description contains numerous adjectives to aid the description, a narrative moves along through the use of **action verbs.**

Narratives may be either **fiction** or **nonfiction. Fiction** means that the writing is based on **imaginary situations and events. Nonfiction** writing concerns **situations and events that really did occur, and characters who are real people.** Sometimes writing bridges the gap between fiction and nonfiction. Memoirs, for instance, are examples of writing that are biographies (life stories) based on actual people and events, but many include conversations or scenes that have been *fictionalized.*

Narratives may take many forms, or genres, which include poetry, short stories, biography, or novels.

Conflict in the Narrative

The idea of a problem or obstacle is inherent in all narratives. These problems are called **conflicts.** There are three basic conflicts: **(1) man against nature**, **(2) man against man**, and **(3) man against himself**. (Note: The term "man" is used to imply both males *and* females.)

In order to understand how conflict works, it is best to focus on a story many of us know. While not everyone has read *The Wonderful Wizard of Oz* published in 1900 by L. Frank Baum, most of us are familiar with the movie, *The Wizard of Oz*, released in 1939, starring the actress and singer Judy Garland. Like *Harry Potter*, both the books and movies, *The Wizard of Oz* is a fantasy about a good-hearted child who has adventures in a place where everything is magical. Using the narrative as it appears in the film, we can focus on the use of conflict.

The Wizard of Oz is a good example of a narrative that has all three basic conflicts. **Man against nature** is clearly evident when Dorothy is swept up by

Courtesy of Photofest.

the tornado, an uncontrollable event created by nature. The **man against man** conflict is present in the feud Dorothy has with the witch, who presents an obstacle against Dorothy's returning home and even her very survival. **Man against himself** is seen in Dorothy's internal struggles when she wants to experience adventures away from home, but is drawn to remain with her family. The Scarecrow, who feels inadequate intellectually, the Tin Man, who struggles with his emotions, and the Cowardly Lion, who doesn't feel as brave as he really is, also experience the **man against himself** conflict.

Elements of the Narrative

All narratives contain some basic elements. We need to examine each of these elements to come to a better understanding and appreciation of each story we read. Continuing with the narrative of *The Wizard of Oz,* let's examine the basic narrative elements: **characters, setting, plot, theme, tone, point of view,** and **moral**.

Characters

These are the figures, which may take the form of people, animals, robots, or other beings, who keep the story moving along. Another name for the main character is **protagonist. Antagonists** are those characters who present obstacles to the main characters. Furthermore, characters may be either **main (major)** or **minor. Main characters** keep the action moving, and, in fact, you could not have a story without them. **Minor characters** simply add interest.

Main or major characters in The *Wizard of Oz* would include Dorothy, the Scarecrow, the Tin Man, the Cowardly Lion, and the Wicked Witch (an antagonist) because without these characters we would not have a story. Minor characters of interest include Auntie Em, the Munchkins, and Toto, the dog.

Setting

The "where" and "when" or **place and time** of the narrative comprise its setting. Often, the setting of the narrative is essential to the story line. Sometimes, it is not important. For example, *The Wizard of Oz* takes place in Kansas and the Land of Oz. Clearly, these **places** are important to the story. Time here is less important. While the film was actually produced in 1939, this fact is not relevant, so we may describe the **time** period as **current**, since the story could have taken place at any time. The action takes place over a period of days, but this information too is not particularly relevant. In historical narratives, of course, time is an essential factor.

Plot

This is the **action** of the story, or "what happens." While it takes some time to review all of the action of the narrative, this element is superficial, and does not explore meaning, consequences, or symbolism.

The plot of *The Wizard of Oz* follows the adventures of Dorothy, a girl living in Kansas, who wishes to explore the rest of the world. After a disagreement with a woman who wishes to take away her dog, Dorothy plans to run away with the carnival. But before she can follow through with her plans, a tornado sweeps up Dorothy and her whole house. In the process, her house kills the Wicked Witch of the East. When the house lands, Dorothy emerges to find herself in Oz, a land inhabited by little people called Munchkins. Good Witch Glenda advises Dorothy that the ruby slippers on her feet had belonged to the Wicked Witch of the East and will now protect Dorothy. The Wicked Witch of the West appears and tries unsuccessfully to take the slippers; she vows vengeance on Dorothy. When Dorothy asks to return home, Glenda and the Munchkins tell her to follow the "yellow brick road" to find the Wizard, who has the capacity to grant all wishes. On the road, Dorothy meets the Scarecrow, who needs a brain; the Tin Man, who wants a heart; and the Cowardly Lion, who desires courage. They accompany her to the Wizard so that he can grant all of their wishes. When the group enters the Emerald City, home to the Wizard, each member is intimidated by the Wizard's awesome presence. The Wizard informs Dorothy that she must bring him the witch's broomstick before he can grant her wish to return home. Helped by her three companions, Dorothy melts the witch by throwing water on her, and she returns with the witch's broomstick to the Wizard. The Wizard tells the Scarecrow, Tin Man, and Cowardly Lion that they have possessed the qualities they were seeking all along, and rewards them with a diploma, watch, and medal, respectively. He then informs Dorothy that she and her dog, Toto, can accompany him in a hot air balloon back to Kansas. However, when they are ready to take off, Toto suddenly leaps out, Dorothy gives chase, and the balloon sails off without them. Just as Dorothy begins to despair, Glenda reappears to ask her what she has learned from her experience. Dorothy replies that she now knows that whatever she wishes for can be found at home. Glenda tells her to simply click the heels of her ruby red slippers together, and she will be on her way home. In the next instant,

Dorothy finds herself back in her bed in Kansas surrounded by her family and the hired hands who look strangely familiar.

Theme

This is the **main idea** of a story. Unlike the plot, it can be stated in one sentence and indicates what the writer is trying to accomplish. When determining the theme, try to think of a sentence that, if placed in a book's table of contents, would help you to easily find the narrative.

The **theme** of *The Wizard of Oz* might be phrased as: A girl dreams of leaving home when a tornado suddenly sweeps her up and she lands in a magical place called Oz, where she has adventures and eventually is happily returned home.

Tone

Another name for tone is the **mood** of the story. What is the feeling you get when reading the story, and how does the writer accomplish this mood? Tone may be classified as **frightening, serious, lighthearted, humorous,** or by numerous other descriptions. **Irony** is a tone we find in many tales. Irony is defined as an unexpected twist. For instance, a story about a soldier who survives many battles only to return home and be killed by a car while he is crossing the street is an example of irony.

There are many different tones in *The Wizard of Oz*. For instance, the tone is scary during the tornado and at the witch's castle. The tone is lighthearted and optimistic as the group ventures along the road to find the Wizard. There is irony too in the fact that all along, Dorothy's friends possessed the characteristics they were seeking. While a movie sets the tone through music, short stories and novels accomplish this through words.

Point of View

This element of the narrative does not refer to a writer's opinion, but rather **who is telling the story.** Generally, there are two types of point of view that we find in the narrative. A story can be written in the **first person** point of view or the **omniscient** point of view.

The **first person** or the "I" point of view is written from the storyteller's standpoint. The narrator is a part of the story and can only relate what he or she sees and feels. It is, therefore, a very personal point of view.

The **omniscient** or "all-knowing" point of view is less confining. It is told from the standpoint of someone *outside* of the action of the story. Therefore, the narrator can convey what is in the minds of all the characters, and can take us to various places (different countries or even outer space) and different time periods (including the past, present, and future). The narrator may also comment on the events that have taken place.

In *The Wizard of Oz,* the point of view is **omniscient** because the camera follows all the characters without Dorothy necessarily being a part of each scene.

Moral

This last element is found in some, *but not all,* narratives. The moral is a lesson that the story teaches us. Children's fairy tales (like Cinderella, which teaches that goodness will be rewarded) usually have morals. But a story need not have a moral for readers to appreciate it.

The Wizard of Oz is one narrative that does have a moral, which becomes clear at the end of the film. The moral is the lesson that Dorothy has learned: *There's no place like home.*

Your Turn—What Did You Learn?   15.1 *Exercise*

1. Another name for writing that tells a story is _____.

2. Stories are mostly comprised of _____ verbs.

3. _____ narratives are realistic, while _____ narratives are imaginative.

4. The three types of conflict found in narratives are man against _____, _____, and _____.

5. The element that deals with the action of a narrative is called _____.

6. The lesson of a narrative is called the _____.

7. The two types of characters found in narratives are _____ and _____.

8. Two types of point of view are _____ and _____.

9. The setting is the _____ and _____ of the narrative.

10. The main idea of a narrative is called its _____.

11. Another name for mood is _____.

12. An unexpected twist is called _____.

Identifying Narrative Elements   15.2 *Exercise*

Like Rowling's *Harry Potter*, beloved children's stories have motivated many of us to become lifelong readers. Do you recognize any of the following fairy tales from your childhood?

Directions: Identify the narrative elements used in the following examples. Write the answer, choosing from *Characters, Setting, Plot, Theme, Tone, Point Of View, Moral.*

1. Little Red Riding Hood traveled into the woods to visit her grandmother's house. _____

2. Cinderella lived with her mean stepmother and stepsisters, and later met her fairy godmother. Eventually, Cinderella got to meet the Prince! _____

© Maugli, 2010. Used under license from Shutterstock, Inc.

3. The first Pig built his house from straw, the second Pig built his house from wooden sticks, and the third Pig used bricks to build his house. The Big Bad Wolf easily blew down the straw and wooden houses, but was unable to blow down the house of bricks. When the Wolf tried to enter through the chimney, he fell into a pot of boiling water and was boiled alive. _____

4. When Snow White entered the deep dark woods, her heart leaped in terror as the wind howled through the trees and eyes appeared to peek at her from the darkness. _____

5. A girl enters the house of Three Bears and tastes their porridge, tries the chairs and bed, but the Bears discover the intruder who quickly runs away. _____

6. My cruel stepmother has tried to trick me and leave me for dead in the woods, but I think I will be safe here with my friends, the dwarfs. _____

7. The story of the Little Red Hen shows us that only those who work hard will be rewarded. _____

8. Two children who are deserted in the forest come upon a gingerbread house where they outwit a witch who tries to eat them. _____

9. Having a good heart will bring happiness, no matter what someone looks like. _____

10. I wish I were a real boy instead of just a marionette. _____

Comprehending Longer Selections 15.3 *Exercise*

Apply what you have learned in this chapter to longer reading selections.

Step One: Before Reading

Vocabulary in Context Practice

Directions: Choose one of the following words to complete each of the sentences below. Use each word only once. Be sure to pay attention to the context clues provided.

contempt—hatred
engrossed—gave total attention
fancy—whim, sudden idea
fond—with a liking for someone or something
gleefully—happily
implicitly—without saying
impressed—said strongly
mutual—for one and other
pursue—follow
spires—pointed towers

1. We knew the feeling was _____ because we both liked each other immediately.

2. Sara _____ opened the presents at her birthday party.

3. Migdalia became so _____ in reading the mystery novel that she forgot what time it was.

4. I am not very _____ of spicy food because it gives me heartburn.

5. Sanjit felt _____ for his boss after he was unfairly fired.

6. Pearl had a _____ for high-heeled shoes, and so she quickly bought the pair she saw in the window of the store.

7. The police had to _____ the bank robber until they caught him.

8. The round _____ of the building could be seen when we looked out the window.

9. The smile on Lucinda's face _____ told him that she would accept his invitation.

10. Professor Jones _____ on his students the need to read the text-book if they wished to pass his class.

Freewrite
Write about a magical skill you wish you had.

Step Two: Read the Selection

Peter Pan, the young boy who never grows up, has often been compared to the heroic Harry Potter. In this reading, a chapter from Peter Pan, Wendy and her brothers, John and Michael, test out their new flying skills and accompany Peter to Neverland where the lost boys who never grow up live.

The Flight (from *Peter Pan*)
By James M. Barrie

1. "Second to the right, and straight on till morning."

2. That, Peter had told Wendy, was the way to the Neverland; but even birds, carrying maps and consulting them at windy corners, could not have sighted it with these instructions. Peter, you see, just said anything that came into his head.

3. At first his companions trusted him implicitly, and so great were the delights of flying that they wasted time circling round church spires or any other tall objects on the way that took their fancy.

4. John and Michael raced, Michael getting a start.

5. They recalled with contempt that not so long ago they had thought themselves fine fellows for being able to fly round a room.

6. Not so long ago. But how long ago? They were flying over the sea before this thought began to disturb Wendy seriously. John thought it was their second sea and their third night.

7. Sometimes it was dark and sometimes light, and now they were very cold and again too warm. Did they really feel hungry at times, or were they

merely pretending because Peter had such a jolly new way of feeding them? His way was to pursue birds who had food in their mouths suitable for humans and snatch it from them; then the birds would follow and snatch it back; and they would all go chasing each other gaily for miles, parting at last with mutual expressions of goodwill. But Wendy noticed with gentle concern that Peter did not seem to know that this was rather an odd way of getting your bread and butter, nor even that there are other ways.

8. Certainly they did not pretend to be sleepy, they were sleepy; and that was a danger, for the moment they popped off, down they fell. The awful thing was that Peter thought this funny.

9. "There he goes again!" he would cry gleefully, as Michael suddenly dropped like a stone.

10. "Save him, save him!" cried Wendy, looking with horror at the cruel sea far below. Eventually Peter would dive through the air, and catch Michael just before he could strike the sea, and it was lovely the way he did it; but he always waited till the last moment, and you felt it was his cleverness that interested him and not the saving of human life. Also he was fond of variety, and the sport that engrossed him one moment would suddenly cease to engage him, so there was always the possibility that the next time you fell he would let you go.

11. He could sleep in the air without falling, by merely lying on his back and floating, but this was, partly at least, because he was so light that if you got behind him and blew he went faster.

12. "Do be more polite to him," Wendy whispered to John, when they were playing "Follow my Leader."

13. "Then tell him to stop showing off," said John.

14. When playing Follow my Leader, Peter would fly close to the water and touch each shark's tail in passing, just as in the street you may run your finger along an iron railing. They could not follow him in this with much success, so perhaps it was rather like showing off, especially as he kept looking behind to see how many tails they missed.

15. "You must be nice to him," Wendy impressed on her brothers. "What would we do if he were to leave us?"

16. "We could go back," Michael said.

17. "How could we ever find our way back without him?"

18. "Well, then, we could go on," said John.

19. "That is the awful thing, John. We should have to go on, for we don't know how to stop."

20. This was true; Peter had forgotten to show them how to stop. (Barrie)

Step Three: Follow-Up Activities

Objective Test on "The Flight"

Directions: Choose the best answer based on the reading.

1. The theme (main idea) of this selection is:
   a. Peter is a show-off.
   b. the group is having a strange, but fun, time flying to Neverland.
   c. Wendy is becoming more worried.
   d. flying over the ocean is dangerous.

2. True or False: Wendy, John, and Michael have the same magical abilities as Peter.

3. Peter's directions to Neverland are:
   a. found on maps.
   b. directed by the sun.
   c. made up.
   d. wrong.

4. Peter gives the children food caught by birds because it is:
   a. nutritious.
   b. fun.
   c. the only food around.
   d. easy to catch.

5. When Peter falls asleep, he:
   a. floats safely.
   b. plays Follow My Leader.
   c. falls like a stone.
   d. plays jokes on the others.

6. True or False: The point of view of this story is omniscient.

7. The moral of this narrative is:
   a. don't follow bad advice.
   b. have fun.
   c. be prepared.
   d. there is no moral.

8. The children probably think that Peter is:
   a. weird but exciting.
   b. someone to be admired.
   c. dangerous.
   d. a good teacher.

9. True or False: Peter has planned the travel to Neverland.

10. True or False: John is worried about how they will get home.

Vocabulary Test on "The Flight"

Directions: Choose one of the meanings to identify the highlighted word as it appears in the selection.

1. They recalled with **contempt** that not so long ago they had thought themselves fine fellows for being able to fly round a room.
   a. curiosity
   b. wonder
   c. awe
   d. hatred

2. At first his companions trusted him **implicitly,** and so great were the delights of flying that they wasted time circling round church spires or any other tall objects on the way that took their fancy.
   a. totally
   b. loudly
   c. without saying
   d. with fear

3. At first his companions trusted him implicitly, and so great were the delights of flying that they wasted time circling round church **spires** or any other tall objects on the way that took their fancy.
   a. bells
   b. pointed towers
   c. rounded towers
   d. roofs

4. At first his companions trusted him implicitly, and so great were the delights of flying that they wasted time circling round church spires or any other tall objects on the way that took their **fancy.**
   a. time
   b. contemplation
   c. whim, sudden idea
   d. delight

5. "You must be nice to him," Wendy **impressed** on her brothers. "What would we do if he were to leave us?"
   a. said strongly
   b. asked
   c. said with doubt
   d. pushed

6. Also he was **fond** of variety, and the sport that engrossed him one moment would suddenly cease to engage him, so there was always the possibility that the next time you fell he would let you go.
   a. aware
   b. with a liking for someone or something
   c. hated
   d. accustomed to

7. Also he was fond of variety, and the sport that **engrossed** him one moment would suddenly cease to engage him, so there was always the possibility that the next time you fell he would let you go.
   a. annoyed
   b. assisted
   c. eluded
   d. gave total attention

8. "There he goes again!" he would cry **gleefully,** as Michael suddenly dropped like a stone.
   a. happily
   b. loudly
   c. fearfully
   d. menacingly

9. His way was to pursue birds who had food in their mouths suitable for humans and snatch it from them; then the birds would follow and snatch it back; and they would all go chasing each other gaily for miles, parting at last with **mutual** expressions of goodwill.
   a. ordered
   b. singular
   c. frustrated
   d. for one and other

10. His way was to **pursue** birds who had food in their mouths suitable for humans and snatch it from them; then the birds would follow and snatch it back; and they would all go chasing each other gaily for miles, parting at last with mutual expressions of goodwill.
    a. anger
    b. harm
    c. follow
    d. sweep up

Questions about "The Flight"

1. Who are the main characters in this selection? Describe each of the characters.

   _____

   _____

   _____

2. Discuss Peter's actions and why he seems unusual.

   _____

   _____

   _____

3. How can you tell that this story is a fantasy, or unrealistic?

   _____

   _____

   _____

4. Does this story have a moral? Explain.

   _____

   _____

   _____

5. What do you think will happen next?

_____

_____

_____

Journal Suggestion

Peter Pan is the story of a boy who never grows up. Imagine if you had the power to remain a child for the rest of your life. In your journal, list the pros and cons of such an experience and then discuss your responses with your group.

Collaborative Activity

Children love reading fantasies like *Peter Pan* and *Harry Potter*. Collaborate with your group to create a short story in which the main character has a superpower. Present your revised story for the class.

Look It Up

1. *Peter Pan* is a classic novel that has been adapted for a number of films. Read the novel and watch one of the film versions. Write a review comparing the book to the movie.

2. Many scholars believe that James M. Barrie used people he knew in his own life as the inspiration for *Peter Pan*. Use the Internet to research this idea. You might want to view the movie *Finding Neverland* to expand your research. Write a paper documenting your findings.

3. Written a century later, *Harry Potter* may be viewed as a modern version of *Peter Pan*. The novels feature heroic boys with magical powers who encounter numerous adventures that spark the imagination of adults and children alike. Read both of these novels (using the original *Harry Potter and the Sorcerer's Stone*). Write a research paper that explores this concept.

Comprehending Longer Selections

15.4 *Exercise*

More Practice

Apply what you have learned in this chapter to longer reading selections.

Step One: Before Reading

Vocabulary in Context Practice

Directions: Choose one of the following words to complete each of the sentences below. Use each word only once. Be sure to pay attention to the context clues provided.

casual—informal, relaxed
cynically—mistrusting
deprived—not having
incredulously—unbelieving
insolently—disrespectfully
lapses—setbacks
raucous—loud, unruly
reassuringly—giving assurance
renounced—gave up
swaggering—walking with confidence

1. The boy was spanked for _____ speaking to his mother.

2. The child was _____ of sweets before dinnertime.

3. The man _____ replied that no candidate will ever lower taxes.

4. Bill _____ eating chili after it gave him heartburn.

5. The boxer who had just won the fight was _____ around the ring.

6. The teacher snapped her fingers to avoid _____ in attention.

7. Upon being told that she won the lottery, she _____ told her friends that nothing like this had ever happened to her before.

8. Wearing _____ clothing to work at the formal firm was strictly not allowed.

9. The old man yelled at the boys whose _____ behavior was disturbing the neighborhood.

10. Mom picked up Steve after he fell, _____ telling him he would be fine.

Freewrite
Write about a time when you had a problem in school, and how you handled it.

Step Two: Read the Selection

Harry Potter doesn't only use magic to get out of a bad situation, but often employs wit and imagination to save the day. Although Laurie is much younger than Harry and has no magical powers to help him, he is just as clever, as we see in the following surprising tale by Shirley Jackson. Shirley Jackson (1916–1965), was a prolific author of short stories that appeared in magazines including Reader's Digest, The New Yorker, and The Saturday Evening Post.

Charles
By Shirley Jackson

1. The day my son Laurie started kindergarten he renounced corduroy overalls with bibs and began wearing blue jeans with a belt; I watched him go off the first morning with the older girl next door, seeing clearly that an era of my life was ended, my sweet-voiced nursery-school tot replaced by a long-trousered, swaggering character who forgot to stop at the corner and wave good-bye to me.

2. He came home the same way, the front door slamming open, his cap on the floor, and the voice suddenly became raucous shouting, "Isn't anybody here?"

3. At lunch he spoke insolently to his father, spilled his baby sister's milk, and remarked that his teacher said we were not to take the name of the Lord in vain.

4. "How was school today?" I asked, elaborately casual.

5. "All right," he said.

6. "Did you learn anything?" his father asked.

7. Laurie regarded his father coldly. "I didn't learn nothing," he said.

8. "Anything," I said. "Didn't learn anything."

9. "The teacher spanked a boy, though," Laurie said, addressing his bread and butter. "For being fresh," he added, with his mouth full.

10. "What did he do?" I asked. "Who was it?"

11. Laurie thought. "It was Charles," he said. "He was fresh. The teacher spanked him and made him stand in a corner. He was awfully fresh."

12. "What did he do?" I asked again, but Laurie slid off his chair, took a cookie, and left, while his father was still saying, "See here, young man."

13. The next day Laurie remarked at lunch, as soon as he sat down, "Well, Charles was bad again today." He grinned enormously and said, "Today Charles hit the teacher."

14. "Good heavens," I said, mindful of the Lord's name, "I suppose he got spanked again?"

15. "He sure did," Laurie said. "Look up," he said to his father.

16. "What?" his father said, looking up.

17. "Look down," Laurie said. "Look at my thumb. Gee, you're dumb." He began to laugh insanely.

18. "Why did Charles hit the teacher?" I asked quickly.

19. "Because she tried to make him color with red crayons," Laurie said. "Charles wanted to color with green crayons so he hit the teacher and she spanked him and said nobody play with Charles but everybody did."

20. The third day—it was Wednesday of the first week—Charles bounced a see-saw onto the head of a little girl and made her bleed, and the teacher made him stay inside all during recess. Thursday Charles had to stand in a corner during story-time because he kept pounding his feet on the floor. Friday Charles was deprived of blackboard privileges because he threw chalk.

21. On Saturday I remarked to my husband, "Do you think kindergarten is too unsettling for Laurie? All this toughness, and bad grammar, and this Charles boy sounds like such a bad influence."

22. "It'll be all right," my husband said reassuringly. "Bound to be people like Charles in the world. Might as well meet them now as later."

23. On Monday Laurie came home late, full of news. "Charles," he shouted as he came up the hill; I was waiting anxiously on the front steps. "Charles," Laurie yelled all the way up the hill, "Charles was bad again."

24. "Come right in," I said, as soon as he came close enough. "Lunch is waiting."

25. "You know what Charles did?" he demanded, following me through the door. "Charles yelled so in school they sent a boy in from first grade to tell the teacher she had to make Charles keep quiet, and Charles had to stay after school. And so all the children stayed to watch him."

26. "What did he do?" I asked.

27. "He just sat there," Laurie said, climbing into his chair at the table. "Hi, Pop, y'old dust mop."

28. "Charles had to stay after school today," I told my husband. "Everyone stayed with him."

29. "What does this Charles look like?" my husband asked Laurie. "What's his other name?"

30. "He's bigger than me," Laurie said. "And he doesn't have any rubbers and he doesn't ever wear a jacket."

31. Monday night was the first Parent-Teachers meeting, and only the fact that the baby had a cold kept me from going; I wanted passionately to meet Charles's mother. On Tuesday Laurie remarked suddenly, "Our teacher had a friend come to see her in school today."

32. "Charles's mother?" my husband and I asked simultaneously.

33. "Naaah," Laurie said. "Charles was so fresh to the teacher's friend he wasn't let do exercises."

34. "Fresh again?" I said.

35. "He kicked the teacher's friend," Laurie said. "The teacher's friend told Charles to touch his toes like I just did and Charles kicked him."

36. "What are they going to do about Charles, do you suppose?" Laurie's father asked him.

37. Laurie shrugged elaborately. "Throw him out of school, I guess," he said.

38. Wednesday and Thursday were routine; Charles yelled during story hour and hit a boy in the stomach and made him cry. On Friday Charles stayed after school again and so did all the other children.

39. With the third week of kindergarten Charles was an institution in our family; the baby was being a Charles when she cried all afternoon; Laurie did a Charles when he filled his wagon full of mud and pulled it through the kitchen; even my husband, when he caught his elbow in the telephone cord and pulled telephone, ashtray, and a bowl of flowers off the table, said, after the first minute, "Looks like Charles."

40. During the third and fourth weeks it looked like a reformation Charles; Laurie reported grimly at lunch on Thursday of the third week, "Charles was so good today the teacher gave him an apple."

41. "What?" I said, and my husband added warily, "You mean Charles?"

42. "Charles," Laurie said. "He gave the crayons around and he picked up the books afterward and the teacher said he was her helper."

43. "What happened?" I asked incredulously.

44. "He was her helper, that's all," Laurie said, and shrugged.

45. "Can this be true, about Charles?" I asked my husband that night. "Can something like this happen?"

46. "Wait and see," my husband said cynically. "When you've got a Charles to deal with, this may mean he's only plotting."

47. He seemed to be wrong. For over a week Charles was the teacher's helper; each day he handed things out and he picked things up; no one had to stay after school.

48. "The P.T.A. meeting's next week again," I told my husband one evening. "I'm going to find Charles's mother there."

49. "Ask her what happened to Charles," my husband said. "I'd like to know."

50. "I'd like to know myself," I said.

51. On Friday of that week things were back to normal. "You know what Charles did today?" Laurie demanded at the lunch table, in a voice slightly awed. "He told a little girl to say a word and she said it and the teacher washed her mouth out with soap and Charles laughed."

52. "What word?" his father asked unwisely, and Laurie said, "I'll have to whisper it to you, it's so bad." He got down off his chair and went around to his father. His father bent his head down and Laurie whispered joyfully. His father's eyes widened.

53. "Did Charles tell the little girl to say that?" he asked respectfully.

54. "She said it twice," Laurie said. "Charles told her to say it twice."

55. "What happened to Charles?" my husband asked.

56. "Nothing," Laurie said. "He was passing out the crayons."

57. Monday morning Charles abandoned the little girl and said the evil word himself three or four times, getting his mouth washed out with soap each time. He also threw chalk.

58. My husband came to the door with me that evening as I set out for the P.T.A. meeting. "Invite her over for a cup of tea after the meeting," he said. "I want to get a look at her."

59. "If only she's there," I said prayerfully.

60. "She'll be there," my husband said. "I don't see how they could hold a P.T.A. meeting without Charles's mother."

61. At the meeting I sat restlessly, scanning each comfortable matronly face, trying to determine which one hid the secret of Charles. None of them looked to me haggard enough. No one stood up in the meeting and apologized for the way her son had been acting. No one mentioned Charles.

62. After the meeting I identified and sought out Laurie's kindergarten teacher. She had a plate with a cup of tea and a piece of chocolate

cake; I had a plate with a cup of tea and a piece of marshmallow cake. We maneuvered up to one another cautiously, and smiled.

63. *"I've been so anxious to meet you," I said. "I'm Laurie's mother."*

64. *"We're all so interested in Laurie," she said.*

65. *"Well, he certainly likes kindergarten," I said. "He talks about it all the time."*

66. *"We had a little trouble adjusting, the first week or so," she said primly, "but now he's a fine little helper. With occasional lapses, of course."*

67. *"Laurie usually adjusts very quickly," I said. "I suppose this time it's Charles's influence."*

68. *"Charles?"*

69. *"Yes," I said, laughing, "you must have your hands full in that kindergarten, with Charles."*

70. *"Charles?" she said. "We don't have any Charles in the kindergarten." (Jackson)*

Step Three: Follow-Up Activities

Objective Test on "Charles"

Directions: Choose the best answer based on the reading.

1. The theme (main idea) of this selection is:
   a. Charles is having a problem with kindergarten.
   b. Laurie is having a problem with kindergarten.
   c. Charles is fooling everyone.
   d. Laurie is having problems and is fooling everyone.

2. True or False: This short story was probably written recently.

3. Laurie stayed late in school because:
   a. the teacher said everyone had to stay with Charles.
   b. he was being punished for misbehaving.
   c. he wanted to fool his parents.
   d. he wanted to see what would happen to Charles.

4. Charles's mother is not in school because:
   a. she doesn't know about her son's behavior.
   b. she doesn't care about her son's behavior.
   c. she is probably sick.
   d. she doesn't exist.

5. Laurie's parents think Charles might be:
   a. a bad influence.   c. suffering from neglect.
   b. a good child.   d. imagined by Laurie.

6. True or False: Laurie is often disrespectful to his parents.

7. Laurie probably makes up lies because:
   a. he likes attention.   c. he wants to shock his parents.
   b. he doesn't want to be blamed. d. a, b, and c are all correct.

8. The ending of this story can best be described as:
   a. sad.   c. surprising.
   b. predictable.   d. funny.

9. True or False: The story contains clues regarding the time period when these events occurred.

10. True or False: Laurie's mother was probably happy to hear the teacher's news about Charles.

Vocabulary Test on "Charles"

Directions: Choose one of the meanings to identify the highlighted word as it appears in the selection.

1. The day my son Laurie started kindergarten he **renounced** corduroy overalls with bibs and began wearing blue jeans with a belt; I watched him go off the first morning with the older girl next door, seeing clearly that an era of my life was ended, my sweet-voiced nursery-school tot replaced by a long-trousered, swaggering character who forgot to stop at the corner and wave good-bye to me.
   a. became attached to
   b. gave up
   c. wore
   d. desired

2. The day my son Laurie started kindergarten he renounced corduroy overalls with bibs and began wearing blue jeans with a belt; I watched him go off the first morning with the older girl next door, seeing clearly that an era of my life was ended, my sweet-voiced nursery-school tot replaced by a long-trousered, **swaggering** character who forgot to stop at the corner and wave good-bye to me.
   a. shaky
   b. walking with confidence
   c. indignant
   d. soft-mannered

3. "It'll be all right," my husband said **reassuringly.**
   a. giving assurance
   b. conceitedly
   c. hesitating
   d. uncertainly

4. With occasional **lapses,** of course.
   a. scoldings
   b. praise
   c. setbacks
   d. corrections

5. At lunch he spoke **insolently** to his father, spilled his baby sister's milk, and remarked that his teacher said we were not to take the name of the Lord in vain.
   a. loudly
   b. laughing
   c. few words
   d. disrespectfully

6. He came home the same way, the front door slamming open, his cap on the floor, and the voice suddenly became **raucous** shouting, "Isn't anybody *here?*"
   a. rough
   b. loud, unruly
   c. unusual
   d. exasperated

7. "Wait and see," my husband said **cynically.** "When you've got a Charles to deal with, this may mean he's only plotting."
   a. wondering
   b. trusting
   c. mistrusting
   d. with confidence

8. Friday Charles was **deprived** of blackboard privileges because he threw chalk.
   a. punished
   b. scolded
   c. given
   d. not having

9. "What happened?" I asked **incredulously.**
   a. unbelieving
   b. shocked
   c. angrily
   d. obstinately

10. "How *was* school today?" I asked, elaborately **casual.**
    a. formal, stilted
    b. informal, relaxed
    c. authentic
    d. concerned

Questions about "Charles"

1. What do Laurie's parents learn about Charles?

   _____

   _____

   _____

2. How does Laurie behave when he is home? Explain.

   _____

   _____

   _____

3. How does the author prepare us with clues for the ending?

   _____

   _____

   _____

4. This story was written over fifty years ago. What clues indicate the time period? How would the story change if it were written for modern times?

   _____

   _____

   _____

5. What kind of discipline does Laurie receive at home? Should the parents have changed the way they react to their son? Explain.

   _____

   _____

   _____

Journal Suggestion

Create your own ending to "Charles." Explain how the parents might have reacted to the teacher's news and how they dealt with his behavior.

Collaborative Activity

Write a skit with other students detailing what happens during the story and what might occur afterward. Have members of your group assume the different roles, and then discuss the possible consequences of Laurie's behavior.

Look It Up

1. Shirley Jackson (1919–1965) was a prolific short story writer whose most significant story was "The Lottery." Read this short story and, using the Internet, research what critics have to say about it. Make a chart comparing similarities and differences in Jackson's "Charles" and "The Lottery." What do both of these stories say about human nature?

2. Using the Internet, research and take notes on some current methods of child discipline. Knowing what we do today about children's behavior, how could parents successfully deal with a child like Laurie? If you were a counselor, what would you advise? How do methods today differ from those fifty years ago?

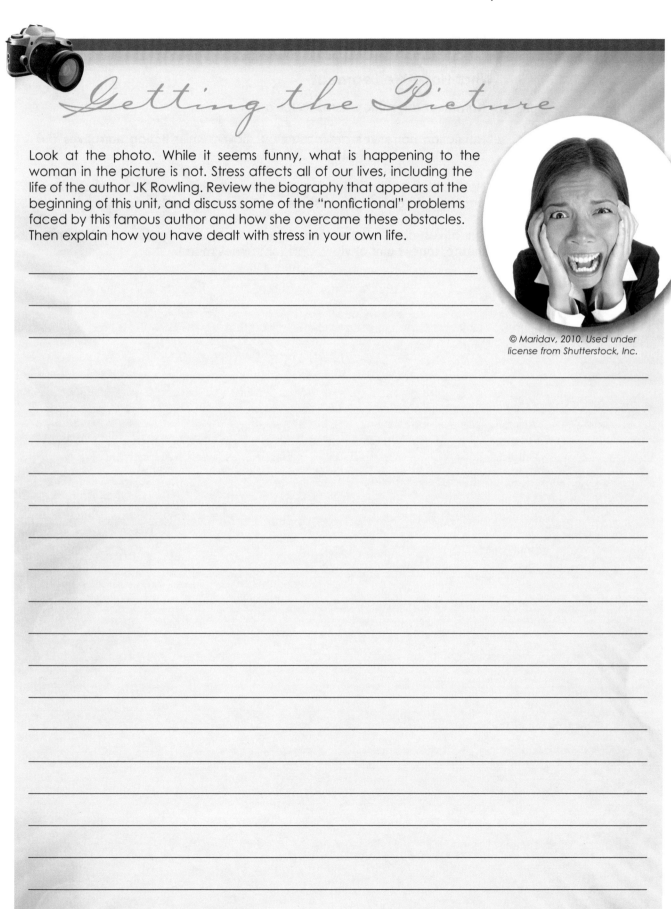

Getting the Picture

Look at the photo. While it seems funny, what is happening to the woman in the picture is not. Stress affects all of our lives, including the life of the author JK Rowling. Review the biography that appears at the beginning of this unit, and discuss some of the "nonfictional" problems faced by this famous author and how she overcame these obstacles. Then explain how you have dealt with stress in your own life.

© Maridav, 2010. Used under license from Shutterstock, Inc.

Chapter Highlights

What Have We Learned?

1. **Narratives** use **action verbs** to tell a story.

2. **Nonfiction narratives** are based on reality, while **fiction narratives** are based on the imagination.

3. Narratives may contain one or more of these types of **conflicts: man against nature, man against man,** and **man against himself.**

4. Narratives contain the following elements: **characters, setting, plot, theme, tone, point of view,** and sometimes **moral.**

Chapter 16

NARRATIVE STRATEGIES

We have learned that reading a good story, or a narrative, can be a very enjoyable activity. Understanding and being able to identify the various story elements can certainly enhance our understanding and appreciation. In this chapter, we will read a few stories and then identify the elements so that we can summarize and respond to what we have read.

This chapter consists of five comprehending longer selections exercises that begin on page 407.

Comprehending Longer Selections

Step One: Before Reading

Vocabulary in Context Practice

Directions: Choose one of the following words to complete each of the sentences below. Use each word only once. Be sure to pay attention to the context clues provided.

elixir—cure-all
elusive—difficult to describe, capture
forestall—prevent
hastened—hurried
illumination—enlightenment
impose—demand, force
persistence—continuation of effort
repression—subduing
trivial—unimportant
tumultuously—with agitation

1. You might not know how to play a piano the first time you try, but with _____, you will eventually be able to play many songs.

2. We _____ to get into our cars since it looked like rain.

3. My interest in drawing is _____ since it is just a hobby.

4. The judge will _____ a fine on Chris for driving without a license.

5. Penicillin is often viewed as a(n) _____ since it can cure many illnesses.

6. That butterfly is so _____ because we can never seem to catch it.

7. Sonya always washes her hands in order to _____ catching a cold.

8. Reading the newspaper provided Frank with _____ so he could understand all current events.

9. Tanya felt a sense of _____ when her parents asked her to be home before midnight.

10. The violent storm made the tree branches shake _____.

Freewrite
Write about a time when you received bad news. How did you react?

Step Two: Read the Selection

J. K. Rowling achieved success as a woman writer because of a society that gave her the freedom to achieve her dreams. But things might have been different had she been born during a more restrictive period, as is the case in the following story by Kate Chopin.

The Story of an Hour
By Kate Chopin

© JupiterImages Corporation

1. Knowing that Mrs. Mallard was afflicted with a heart trouble, great care was taken to break to her as gently as possible the news of her husband's death.

2. It was her sister Josephine who told her, in broken sentences, with hints that revealed in half concealing. Her husband's friend Richards was there, too, near her. It was he who had been in the newspaper office when intelligence of the railroad disaster was received, with Brently Mallard's name leading the list of "killed." He had only taken the time to assure himself of its truth by a second telegram, and had hastened to forestall any less careful, less tender friend in bearing the sad message.

3. She did not hear the story as many women have heard the same, with a paralyzed inability to accept its significance. She wept at once, with sudden, wild abandonment, in her sister's arms. When the storm of grief had spent itself she went away to her room alone. She would have no one follow her.

4. There stood, facing the open window, a comfortable, roomy armchair. Into this she sank, pressed down by a physical exhaustion that haunted her body and seemed to reach into her soul.

5. She could see in the open square before her house the tops of trees that were all aquiver with the new spring life. The delicious breath of rain was in the air. In the street below a peddler was crying his wares. The notes of a distant song which someone was singing reached her faintly, and countless sparrows were twittering in the eaves.

6. There were patches of blue sky showing here and there through the clouds that had met and piled above the other in the west facing her window.

7. She sat with her head thrown back upon the cushion of the chair, quite motionless, except when a sob came up into her throat and shook her, as a child who has cried itself to sleep continues to sob in its dreams.

8. She was young, with a fair, calm face, whose lines bespoke repression and even a certain strength. But now there was a dull stare in her eyes, whose gaze was fixed away off yonder on one of those patches of blue sky. It was not a glance of reflection, but rather indicated a suspension of intelligent thought.

9. There was something coming to her and she was waiting for it fearfully. What was it? She did not know; it was too subtle and elusive to name. But she felt it, creeping out of the sky, reaching toward her through the wounds, the scents, the color that filled the air.

10. Now her bosom rose and fell tumultuously. She was beginning to recognize this thing that was approaching to possess her, and she was striving to beat it back with her will—as powerless as her two white slender hands would have been.

11. When she abandoned herself, a little whispered word escaped her slightly parted lips. She said it over and over under her breath: "Free, free, free!" The vacant stare and the look of terror that had followed it went from her eyes. They stayed keen and bright. Her pulse beat fast, and the coursing blood warmed and relaxed every inch of her body.

12. She did not stop to ask if it were or were not a monstrous joy that held her. A clear and exalted perception enabled her to dismiss the suggestion as trivial.

13. She knew that she would weep again when she saw the kind, tender hands folded in death; the face that had never looked save with love upon her, fixed and gray and dead. But she saw beyond that bitter moment a long procession of years to come that would belong to her absolutely. And she opened and spread her arms out to them in welcome.

14. There would be no one to live for her during those coming years; she would live for herself. There would be no powerful will bending her to that blind persistence with which men and women believe they have a right to impose a private will upon a fellow-creature. A kind intention or a cruel intention made the act seem no less a crime as she looked upon it in that brief moment of illumination.

15. And yet she had loved him—sometimes. Often she had not. What did it matter! What could love, the unsolved mystery, count for in face of this possession of self-assertion which she suddenly recognized as the strongest impulse of her being!

16. "Free! Body and soul free!" she kept whispering.

17. Josephine was kneeling before the closed door with her lips to the keyhole, imploring for admission, "Louise, open the door! I beg; open the door—you will make yourself ill. What are you doing, Louise? For heaven's sake open the door."

18. "Go away. I am not making myself ill." No; she was drinking in a very elixir of life through that open window.

19. Her fancy was running riot along those days ahead of her. Spring days, and summer days, and all sorts of days that would be her own. She breathed a quick prayer that life might be long. It was only yesterday she had thought with a shudder that life might be long.

20. She arose at length and opened the door to her sister's importunities. There was a feverish triumph in her eyes, and she carried herself unwittingly like a goddess of Victory. She clasped her sister's waist, and together they descended the stairs. Richards stood waiting for them at the bottom.

21. Someone was opening the front door with a latchkey. It was Brently Mallard who entered, a little travel-stained, composedly carrying his gripsack and umbrella. He had been far from the scene of accident, and did not even know there had been one. He stood amazed at Josephine's piercing cry; at Richards' quick motion to screen him from the view of his wife.

22. But Richards was too late.

23. When the doctors came they said she had died of heart disease—of joy that kills. (Chopin)

Kate Chopin (1851–1904), was a writer known for her depiction of the inner feelings of women. Criticized during her lifetime for her honest portrayal of women's sexuality, Chopin is now regarded as a feminist author of note.

The Short Story Worksheet: "The Story of an Hour"
Directions: Fill in the narrative elements for the story you just read:

1. **Characters:** List the major characters, with a short description of each. List minor characters:

   _____

   _____

   _____

2. **Setting:** Describe the setting (time and place).

   _____

   _____

   _____

3. **Plot:** Explain the series of events.

   _____

   _____

   _____

4. **Theme:** State the main idea.

   _____

   _____

   _____

5. **Tone:** Discuss how mood is created. How is humor, fear, irony, etc., conveyed? Be specific.

   _____

   _____

   _____

6. **Point of View:** State the author's point of view.

   _____

   _____

   _____

7. **Moral:** Is there a lesson, if so, what is it?

   _____

   _____

   _____

   What is your reaction to the story? Why did you or didn't you like it? Explain your answer.

   _____

   _____

   _____

Now, write a short story report (one to two pages) using the answers to the above questions.

Step Three: Follow-Up Activities

Objective Test on "The Story of an Hour"

Directions: Choose the best answer based on the reading.

1. Mrs. Mallard suffered from:
   - a. a heart problem.
   - b. a nervous problem.
   - c. extreme shyness.
   - d. nothing but good health.

2. The story takes place during:
   - a. winter.
   - b. spring.
   - c. summer.
   - d. fall.

3. Brently Mallard is:
   - a. alive.
   - b. killed in a train accident.
   - c. hit by a car.
   - d. saved from a train accident.

4. When she hears about her husband, after a while Mrs. Mallard feels:
   - a. sad.
   - b. relieved.
   - c. depressed.
   - d. triumphant.

5. She believes that her husband:
   - a. hates her.
   - b. loves her.
   - c. has no feeling for her.
   - d. is too materialistic.

6. Mrs. Mallard:
   - a. totally loved her husband.
   - b. totally hated her husband.
   - c. sometimes loved her husband.
   - d. learned to love her husband.

7. Mrs. Mallard prays for:
   - a. the death of her husband.
   - b. the survival of her husband.
   - c. freedom.
   - d. long life.

8. When Louise Mallard goes downstairs, she becomes:
   - a. calmer.
   - b. shocked.
   - c. resolved.
   - d. forlorn.

9. The line "joy that kills" indicates that the story is:
   - a. shocking.
   - b. predictable.
   - c. ironic.
   - d. descriptive.

10. This story would hold the most appeal for:
    - a. children.
    - b. romantics.
    - c. mystery lovers.
    - d. feminists.

Vocabulary Test on "The Story of an Hour"

Directions: Choose one of the meanings to identify the highlighted word as it appears in the selection.

1. He had only taken the time to assure himself of its truth by a second telegram, and had **hastened** to forestall any less careful, less tender friend in bearing the sad message.
   - a. worried
   - b. sneaked
   - c. hurried
   - d. liked

2. He had only taken the time to assure himself of its truth by a second telegram, and had hastened to **forestall** any less careful, less tender friend in bearing the sad message.
   - a. prevent
   - b. secure
   - c. rush
   - d. send

3. No; she was drinking in a very **elixir** of life through that open window.
   a. air   c. cure-all
   b. water   d. springtime

4. There would be no powerful will bending her to that blind **persistence** with which men and women believe they have a right to impose a private will upon a fellow-creature.
   a. continuation   c. horror
   b. anger   d. relationship

5. There would be no powerful will bending her to that blind persistence with which men and women believe they have a right to **impose** a private will upon a fellow-creature.
   a. direct   c. correct
   b. create   d. demand, force

6. A clear and exalted perception enabled her to dismiss the suggestion as **trivial.**
   a. ridiculous   c. unimportant
   b. important   d. forgotten

7. A kind intention or a cruel intention made the act seem no less a crime as she looked upon it in that brief moment of **illumination.**
   a. curiosity   c. void
   b. sameness   d. enlightenment

8. She was young, with a fair, calm face, whose lines bespoke **repression** and even a certain strength.
   a. subduing   c. beauty
   b. openness   d. knowledge

9. Now her bosom rose and fell **tumultuously.**
   a. softly   c. with agitation
   b. quickly   d. with pain

10. She did not know; it was too subtle and **elusive** to name.
    a. abhorrent   c. small
    b. difficult to describe, capture   d. confusing

Questions about "The Story of an Hour"

1. How does Mrs. Mallard react when she first hears of her husband's "death"?

   _____

   _____

   _____

2. How do her feelings change once she is alone in her room?

   _____

   _____

   _____

3. Why does she think she loved her husband "sometimes"?

   _____

   _____

   _____

4. What really happens to Brently Mallard?

_____

_____

_____

5. What really causes Mrs. Mallard's death?

_____

_____

_____

Journal Suggestions

1. At the end of the story, we learn that Louise Mallard "died of joy that kills." Discuss the meaning of this statement. Was Mrs. Mallard really happy to learn that her husband was alive? Is it possible to die of joy? How do you think she really felt? Define irony. How is the ending of this story ironic?

2. The story takes place during the spring season. Discuss how the setting aids the theme.

3. Upon learning of her husband's "death," Mrs. Mallard feels a sense of freedom. Discuss why she feels this way. Suppose Mrs. Mallard had remained alive. Write an ending showing what might happen to the couple in the next few years.

Collaborative Activity

Working with others, compose a story about the events of "The Story of an Hour" written from the point of view of Louise Mallard's husband or sister.

Look It Up

1. Use the Internet to research the period of time in which Kate Chopin lived. What was life like for women then? What types of job opportunities did women have? What was their life at home like? Write an extended essay describing the results of your research.

2. The works of Kate Chopin (1851–1904) were considered rebellious and frowned upon by a conservative Victorian society; however, modern society has come to regard Chopin as a respected and iconoclastic writer. Using the Internet, research her life and compare the themes of "The Story of an Hour" to Chopin's novel *The Awakening,* as well as other short stories by the author.

Comprehending Longer Selections

More Practice
Step One: Before Reading
Vocabulary in Context Practice
Directions: Choose one of the following words to complete each of the sentences below. Use each word only once. Be sure to pay attention to the context clues provided.

accompaniment—going along with
benignly—innocently, nicely
disrupt—disturb
frayed—torn at edges
haunts—places usually visited
noose—tied rope
random—without order
shallow—not deep
sharecropper—tenant farmer who pays rent in crops
tremors—quiverings

1. The honking of a car outdoors began to _____ our study session.

2. That lake is so _____ that your feet can touch bottom when standing.

3. Mandy's skirt became _____ when she caught it on the hook.

4. The neighborhood playground and the library were my favorite _____ when I was a child.

5. José sang while his sister played the guitar for _____.

6. Hanna's great-great grandfather was a _____ and worked hard to raise the crops he gave to his landlord.

7. Sameer's choice of players for the softball team was completely _____; he just picked their names out of a hat.

8. When Alissa becomes nervous, the _____ in her hand are so bad that she can't even hold a pencil.

9. When the dog approached us _____, we could tell that he was friendly.

10. The sailor tightened the _____ to secure the boat.

Freewrite
Have you ever witnessed a scene that shocked you? Write about your experience.

Step Two: Read the Selection

Rowling's Harry Potter and the Sorcerer's Stone begins with the horrifying event of the murder of Harry's parents. This short story by Alice Walker also contains a shocking incident, but the manner in which it is presented makes the story a memorable one.

Flowers
By Alice Walker

1. *It seemed to Myop as she skipped lightly from hen house to pigpen to smokehouse that the days had never been as beautiful as these. The air held a keenness that made her nose twitch. The harvesting of the corn and cotton, peanuts and squash, made each day a golden surprise that caused excited little tremors to run up her jaws.*

2. *Myop carried a short, knobby stick. She struck out at random at chickens she liked, and worked out the beat of a song on the fence around the pigpen. She felt light and good in the warm sun. She was ten, and nothing existed for her but her song, the stick clutched in her dark brown hand, and the tat-de-ta-ta-ta of accompaniment.*

3. *Turning her back on the rusty boards of her family's sharecropper cabin, Myop walked along the fence till it ran into the stream made by the spring. Around the spring, where the family got drinking water, silver ferns and wildflowers grew. Along the shallow banks pigs rooted. Myop watched the tiny white bubbles disrupt the thin black scale of soil and the water that silently rose and slid away down the stream.*

4. *She had explored the woods behind the house many times. Often, in late autumn, her mother took her to gather nuts among the fallen leaves. Today she made her own path, bouncing this way and that way, vaguely keeping an eye out for snakes. She found, in addition to various common but pretty ferns and leaves, an armful of strange blue flowers with velvety ridges and a sweetsuds bush full of the brown, fragrant buds.*

5. *By twelve o'clock, her arms laden with sprigs of her findings, she was a mile or more from home. She had often been as far before, but the strangeness of the land made it not as pleasant as her usual haunts. It seemed gloomy in the little cove in which she found herself. The air was damp, the silence close and deep.*

6. *Myop began to circle back to the house, back to the peacefulness of the morning. It was then she stepped smack into his eyes. Her heel became lodged in the broken ridge between brow and nose, and she*

© JupiterImages Corporation

"The Flowers" from In Love & Trouble: Stories of Black Women, copyright © 1973 by Alice Walker, reprinted by permission of Houghton Mifflin Harcourt Publishing Company.

reached down quickly, unafraid, to free herself. It was only when she saw his naked grin that she gave a little yelp of surprise.

7. He had been a tall man. From feet to neck covered a long space. His head lay beside him. When she pushed back the leaves and layers of earth and debris, Myop saw that he'd had large white teeth, all of them cracked or broken, long fingers, and very big bones. All his clothes had rotted away except some threads of blue denim from his overalls. The buckles of the overalls had turned green.

8. Myop gazed around the spot with interest. Very near where she'd stepped into the head was a wild pink rose. As she picked it to add to her bundle she noticed a raised mound, a ring, around the rose's root. It was the rotted remains of a noose, a bit of shredding plowline, now blending benignly into the soil. Around an overhanging limb of a great spreading oak clung another piece. Frayed, rotted, bleached, and frazzled—barely there—but spinning restlessly in the breeze. Myop laid down her flowers.

9. And the summer was over. (Walker 119–120)

Alice Walker (1944–) is best known for her novel The Color Purple, for which she won the Pulitzer Prize. The novel, which highlights the struggles of African-American women, was produced as a major motion picture by Steven Spielberg.

The Short Story Worksheet: "Flowers"

Directions: Fill in the narrative elements for the story you just read:

1. **Characters:** List the major characters, with a short description of each. List minor characters:

   _____

   _____

   _____

2. **Setting:** Describe the setting (time and place).

   _____

   _____

   _____

3. **Plot:** Explain the series of events.

   _____

   _____

   _____

4. **Theme:** State the main idea.

   _____

   _____

   _____

5. **Tone:** Discuss how mood is created. How is humor, fear, irony, etc., conveyed? Be specific.

   _____

   _____

   _____

6. **Point of View:** State the author's point of view.

_____

_____

_____

7. **Moral:** Is there a lesson, if so, what is it?

_____

_____

_____

What is your reaction to the story? Why did you or didn't you like it? Explain your answer.

_____

_____

_____

Now, write a short story report (one to two pages) using the answers to the above questions.

Step Three: Follow-Up Activities

Objective Test on "Flowers"

Directions: Choose the best answer based on the reading.

1. The season in which this story takes place is probably:
   a. winter.   c. summer.
   b. spring.   d. fall.

2. Myop's father is probably a:
   a. laborer.   c. soldier.
   b. coal miner.   d. sharecropper.

3. Myop is probably walking because she:
   a. needs to collect nuts.   c. has nothing better to do.
   b. wants to find roses.   d. is looking for a man.

4. At the beginning of the story, Myop is probably:
   a. tired.   c. sad.
   b. nervous.   d. happy.

5. Myop's musical instrument is her:
   a. flute.   c. stick.
   b. rock.   d. drum.

6. Myop wanders:
   a. into her backyard.   c. close to home.
   b. behind her friend's home. d. over a mile from home.

7. When she wanders into a new area, Myop usually feels:
   a. excited.   c. sleepy.
   b. uncomfortable.   d. angry.

8. Myop is stopped by:
   a. her heel being caught.   c. her mother calling her.
   b. a strange noise.   d. a peculiar feeling.

9. The dead man had probably been there for:
   a. a few hours.   c. a week.
   b. a day.   d. a long time.

10. The man probably died because of a:
    a. cut throat.   c. heart attack.
    b. lynching.   d. fight.

Vocabulary Test on "Flowers"

Directions: Choose one of the meanings to identify the highlighted word as it appears in the selection.

1. It was the rotted remains of a **noose,** a bit of shredding plowline, now blending benignly into the soil.
   a. necktie.   c. scarf.
   b. lock.   d. tied rope.

2. It was the rotted remains of a noose, a bit of shredding plowline, now blending **benignly** into the soil.
   a. frighteningly.   c. secretively.
   b. innocently, nicely.   d. assuredly.

3. Along the **shallow** banks pigs rooted.
   a. deep   c. marsh-like
   b. not deep   d. weedy

4. She was ten, and nothing existed for her but her song, the stick clutched in her dark brown hand, and the tat-de-ta-ta-ta of **accompaniment.**
   a. music   c. noise
   b. going along with   d. musical notes

5. Turning her back on the rusty boards of her family's **sharecropper** cabin, Myop walked along the fence till it ran into the stream made by the spring.
   a. farmer who grows crops
   b. agriculturalist
   c. tenant farmer who pays rent in crops
   d. carpenter

6. Myop watched the tiny white bubbles **disrupt** the thin black scale of soil and the water that silently rose and slid away down the stream.
   a. push down   c. uncover
   b. cover   d. disturb

7. The harvesting of the corn and cotton, peanuts and squash, made each day a golden surprise that caused excited little **tremors** to run up her jaws.
   a. red lines   c. quiverings
   b. frowns   d. hollows

8. She struck out at **random** at chickens she liked, and worked out the beat of a song on the fence around the pigpen.
   a. in order   c. energetically
   b. without order   d. methodically

9. **Frayed,** rotted, bleached, and frazzled—barely there—but spinning restlessly in the breeze.
   a. torn at edges   c. discolored
   b. destroyed   d. rumpled

10. She had often been as far before, but the strangeness of the land made it not as pleasant as her usual **haunts.**
    a. scary places   c. places usually visited
    b. dark places   d. foreign

Questions about "Flowers"

1. Who is Myop? Why is she walking through the woods?

   _____

   _____

   _____

2. What is Myop doing as she walks through the woods? What stops her?

   _____

   _____

   _____

3. Describe what Myop suddenly finds during her walk.

   _____

   _____

   _____

4. What do you think happened to the man?

   _____

   _____

   _____

5. How does Myop feel about what she has found? Do you think her reaction is unusual? Why or why not?

   _____

   _____

   _____

Journal Suggestion

"Flowers" is often perceived as a story about the loss of innocence. In what ways is Myop shown as an innocent child? What event shatters that innocence? How do you think Myop is changed by what she has seen? Write about your observations.

Collaborative Activities

1. In short stories like "Flowers," each image carries weight. Examine the sensory images that show what things look like ("tiny white bubbles"), sound like ("tat-de-ta-ta-ta"), smell like ("fragrant buds"), and feel like ("warm sun"). Write your thoughts in a journal about how these images help to convey the writer's message. Discuss your answers with others in your group.

2. Introductions and conclusions are always important, especially in short stories. Examine the first and last paragraphs of "Flowers." Why does Walker choose to begin and end with these particular lines? Discuss your answers with your group.

3. The story ends with the line, "And the summer was over." What do you think might have happened after Myop returns home? With others, write a continuation of the story.

4. The power of what Myop sees lies in what is not said. Invent a story detailing what might have happened to the corpse she discovers. What do you think the circumstances were that caused his hanging? Did he have a family? What were his dreams? Share your story with others.

Look It Up
Myop discovers a horrifying scene. Use the Internet to research the period of time in the South when racism was rampant and hangings were numerous. Write a report based on your findings.

Comprehending Longer Selections

16.3   Exercise

More Practice
Step One: Before Reading
Vocabulary in Context Practice
Directions: Choose one of the following words to complete each of the sentences below. Use each word only once. Be sure to pay attention to the context clues provided.

assures—makes certain
dawdles—wastes time
emerge—come out
glimpse—peek at
manna—food of divine origin
ominous—scary
overseer—person in charge
ruddy—reddish
savor—enjoy the taste
shrill—sharp

1. "The clouds look _____," said Billy, "we had better go inside before it starts to storm!"

2. Mother always _____ the children that monsters don't really exist.

3. The _____ made sure the factory workers finished putting together all of the parts of the machine.

4. Kathy had to _____ over her brother's shoulder to get a better view of what he was writing.

5. It was so exciting to watch the baby chicks _____ from the egg!

6. Rachel held the last spoonfuls of chocolate ice cream in her mouth to _____ the wonderful taste.

7. The _____ sound of the camp director's whistle caused us to cover our ears.

8. Henry always _____, taking his time to come back inside from recess.

9. Janet's job as a ski instructor has caused her complexion to become quite _____.

10. After fleeing from Egypt, the ancient Israelites enjoyed the sweet-tasting _____, which they believed was sent from heaven.

Step Two: Read the Selection

Fear and suspense are often the hallmarks of crafting a good story. The tone of a story often keeps the reader's interest, as it does with the Harry Potter tales. Here, in this excerpt from Shirley Russak Wachtel's The Story of Blima—A Holocaust Survivor, *which is a true account of the experiences of the author's mother, the tone peaks our interest.*

Darkness Falls
By Shirley Russak Wachtel

1. *Four AM. A shrill whistle shocks us awake. We jump down from our cubicles and line up for roll call.*

2. *"Pinch your cheeks," someone whispers, and word goes down the line. We pinch until it hurts and pray for the tinge we had only days ago to return. When the woman commandant turns to inspect the others, we wait, shoulders back, standing tall. Looking at the girls opposite us, I surmise we are a sorry bunch.*

© posztos (colorlab.hu), 2010. Used under license from Shutterstock, Inc.

3. *The commandant must be a man, I think, for I find no trace of femininity, no softness in her long face. Her dark hair is cut short and her body is tightly wrapped in a thick coat with gold buttons. In one hand she holds a whip, in the other a leash holding a large German Shepherd she calls Otto. A dog is given a name, I think, but we ourselves are but numbers. As the commandant walks down the line for inspection, I try to glimpse her eyes. But I am unable to tell their color. If there is such a hue as muddied steel, I decide they are that. Certainly they hold no clue to a soul. When she walks past me, I look away.*

4. *She sits down with the dog beside her and begins to call numbers. I have never memorized mine, and I quickly look down. 44703. The girl who has been assigned as our leader pulls out any girl who dawdles.*

5. *"44703!"*

6. *I jump forward as if by a spark and join the others. I don't know if hearing my number is a good thing, but then our group of about 25 begins to march toward the main barracks where I can already smell the cooking of soup. When we enter, my hopes are born out. I am given a portion of bread and a cup of tasteless soup. The black bread is not like Tante Rachel's even on the eighth day. Yet I devour both quickly as if they were manna from heaven. Only much later do I think I must not rush so, for the food hits my stomach ferociously. I must learn to eat more slowly, not savor exactly, but give my system a chance to digest properly. We go to the toilet, mere holes in the ground, and relieve ourselves. We are given ice water which we pour quickly over ourselves, happy at last to feel refreshed. And then we march.*

7. *The sun, the same sun I would see from my room at home, rises full and proud over the mountains. The air has a crispness from the last traces of winter's frost, and, as we march, I see the mountains, first a dusty blue, emerge from the clouds. As we draw closer, I see each hillock ringed by the promise of green, and I take comfort in the fact that the earth is still here. I try not to think of my swollen knees, the tiny pebbles beneath the wooden soles that attack me mercilessly with each step. Earth is still here, and so is the sun. Everything is the same, and for a moment I see myself walking up the steps to the home of my parents, coming to the door. My only worry is that it will be closed.*

8. *A girl three people in front of me trips on a pebble and the lash comes swiftly down. I see her standing up and marching again as if bothered only momentarily by a fly. The lady commandant in the heavy boots laughs and calls her a stupid cow.*

9. *We arrive at the factory where there are two women overseers. One is short with sacks of ruddy flesh on her cheeks and under her chin. Her short white hair is sleeked away from her face, giving it the appearance of a tennis ball. She walks up and down the rows of girls with much effort, and when she stops in front of me, I notice a nervous tick in her right eye. She smiles, but it seems like an evil smile. She even tells us her name, Helga, and assures us of our good fortune in being chosen for this labor.*

10. *But it is the other overseer who inspires fear in me. She is tall, taller than any of the girls or the guards, for that matter. Unlike Frau Helga who wears a simple blouse and long skirt, Frau Gizella wears a jumper with huge pockets. The pockets seem to be full, and I can see what I believe to be a thick rope emerging from one of them. Her platinum blonde hair sits atop her head like a crown. From the moment I enter the factory, the eyes never leave my face.*

11. *"Can you sew?" she asks me the same question she has asked of other girls down the line.*

12. *I remember Clara's words and swiftly reply, "Yes, Commandant." I have no clue how to sew even a sock, but here I tell her I can. The ominous-looking black sewing machines wait, row by row, in the vast factory. If only I had watched Mama more carefully! If only I had paid attention. If only . . .*

13. *The girls who say they have no skills are led out of the factory through what appears to be a long tunnel. The rest of us sit down, each at a machine piled with sturdy brown tweed uniforms, perhaps thirty in all. I lift the spool of thread and try to attach it to the bobbin. It slips from my hand and rolls to the floor, but no one notices as I quickly retrieve it.*

14. *One of the girls has been found out, and I watch as Frau Helga stomps quickly toward her and grabs her by the neck. The pity is she had no hair to be pulled.*

15. *"What is wrong with you?" Frau Helga cries, dragging her toward the door through which the others had disappeared. The girl, a skinny one of no more than sixteen, has learned and makes no sound as she proceeds down the long tunnel. When the doors have closed, Helga rubs her chubby hands together as if to cleanse them of some vermin.*

16. *"To work, to work!" she snickers, eying each of us.*

17. *I return to the thread and bobbin, which I somehow master. I am trying to position a collar to be sewn at the neck of a uniform when suddenly I look forward and see two huge pockets before me.*

18. *Frau Gizella places large but surprisingly smooth hands on the machine, bends her head and peers directly into my eyes. I remember the rope in her pocket, and for a moment my heart stops.*

19. *"Your name?" she asks. I recite my number.*

20. *Gizella closes her eyes and shakes her head slowly. The other girls have begun their work and take no notice.*

21. *"Your name," she repeats. I swallow. I try not to look at the thick blonde eyebrows that shadow her eyes.*

22. *"Blima. Blima Weisstuch."*

23. *"Where are you from, Blima Weisstuch?"*

24. *"Dombrowa, Madam."*

25. *She considers this a moment.*

26. *"Dombrowa. I have not heard of that town."*

27. *I sit frozen before the machine, unable to take up the collar.*

28. *"Can you sew, Blima Weisstuch?" she asks, her voice lower.*

29. *I nod, even though it is clear that I haven't a single notion of how to proceed. She stretches her massive hand forward as I ready myself for the pull at the neck. Incredibly, she begins to regulate the bobbin and fix the collar in the proper place. The girls' heads are all down as she straightens herself to full height and, with not another word, walks away. I begin to sew. (Wachtel)*

Shirley Russak Wachtel (1951–) wrote The Story of Blima, a memoir of her mother, for her doctoral dissertation. The novel is a portion of a larger work, My Mother's Shoes, which details the lives of mother and daughter. Wachtel is also the author of several children's books as well as textbooks for college students.

The Short Story Worksheet: "Darkness Falls"
Directions: Fill in the narrative elements for the story you just read:

1. **Characters:** List the major characters, with a short description of each. List minor characters.

   _____

   _____

   _____

2. **Setting:** Describe the setting (time and place).

   _____

   _____

   _____

3. **Plot:** Explain the series of events.

   _____

   _____

   _____

4. **Theme:** State the main idea.

   _____

   _____

   _____

5. **Tone:** Discuss how mood is created. How is humor, fear, irony, etc., conveyed? Be specific.

_____

_____

_____

6. **Point of View:** State the author's point of view.

_____

_____

_____

7. **Moral:** Is there a lesson, if so, what is it?

_____

_____

_____

8. What is your reaction to the story? Why did you or didn't you like it? Explain your answer.

_____

_____

_____

Now, write a short story report (one to two pages) using the answers to the above questions.

Step Three: Follow-Up Activities

Objective Test on "Darkness Falls"
Directions: Choose the best answer based on the reading.

1. The story takes place in a:
   a. cabin.
   b. home.
   c. jail.
   d. concentration camp.

2. The commandant can best be described as:
   a. sweet.
   b. personable.
   c. frightening.
   d. distant.

3. The narrator eats all of the soup because:
   a. she is hungry.
   b. it is good.
   c. she will be punished if she doesn't eat it.
   d. it reminds her of her aunt's cooking.

4. The two women overseers:
   a. look alike.
   b. look different.
   c. seem friendly.
   d. never speak.

5. The narrator wishes she had paid more attention to:
   a. the guards.
   b. her mother's sewing.
   c. her aunt's cooking.
   d. her language skills.

6. Girls who cannot sew are:
   a. punished.
   b. whipped.
   c. sent down a long tunnel.
   d. shipped home.

7. The narrator is nervous because she:
   a. misses her family.
   b. is hungry.
   c. can't sew.
   d. doesn't like the overseers.

8. Blima is frightened of the:
   a. dogs.
   b. number.
   c. chains.
   d. rope.

9. When Gizella asks if she can sew, Blima:
   a. lies.
   b. tells the truth.
   c. boasts.
   d. is silent.

10. Gizella's actions show that she is:
    a. mean.
    b. uncertain.
    c. frightening.
    d. kind.

Vocabulary Test on "Darkness Falls"

Directions: Choose one of the meanings to identify the highlighted word as it appears in the selection.

1. Yet I devour both quickly as if they were **manna** from heaven.
   a. inspiration
   b. food of divine origin
   c. bread
   d. pudding

2. The air has a crispness from the last traces of winter's frost, and, as we march, I see the mountains, first a dusty blue, **emerge** from the clouds.
   a. rise above
   b. come out
   c. tear
   d. hide

3. She even tells us her name, Helga, and **assures** us of our good fortune in being chosen for this labor.
   a. denies
   b. condemns
   c. makes certain
   d. assaults

4. I must learn to eat more slowly, not **savor** exactly, but give my system a chance to digest properly.
   a. devour
   b. swallow
   c. gobble
   d. enjoy the taste

5. But it is the other **overseer** who inspires fear in me.
   a. guard
   b. mistress
   c. person in charge
   d. employer

6. As the commandant walks down the line for inspection, I try to **glimpse** her eyes.
   a. peek at
   b. hide from
   c. find answers
   d. avert

7. A **shrill** whistle shocks us awake.
   a. noisy
   b. soprano
   c. sharp
   d. dull

8. The girl who has been assigned as our leader pulls out any girl who **dawdles.**
   a. becomes nervous
   b. wastes time
   c. calls out
   d. fails

9. The **ominous**-looking black sewing machines wait, row by row, in the vast factory.
   - a. scary
   - b. large
   - c. curious
   - d. omniscient

10. One is short with sacks of **ruddy** flesh on her cheeks and under her chin.
    - a. chubby
    - b. wrinkled
    - c. pimpled
    - d. reddish

Questions about "Darkness Falls"

1. Who is Blima? Where is she?

   _____

   _____

   _____

2. What things in Blima's life are still "the same" and what things are different?

   _____

   _____

   _____

3. Compare the two overseers and their reactions to the prisoners.

   _____

   _____

   _____

4. Why does Blima lie about having sewing abilities?

   _____

   _____

   _____

5. Why is Blima surprised about Gizella's behavior?

   _____

   _____

   _____

Journal Suggestions

1. Tone is an important element in any story. Examine the chapter you just read and circle any words or phrases that help to create a suspenseful and frightening mood. Compare this chapter to a chapter in *Harry Potter and the Sorcerer's Stone* to see how a writer builds a feeling of suspense.

2. The chapter you just read is from the book *The Story of Blima—A Holocaust Survivor,* one of many books written about the Holocaust. The Holocaust was an unimaginable, tragic period during the 1940s when Adolf Hitler and the Nazi Party of Germany caused the imprisonment and

deaths of millions of Jews and other people. Make a list of the things you know about the Holocaust and share it with your group. Do you think an event like the Holocaust could ever happen again?

Collaborative Activity

What can we infer about Blima's personality and her life from this short chapter? What do you think her life was like before World War II? Can you guess what will happen to her? Write some responses in your journal, and share and discuss them with your group.

Look It Up

1. *The Story of Blima* is a memoir. Research how a memoir differs from a biography or a work of fiction. Write a paper about the differences, citing examples like *The Story of Blima,* a biography (or autobiography) about an American president, and one of the Harry Potter novels.

2. Use the Internet to research the Holocaust, its causes and effects. To see how ordinary people were affected, read *The Story of Blima—A Holocaust Survivor* by Shirley Russak Wachtel, *Night* by Eli Weisel, and *The Diary of Anne Frank*. Write a paper comparing the experiences of each of these individuals.

3. The Holocaust has been the subject of many movies. Watch *Schindler's List*, *The Pianist*, or the documentary *Paper Clips*. Write a paper or make an oral presentation that provides a summary and reaction to what you have seen.

Comprehending Longer Selections   16.4   *Exercise*

More Practice
Step One: Before Reading
Vocabulary in Context Practice
Directions: Choose one of the following words to complete each of the sentences below. Use each word only once. Be sure to pay attention to the context clues provided.

apprehension—fear of what is to come
clenched—tightly closed
contemptible—hateful
critical—most important, serious
diagnosis—medical explanation
dread—fear
fury—wild anger
heifer—young cow
membrane—thin layer of tissue
splinters—tiny slivers of wood

1. When Mary's husband flirted with another woman, Mary became angry over such a _____ act.

2. He worried that he might have the flu, but the _____ was that it was just a bad cold.

3. Derek hit the ball so hard that the bat broke into a thousand _____.

4. Lorraine had a sense of _____ over the biology final next week because she hadn't studied.

5. Cole shivered with _____ when the vampire appeared on screen.

6. The boxer _____ his fist and began to pound his opponent.

7. On the farm we noticed a _____ standing next to the older cows.

8. After being insulted repeatedly, Rolando turned to his abuser with _____ in his eyes.

9. Passing a road test is _____ if you want to get a driver's license.

10. While gardening, Patty mistakenly cut the _____ of the plant's stalk.

Step Two: Read the Selection

Rowling's Harry Potter possesses amazing magical powers. Here's a tale by William Carlos Williams in which the doctor might have wished for his own magical abilities.

The Use of Force
By William Carlos Williams

1. They were new patients to me, all I had was the name, Olson. Please come down as soon as you can, my daughter is very sick. When I arrived I was met by the mother, a big startled looking woman, very clean and apologetic who merely said, Is this the doctor? And let me in. In the back, she added. You must excuse us, doctor, we have her in the kitchen where it is warm. It is very damp here sometimes.

2. The child was fully dressed and sitting on her father's lap near the kitchen table. He tried to get up, but I motioned for him not to bother, took off my overcoat and started to look things over. I could see that they were all very nervous, eyeing me up and down distrustfully. As often, in such cases, they weren't telling me more than they had to, it was up to me to tell them; that's why they were spending three dollars on me.

3. The child was fairly eating me up with her cold, steady eyes, and no expression to her face whatever. She did not move and seemed, inwardly, quiet; an unusually attractive little thing, and as strong as a heifer in appearance. But her face was flushed, she was breathing rapidly, and I realized that she had a high fever. She had magnificent blonde hair, in profusion. One of those picture children often reproduced in advertising leaflets and the photo-gravure sections of the Sunday papers.

4. She's had a fever for three days, began the father and we don't know what it comes from. My wife has given her things, you know, like people do, but it don't do no good. And there's been a lot of sickness around. So we tho't you'd better look her over and tell us what is the matter.

5. As doctors often do I took a trial shot at it as a point of departure. Has she had a sore throat?

6. Both parents answered me together, No . . . No, she says her throat don't hurt her.

7. Does your throat hurt you? Added the mother to the child. But the little girl's expression didn't change nor did she move her eyes from my face.

8. Have you looked?

9. I tried to, said the mother, but I couldn't see.

10. As it happens we had been having a number of cases of diphtheria in the school to which this child went during that month and we were all, quite apparently, thinking of that, though no one had as yet spoken of the thing.

© Jupiterimages Corporation

11. Well, I said, suppose we take a look at the throat first. I smiled in my best professional manner and asking for the child's first name I said, come on, Mathilda, open your mouth and let's take a look at your throat.

12. Nothing doing.

13. Aw, come on, I coaxed, just open your mouth wide and let me take a look. Look, I said opening both hands wide, I haven't anything in my hands. Just open up and let me see.

14. Such a nice man, put in the mother. Look how kind he is to you. Come on, do what he tells you to. He won't hurt you.

15. At that I ground my teeth in disgust. If only they wouldn't use the word "hurt" I might be able to get somewhere. But I did not allow myself to be hurried or disturbed but speaking quietly and slowly I approached the child again.

16. As I moved my chair a little nearer suddenly with one catlike movement both her hands clawed instinctively for my eyes and she almost reached them too. In fact she knocked my glasses flying and they fell, though unbroken, several feet away from me on the kitchen floor.

17. Both the mother and father almost turned themselves inside out in embarrassment and apology. You bad girl, said the mother, taking her and shaking her by one arm. Look what you've done. The nice man . . .

18. For heaven's sake, I broke in. Don't call me a nice man to her. I'm here to look at her throat on the chance that she might have diphtheria and possibly die of it. But that's nothing to her. Look here, I said to the child, we're going to look at your throat. You're old enough to understand what I'm saying. Will you open it now by yourself or shall we have to open it for you?

19. Not a move. Even her expression hadn't changed. Her breaths however were coming faster and faster. Then the battle began. I had to do it. I had to have a throat culture for her own protection. But first I told the parents that it was entirely up to them. I explained the danger but said that I would not insist on a throat examination so long as they would take the responsibility.

20. If you don't do what the doctor says you'll have to go to the hospital, the mother admonished her severely.

21. Oh yeah? I had to smile to myself. After all, I had already fallen in love with the savage brat, the parents were contemptible to me. In the ensuing struggle they grew more and more abject, crushed, exhausted while she surely rose to magnificent heights of insane fury of effort bred of her terror of me.

22. The father tried his best, and he was a big man but the fact that she was his daughter, his shame at her behavior and his dread of hurting her made him release her just at the critical times when I had almost achieved success, till I wanted to kill him. But his dread also that she might have diphtheria made him tell me to go on, go on though he himself was almost fainting, while the mother moved back and forth behind us raising and lowering her hands in an agony of apprehension.

23. Put her in front of you on your lap, I ordered, and hold both her wrists.

24. But as soon as he did the child let out a scream. Don't, you're hurting me. Let go of my hands. Let them go I tell you. Then she shrieked terrifyingly, hysterically. Stop it! Stop it! You're killing me!

25. Do you think she can stand it, doctor! said the mother.

26. You get out, said the husband to his wife. Do you want her to die of diphtheria?

27. Come on now, hold her, I said.

28. Then I grasped the child's head with my left hand and tried to get the wooden tongue depressor between her teeth. She fought, with clenched teeth, desperately! But now I also had grown furious—at a child. I tried to hold myself down but I couldn't. I know how to expose a throat for inspection. And I did my best. When finally I got the wooden spatula behind the last teeth and just the point of it into the mouth cavity, she opened up for an instant but before I could see anything she came down again and gripped the wooden blade between her molars. She reduced it to splinters before I could get it out again.

29. Aren't you ashamed, the mother yelled at her. Aren't you ashamed to act like that in front of the doctor?

30. Get me a smooth-handled spoon of some sort, I told the mother. We're going through with this. The child's mouth was already bleeding. Her tongue was cut and she was screaming in wild hysterical shrieks. Perhaps I should have desisted and come back in an hour or more. No doubt it would have been better. But I have seen at least two children lying dead in bed of neglect in such cases, and feeling that I must get a diagnosis now or never I went at it again. But the worst of it was that I too had got beyond reason. I could have torn the child apart in my own fury and enjoyed it. It was a pleasure to attack her. My face was burning with it.

31. The damned little brat must be protected against her own idiocy, one says to oneself at such times. Others must be protected against her. It is a social necessity. And all these things are true. But a blind fury, a feeling of adult shame, bred of a longing for muscular release are the operatives. One goes on to the end.

32. In the final unreasoning assault I overpowered the child's neck and jaws. I forced the heavy silver spoon back of her teeth and down her throat till she gagged. And there it was—both tonsils covered with membrane. She had fought valiantly to keep me from knowing her secret. She had been hiding that sore throat for three days at least and lying to her parents in order to escape just such an outcome as this.

33. Now truly she was furious. She had been on the defensive before but now she attacked. Tried to get off her father's lap and fly at me while tears of defeat blinded her eyes. (Williams 56–60)

William Carlos Williams (1863–1963) was a physician as well as a writer. Best known for his poems, he wrote in a simple style about everyday objects.

The Short Story Worksheet: "The Use of Force"

Directions: Fill in the narrative elements for the story you just read:

1. **Characters:** List the major characters, with a short description of each. List minor characters:

   _____

   _____

   _____

2. **Setting:** Describe the setting (time and place).

   _____

   _____

   _____

3. **Plot:** Explain the series of events.

_____

_____

_____

4. **Theme:** State the main idea.

_____

_____

_____

5. **Tone:** Discuss how mood is created. How is humor, fear, irony, etc., conveyed? Be specific.

_____

_____

_____

6. **Point of View:** State the author's point of view.

_____

_____

_____

7. **Moral:** Is there a lesson, if so, what is it?

_____

_____

_____

8. What is your reaction to the story? Why did you or didn't you like it? Explain your answer.

_____

_____

_____

Now, write a short story report (one to two pages) using the answers to the above questions.

Step Three: Follow-Up Activities

Objective Test on "The Use of Force"

Directions: Choose the best answer based on the reading.

1. The story probably takes place in:
   a. the present.　　　　　　　c. the future.
   b. the past.　　　　　　　　d. cannot tell.

2. The girl is in the kitchen because:
   a. she won't stay in bed.　　c. she needs to eat.
   b. it is warm.　　　　　　　d. there are chairs.

3. The girl's parents:
   a. know how to handle her.　c. become angry.
   b. punish her too much.　　　d. are frustrated and uncertain.

4. The doctor:
   a. admires the girl and her parents.
   b. admires the parents, but not the girl.
   c. admires the girl and not the parents.
   d. dislikes everyone.

5. The doctor uses force because he:
   a. wants to overpower the girl.   c. fears he might be sued.
   b. is afraid the girl has diphtheria.   d. has become angry with the girl.

6. The doctor uses a metal spoon to open her mouth because:
   a. she broke the wooden tongue depressor.
   b. it is a medical instrument.
   c. he can scoop out mucus with it.
   d. it helps him see better.

7. During the encounter, the girl becomes:
   a. quieter.   c. sicker.
   b. more upset.   d. understanding.

8. During the encounter, the doctor becomes:
   a. happier.   c. prouder.
   b. sadder.   d. angrier.

9. After successfully opening her mouth, the doctor feels:
   a. strong.   c. ashamed.
   b. proud.   d. frustrated.

10. The girl's secret is that she:
   a. has a sore throat.   c. needs to go to a hospital.
   b. was pretending.   d. is very sick.

Vocabulary Test on "The Use of Force"

Directions: Choose one of the meanings to identify the highlighted word as it appears in the selection.

1. But I have seen at least two children lying dead in bed of neglect in such cases, and feeling that I must get a **diagnosis** now or never, I went at it again.
   a. prognosis   c. medical explanation
   b. symptoms   d. understanding

2. The father tried his best, and he was a big man but the fact that she was his daughter, his shame at her behavior and his **dread** of hurting her made him release her just at the critical times when I had almost achieved success, till I wanted to kill him.
   a. dismay   c. disgust
   b. desire   d. fear

3. The father tried his best, and he was a big man but the fact that she was his daughter, his shame at her behavior and his dread of hurting her made him release her just at the **critical** times when I had almost achieved success, till I wanted to kill him.
   a. most important, serious   c. fearful
   b. disturbing   d. easy

4. She fought, with **clenched** teeth, desperately!
   a. bared   c. sharp
   b. exposed   d. tightly closed

5. But his dread also that she might have diphtheria made him tell me to go on, go on though he himself was almost fainting, while the mother moved back and forth behind us raising and lowering her hands in an agony of **apprehension**.
   a. appreciation
   b. assault
   c. dismay
   d. fear of what is to come

6. She reduced it to **splinters** before I could get it out again.
   a. tiny slivers of wood
   b. garbage
   c. cuts
   d. tears

7. And there it was—both tonsils covered with **membrane**.
   a. fungus
   b. thin layer of tissue
   c. bacteria
   d. germs

8. After all, I had already fallen in love with the savage brat, the parents were **contemptible** to me.
   a. contrite
   b. hateful
   c. sympathetic
   d. helpful

9. In the ensuing struggle they grew more and more abject, crushed, exhausted while she surely rose to magnificent heights of insane **fury** of effort bred of her terror of me.
   a. terror
   b. wild anger
   c. sobbing
   d. desperation

10. She did not move and seemed, inwardly, quiet; an unusually attractive little thing, and as strong as a **heifer** in appearance.
    a. goat
    b. young cow
    c. lamb
    d. sheep

Questions about "The Use of Force"

1. Why does the doctor visit the girl and her parents?

   _____

   _____

   _____

2. Describe how the girl reacts to the doctor.

   _____

   _____

   _____

3. Why does the doctor use force?

   _____

   _____

   _____

4. What is his opinion of the girl, and of her parents?

   _____

   _____

   _____

5. What secret is the girl hiding?

_____

_____

_____

Journal Suggestion

"The Use of Force" is a story that may be interpreted from a psychological point of view. Review the story and respond in your journal to the following questions: (a) why does the girl refuse to cooperate? (b) why does the doctor admire her and dislike the parents? c) why does the doctor say, "it was a pleasure to attack her"? Discuss your answers with your group.

Collaborative Activities

1. What do you think about the doctor's use of force? Could the situation have been handled any other way or was force the only choice? Discuss your thoughts with others.

2. The story ends rather abruptly. What do you think happened after the doctor left? Write your own ending and share it with your group.

3. This story is written in the first person point of view and reveals an interesting experience about a day in the life of a doctor. Write about an unusual experience you have had on the job or within your household. Share your story with the class.

Look It Up

1. Diphtheria is one of several diseases that became an epidemic, or widespread, before an immunization was found. Using the Internet, research and report on information on this disease or another serious illness like polio or typhoid fever. Or, you might want to focus on a modern-day epidemic like AIDS, and report on advances being made to eradicate this or other diseases.

2. Besides being a short story writer, novelist, and pediatrician, William Carlos Williams is probably best known for his poems. Use the Internet to research his life and literary works. Is his position as a doctor reflected in any of his other works? You might want to consult his autobiography in your research. Write a paper detailing what you have found.

Comprehending Longer Selections   16.5   *Exercise*

More Practice
Step One: Before Reading
Vocabulary in Context Practice
Directions: Choose one of the following words to complete each of the sentences below. Use each word only once. Be sure to pay attention to the context clues provided.

acute—sharp
concealment—hiding
dissemble—pretend
distinct—clear
foresight—knowledge of what is to come
hypocritical—phony
precisely—exactly
premises—habitation
sagacity—wisdom
suppositions—guessing

1. Leo's eyesight is so _____ that he can see things a mile away!

2. Even though it was foggy, Marian's hat was so _____ that we knew it was she.

3. Mark seems to know about everything so that sometimes I think he has the _____ of King Solomon!

4. People who caution against smoking cigarettes but smoke themselves may be viewed as _____.

5. To thread a needle you must place the cotton _____ through the eye.

6. We looked for Andy for an hour before realizing his _____ behind the door.

7. Even though we didn't like the painting we had to _____ an interest in it so we wouldn't hurt the artist's feelings.

8. Forgetting her umbrella showed a lack of _____ when Sara walked out on a cloudy day.

9. When Mr. Jones could no longer pay his rent, the landlord told him to leave the _____.

10. Mike's _____ turned out to be correct when the man he suspected of the robbery was later convicted.

Step Two: Read the Selection

Many of us feel scared, even terrified, when we enter the world of Harry Potter books and movies. However, even J. K. Rowling would have to acknowledge that the master of terror is Edgar Allan Poe. Here is one of his most famous and terrifying tales.

The Tell-Tale Heart
By Edgar Allan Poe

1. True! Nervous—very, very dreadfully nervous I had been and am but why will you say that I am mad? The disease had sharpened my senses—not destroyed—not dulled them. Above all was the sense of hearing acute. I heard all things in the heaven and in the earth. I heard many things in hell. How, then, am I mad? Hearken! and observe how healthily—how calmly I can tell you the whole story.

2. It is impossible to say how first the idea entered my brain; but once conceived, it haunted me day and night. Object there was none. Passion there was none. I loved the old man. He had never wronged me. He had never given me insult. For his gold I had no desire. I think it was his eye! Yes, it was this! He had the eye of a vulture—a pale blue eye with a film over it. Whenever it fell upon me, my blood ran cold, and so by degrees—very gradually—I made up my mind to take the life of the old man, and thus rid myself of the eye forever.

3. Now this is the point. You fancy me mad. Madmen know nothing. But you should have seen me. You should have seen how wisely I proceeded—with what caution—with what foresight—with what dissimulation I went to work! I was never kinder to the old man than during the whole week before I killed him. And every night, about midnight, I turned the latch of his door and opened it—ah, so gently! And then, when I had made an opening sufficient for my head, I put in a dark lantern, all closed, closed, so that no light shone out, and then I thrust it in! I moved it slowly—very, very slowly, so that I might not disturb the old man's sleep. It took me an hour to place my whole head within the opening so far that I could see him as he lay upon his bed. Ha!—would a madman have been so wise as this? And then, when my head was well in the room, I undid the lantern cautiously—oh, so cautiously—cautiously (for the hinges creaked)—I undid it just so much that a single thin ray fell upon the vulture eye. And this I did for seven long nights—every night just at midnight—but I found the eye always closed; and so it was impossible to do the work; for it was not the old man who vexed me, but his Evil Eye. And every morning, when the day broke, I went boldly into the chamber, and spoke courageously to him, calling

him by name in a hearty tone, and inquiring how he had passed the night. So you see he would have been a very profound old man, indeed, to suspect that every night, just at twelve, I looked in upon him while he slept.

4. Upon the eighth night I was more than usually cautious in opening the door. A watch's minute hand moves more quickly than did mine. Never, before that night, had I felt the extent of my own powers—of my sagacity. I could scarcely contain my feelings of triumph. To think that there I was, opening the door, little by little, and he not even to dream of my secret deeds or thoughts. I fairly chuckled at the idea; and perhaps he heard me; for he moved on the bed suddenly, as if startled. Now you may think that I drew back—but no. His room was as black as pitch with the thick darkness (for the shutters were close fastened, through fear of robbers), and so I knew that he could not see the opening of the door, and I kept pushing it on steadily, steadily.

© JupiterImages Corporation

5. I had my head in, and was about to open the lantern, when my thumb slipped upon the tin fastening, and the old man sprang up in bed, crying out, "Who's there?" I kept quite still and said nothing. For a whole hour I did not move a muscle, and in the meantime I did not hear him lie down. He was still sitting up in the bed listening—just as I have done, night after night, hearkening to the death watches in the wall.

6. Presently I heard a slight groan, and I knew it was the groan of mortal terror. It was not a groan of pain or of grief—oh, no!—it was the low stifled sound that rises from the bottom of the soul when overcharged with awe. I knew the sound well. Many a night, just at midnight, when all the world slept, it has welled up from my own bosom, deepening, with its dreadful echo, the terrors that distracted me. I say I knew it well. I knew what the old man felt, and pitied him, although I chuckled at heart. I knew that he had been lying awake ever since the first slight noise, when he had turned in his bed. His fears had been ever since growing upon him. He had been trying to fancy them causeless, but could not. He had been saying to himself— "It is nothing but the wind in the chimney—it is, only a mouse crossing the floor," or "It is merely a cricket which has made a single chirp." Yes, he had been trying to comfort himself with these suppositions: but he had found all in vain. All in vain; because Death, in approaching him, had stalked with his mournful influence of the unperceived shadow that caused him to feel—although he neither saw nor heard—to feel the presence of my head within the room.

7. When I had waited a long time, very patiently, without hearing him lie down, I resolved to open a little—a very, very little crevice in the lantern. So I opened it—you cannot imagine it—you cannot imagine how stealthily, stealthily—until at length a single dim ray, like the thread of the spider, shot from out the crevice and fell upon the vulture eye.

8. It was open—wide, wide open—and I grew furious as I gazed upon it. I saw it with perfect distinctiveness—all a dull blue, with a hideous veil over it that chilled the very marrow in my bones; but I could see nothing else

of the old man's face or person; for I had directed the ray as if by instinct, precisely upon the damned spot.

9. And have I not told you that what you mistake for madness is but overacuteness of the senses?—Now, I say, there came to my ears a low, dull, quick sound, such as a watch makes when enveloped in cotton. I knew that sound well, too. It was the beating of the old man's heart. It increased my fury, as the beating of a drum stimulates the soldier into courage.

10. But even yet I refrained and kept still. I scarcely breathed. I held the lantern motionless. I tried how steadily I could maintain the ray upon the eye. Meantime the hellish tattoo of the heart increased. It grew quicker and quicker, and louder and louder every instant. The old man's terror must have been extreme! It grew louder, I say louder every moment!—do you mark me well? I have told you that I am nervous: so I am. And now at the dead hour of the night, amid the dreadful silence of that old house, so strange a noise as this excited me to uncontrol. But the beating grew louder, louder. I thought the heart must burst. And now a new anxiety seized me—the sound would be heard by a neighbor! The old man's hour had come! With a loud yell, I threw open the lantern and leaped into the room. He shrieked once—once only. In an instant I dragged him to the floor, and pulled the heavy bed over him. I then smiled gaily, to find the deed so far done. But, for many minutes, the heart beat on with a muffled sound. This, however, did not vex me; it would not be heard through the wall. At length it ceased. The old man was dead. I removed the bed and examined the corpse. Yes, he as stone, stone dead. I placed my hand upon the heart and held it there many minutes. There was no pulsation. He was stone dead. His eye would trouble me no more.

11. If still you think me mad, you will think so no longer when I describe the wise precautions I took for the concealment of the body. The night waned, and I worked hastily, but in silence. First of all I dismembered the corpse. I cut off the head and the arms and the legs.

12. I then took up three planks from the flooring of the chamber, and deposited all between the scantlings. I then replaced the boards so cleverly, so cunningly, that no human eye—not even his—could have detected anything wrong. There was nothing to wash out—no stain of any kind—no blood spot whatever. I had been too wary for that. A tub had caught all—ha! Ha!

13. When I had made an end of these labors, it was four o'clock—still dark as midnight. As the bell sounded the hour, there came a knocking at the street door. I went down to open it with a light heart—for what had I now to fear? There entered three men, who introduced themselves, with perfect suavity, as officers of the police. A shriek had been heard by a neighbor during the night; suspicion of foul play had been aroused; information had been lodged at the police office, and they (the officers) had been deputed to search the premises.

14. I smiled—for what had I to fear? I bade the gentlemen welcome. The shriek, I said, was my own in a dream. The old man, I mentioned, was absent in the country. I took my visitors all over the house. I bade them search—search well. I led them, at length, to his chamber. I showed them his treasures, secure, undisturbed. In the enthusiasm of my confidence, I brought chairs to the room, and desired them here to rest from their fatigues, while I myself, in the wild audacity of my perfect triumph, placed my own seat upon the very spot beneath which reposed the corpse of the victim.

15. The officers were satisfied. My manner had convinced them. I was singularly at ease. They sat, and while I answered cheerily, they chatted of familiar things. But, erelong, I felt myself getting pale and wished them gone. My head ached, and I fancied a ringing in my ears; but still they sat and still chatted. The ringing became more distinct—it continued and became more distinct; I talked more freely to get rid of the feeling; but it continued and gained definiteness—until, at length, I found that the noise was not within my ears.

16. No doubt I now grew very pale—but I talked more fluently, and with a heightened voice. Yet the sound increased—and what could I do? It was a low, dull, quick sound—much such a sound as a watch makes when enveloped in cotton. I gasped for breath—and yet the officers heard it not. I talked more quickly—more vehemently; but the noise steadily increased. Oh, God! What could I do? I foamed—I raved—I swore! I swung the chair upon which I had been sitting, and grated it upon the boards, but the noise arose over all and continually increased. It grew louder—louder—louder! And still the men chatted pleasantly, and smiled. Was it possible they heard not? Almighty God!—no, no! They heard!—they suspected!—they knew!—they were making a mockery of my horror!—this I thought, and this I think. But anything was better than this agony! Anything was more tolerable than derision! I could bear those hypocritical smiles no longer! I felt that I must scream or die! And now—again!—hark! louder! louder! louder! louder!

17. "Villains!" I shrieked, "dissemble no more! I admit the deed!—tear up the planks! Here, here!—it is the beating of his hideous heart!" (Poe)

Edgar Allan Poe (1809–1849) is probably best known for his astonishing works of horror. Among his stories are "The Cask of Amontillado" and "The Masque of the Red Death." His poems include the haunting "The Bells" and "Annabel Lee."

The Short Story Worksheet: "The Tell-Tale Heart"
Directions: Fill in the narrative elements for the story you just read:

1. **Characters:** List the major characters, with a short description of each. List minor characters:

   _____
   _____
   _____

2. **Setting:** Describe the setting (time and place).

   _____
   _____
   _____

3. **Plot:** Explain the series of events.

   _____
   _____
   _____

4. **Theme:** State the main idea.

   _____
   _____
   _____

5. **Tone:** Discuss how mood is created. How is humor, fear, irony, etc., conveyed? Be specific.

_____

_____

_____

6. **Point of View:** State the author's point of view.

_____

_____

_____

7. **Moral:** Is there a lesson, if so, what is it?

_____

_____

_____

8. What is your reaction to the story? Why did you or didn't you like it? Explain your answer.

_____

_____

_____

Now, write a short story report (one to two pages) using the answers to the above questions.

Step Three: Follow-Up Activities

Objective Test on "The Tell-Tale Heart"
Directions: Choose the best answer based on the reading.

1. The story is probably called "The Tell-Tale Heart" because of:
   a. the beating of the old man's heart.
   b. the narrator believes he can hear the old man's heart still beating.
   c. the narrator's heart stops.
   d. the police hear a heart beating.

2. The theme of the story deals with:
   a. the insanity that causes killing and confession.
   b. the insanity that results in a police discovery.
   c. the evil nature of an old man.
   d. a clever deception.

3. The narrator is:
   a. the old man.   c. a child.
   b. a detective.   d. a killer.

4. The narrator denies:
   a. the murder.
   b. his madness.
   c. the fact that he owes the old man money.
   d. his love for the old man.

5. The old man is killed because of his:
   a. money.
   b. gold.
   c. eye.
   d. bad attitude.

6. The killer gets ready for the murder by:
   a. looking into the old man's bedroom.
   b. sharpening his knives.
   c. stealing the old man's money.
   d. creeping up behind the old man while he's reading.

7. The old man knows:
   a. his killer hates him.
   b. the day he will die.
   c. someone is in the room.
   d. he will give the killer away.

8. The killer pounces on the old man because he is afraid that:
   a. neighbors will hear the man's heart beating.
   b. neighbors will hear the man's screaming.
   c. he will be attacked.
   d. he hears police.

9. The body is hid:
   a. in a deep grave.
   b. under the floor.
   c. in a closet.
   d. under the mattress.

10. Police enter the house because:
    a. neighbors heard a shriek.
    b. the killer wanted to confess.
    c. they suspect the real killer.
    d. they heard the old man's heart beating.

Vocabulary Test on "The Tell-Tale Heart"

Directions: Choose one of the meanings to identify the highlighted word as it appears in the selection.

1. You should have seen how wisely I proceeded—with what caution—with what **foresight**—with what dissimulation I went to work!
   a. intellect
   b. curiosity
   c. knowledge of what is to come
   d. secrecy

2. Never, before that night, had I *felt* the extent of my own powers—of my **sagacity.**
   a. wisdom
   b. madness
   c. cunning
   d. arm

3. The ringing became more **distinct**—it continued and became more distinct; I talked more freely to get rid of the feeling; but it continued and gained definiteness—until, at length, I found that the noise was *not* within my ears.
   a. clear
   b. fearsome
   c. shrill
   d. unusual

4. I saw it with perfect distinctiveness—all a dull blue, with a hideous veil over it that chilled the very marrow in my bones; but I could see nothing else of the old man's face or person; for I had directed the ray as if by instinct, **precisely** upon the damned spot.
   a. preciously
   b. exactly
   c. assuredly
   d. understandably

5. If still you think me mad, you will think so no longer when I describe the wise precautions I took for the **concealment** of the body.
   - a. security
   - b. cleanliness
   - c. hiding
   - d. procedure

6. A shriek had been heard by a neighbor during the night; suspicion of foul play had been aroused; information had been lodged at the police office, and they (the officers) had been deputed to search the **premises.**
   - a. flooring
   - b. neighborhood
   - c. closets
   - d. habitation

7. "Villains!" I shrieked, "**dissemble** no more!"
   - a. annoy
   - b. make noise
   - c. pretend
   - d. investigate

8. I could bear those **hypocritical** smiles no longer!
   - a. happy
   - b. challenging
   - c. understanding
   - d. phony

9. Yes, he had been trying to comfort himself with these **suppositions:** but he had found all in vain.
   - a. ideas
   - b. guessing
   - c. dreams
   - d. juxtapositions

10. Above all was the sense of hearing **acute.**
   - a. sharp
   - b. low
   - c. disturbing
   - d. deep

Questions about "The Tell-Tale Heart"

1. Who is the narrator?

   _____

   _____

   _____

2. Why is the old man murdered?

   _____

   _____

   _____

3. How is the old man murdered?

   _____

   _____

   _____

4. Why does the killer confess?

   _____

   _____

   _____

5. How can we tell that the killer is insane?

_____

_____

_____

Journal Suggestions

1. Irony is used to good effect in "The Tell-Tale Heart." Irony is the tone of a tale characterized by an unexpected twist, or the opposite of what is expected. In your journal, list the ways Poe uses irony in this bleak story. Share your results with your group.

2. Challenge yourself! Write your own "scary story" and share it with your group.

Collaborative Activity

"The Tell-Tale Heart" ends with the narrator's confession. What do you think will happen to this character? Will he be convicted? Can he plead not guilty on the basis of insanity when he repeatedly insists that he is sane? Conduct a mock trial with others in your group, each person assuming a different role (narrator, lawyer, neighbor, etc.) to find out the results.

Look It Up

1. The narrators in Poe's stories are often bizarre characters with evil intentions. Compare the narrator in "The Tell-Tale Heart" to the narrator of "The Cask of Amontillado," another Poe tale. Research the website www.poedecoder.com to find out what others have to say, and write a short paper about the role of the narrator.

2. Edgar Allan Poe is famous for his poetry (also often dark in nature) as well as his short stories. On the Internet, find some of Poe's poetry, including "The Raven" and "Annabel Lee." Write a paper comparing the themes of these poems.

3. Many people believe that Poe's life was just as fascinating as his literature. Research the biography of Poe. What impact, if any, did his life's experiences have on his works? Write a paper about this topic and share your results with others.

Getting the Picture

Look carefully at the picture of Great Hall, Oxford, a setting in a Harry Potter movie. Use your imagination to invent a story about Harry Potter's next adventure. Write your fictional story on the following lines.

© Chris Sargent, 2010. Used under license from Shutterstock, Inc.

_____

_____

_____

_____

_____

_____

_____

_____

_____

_____

_____

_____

_____

_____

_____

_____

_____

_____

_____

_____

_____

_____

Chapter Highlights

What Have We Learned?

In this chapter, we have practiced identifying the elements of the **narrative,** including **characters, setting, plot, theme, tone, point of view,** and sometimes **moral.** With increased practice in identification and discussion, we can continue to read and appreciate a variety of short stories and novels.

CAN I REALLY ENJOY READING POETRY?

CHAPTER 17 Analogies and Figures of Speech
CHAPTER 18 Poetic Figures of Speech and Imagery

Comprehending the narrative and its various elements certainly increases appreciation of the written word. Now that you have a critical understanding, you are ready to explore affective comprehension—the real reason people love to read.

Spotlight on

Avril Lavigne (1984–)

Avril Ramona Lavigne, born on September 27, 1984 in Belleville, Ontario, Canada, is a popular singer and songwriter who has sold over 30 million copies of her albums worldwide. Lavigne began singing and playing the guitar in her church choir, and was later discovered singing country covers. In 2002, she signed with Arista Records where she released her first album, *Let Go*, ultimately selling 15 million copies. The single "Complicated" gained fame throughout the world. *Under My Skin* was released in 2004; this album won two World Music Awards for World's Best Pop/Rock Artist and World's Best Selling Canadian Artist. In 2007, Lavigne came out with *The Best Damn Thing*, which reached number one on the charts with songs like "Hot," "Girlfriend," and "When You're Gone." Lavigne was married to fellow rocker Deryck Whibley from July 2006 to October 2009, but afterwards the two continued to work together, as Whibley produced her fourth album, as well as her single,"Alice," which was written for Tim Burton's *Alice in Wonderland*. Lavigne launched her first fragrance, Dark Star, in July 2009. The singer is also known for her charitable works, recording a cover of John Lennon's "Imagine" which appeared in the album, *Instant Karma: The Amnesty International Campaign to Save Darfur*, released in 2007. Lavigne has also contributed to various charities like Amnesty International, the Make-A-Wish Foundation, and Youth AIDS, for which she appeared in ALDO ads to raise funds to educate about HIV/AIDS.

© Mario Anzuoni/Reuters/Corbis

Chapter 17

ANALOGIES AND FIGURES OF SPEECH

The songwriter Avril Lavigne, like any fine poet or writer, can provoke an emotional reaction in those who hear her work. Whenever we listen to or read something that makes us cry or laugh or become frightened or forces us to think about something in a new way, we are reacting "affectively." **Affective comprehension** is, simply put, *how we are "affected" by what we read*. This response, which can be emotional as well as mental, is the primary reason people love to read. Perhaps you know someone who is always reading a novel or attending poetry readings. That individual enjoys these activities because of the *affective* reaction they spark. Of course, you must have a basic understanding (literal comprehension) and interpretation (critical comprehension) before you can react in an "affective" way. All readers agree, however, that a strong affective reaction is ultimately what makes reading worthwhile.

Before we can understand how we use *affective comprehension* when reading literature including short stories and poetry, we need to explore devices used in writing or even everyday language that enhance our appreciation of what we read. Many individuals avoid reading poetry for the same reason some people reject abstract art. This is because we do not quite understand these forms of communication. Ironically, the point of both abstract art and poetry is to condense a message, get to the "heart" of it by making it as simple as possible. For example, portraits by the artist Picasso do not represent human figures in the least, and that is because he was trying to convey the energy or spirit *inside* the physical body. Poets often use as few words as possible because each word carries multiple meanings, which are subject to individual interpretation. For example, take a look at the following line:

The river flows, upstream, downstream.

You might view it as part of a description of an area in the woods. Probably, you wouldn't pay much attention to it. Now, let's view the same line in the context of a poem.

Life
the river
flows
upstream
downstream

The title, placement of the words, and lack of punctuation indicate that this is a poem. Each word now carries a greater meaning, a meaning that may be different for each reader. The river is no longer just viewed as a body of water, but may now be a symbol for life which, like a river, has its ups and downs. Reading affectively, then, can open up new meanings for us, making our understanding and appreciation of what we read clearer.

When we read anything on a literal level (as we did in the first "river" example), we are reading for **denotative** meaning. We are interpreting what we read for its dictionary definition. For example, if you were to look up the word *blue* in the dictionary, it would be defined as a primary color. However, the word *blue* may also be used in other ways. If a friend were to tell you that you looked "blue," you probably would not rush out for an oxygen mask! Instead, you would interpret the word as meaning "sad" or "gloomy." These suggested interpretations are called **connotative** meanings. Connotative meanings are often used in everyday language as well as literature, to make meanings clearer.

Analogies are often used in *connotative* expression. An **analogy** is a comparison of two different ideas in order to project an image that is as clear as possible. For example, the line "Cathy turned pale" becomes much clearer when it becomes the analogy "Cathy turned as pale as a ghost," creating an image that is more horrifying. Similarly, the sentence "Henry gave his girlfriend a hug" is not nearly as clear as "Henry gave his girlfriend a bear hug." The "bear" hug suggests a connotative meaning using the analogy of an embrace to that of a squeeze by a bear. It presents a better image in our minds. Analogies are sometimes referred to as **figurative language.**

Whether we realize it or not, we use analogies, or figurative language, in our speech everyday. These types of analogies are called **figures of speech,** or idioms. English is not the only language that has figures of speech, but these expressions are present in all languages, often making new languages difficult to learn. Nevertheless, figures of speech add color and interest to our language while often making the meaning clearer. Figures of speech *are analogies that are always interpreted in a connotative, or suggested, way.* If we were to interpret these phrases literally (e.g., "the check bounced"), or in a denotative way, they simply would not make sense. Let's see if you can recognize how figurative language is used—in both everyday language and in poetry—in the following exercises.

Exercise 17.1 Your Turn—What Did You Learn?

1. Whenever we read something that makes us laugh, cry, or become fearful, we are reacting on a(n) _____ level.

2. A _____ is usually a short kind of writing that may or may not rhyme, and which can be interpreted on different levels.

3. _____ are comparisons that make the image clearer.

4. A(n) _____ meaning of a word is the definition we would find in the dictionary.

5. The suggested meaning of a word is often referred to as its _____ meaning.

6. _____ language uses analogies to make the meaning as clear as possible.

7. Two other names for figurative language used in everyday speech are _____ and _____.

8. Figurative language must always be interpreted in a _____ way.

Identifying Figurative Language

17.2 *Exercise*

One of the reasons for Avril Lavigne's popularity is that the words she uses in her songs help others to identify with her feelings and ideas. She accomplishes this by using everyday expressions that are easily recognizable. See if you can identify the figurative language (figures of speech) in the following exercise.

Directions: Write "L" for expressions that are interpreted literally (denotatively), and "F" for those that are interpreted figuratively (connotatively).

1. _____ Last night, we slept at John's house.
2. _____ Working is sometimes a pain in the neck.
3. _____ Emily has her eye on a new car.
4. _____ I heard Wayne got kicked out of his parents' house.
5. _____ When are we going to the park?
6. _____ That stock is a rock solid investment.
7. _____ If Paul is going to get anywhere in life, he'd better pull himself up by his bootstraps.
8. _____ If Harriet keeps eating cupcakes, she is going to get fat.
9. _____ Neil is so quiet, we wondered if the cat got his tongue.
10. _____ All the boys thought Laura looked hot in that low-cut outfit.

Identifying Figurative Language in Idioms

17.3 *Exercise*

Now that you have identified figurative language, try to define some popular expressions, or idioms, and come up with a few figures of speech that you have heard.

A. Directions: Write the meaning of the italicized popular expressions as used in the following sentences:

1. Look at what Sam is wearing. He must be *off his rocker!*

   _____

2. If Tammy doesn't stop talking, she is going to *spill the beans*.

   _____

3. Mike's project design is really *cool*.

   _____

4. Mayor Rodell won the election *by a landslide*.

_____

5. We are going to *raise the roof* at this party!

_____

B. Directions: Using the clue word provided in the parentheses, write a figure of speech as an idiom to make the meaning clearer in the following sentences:

1. Walter's plan doesn't make sense at all. I think he is not thinking clearly. (marbles)

_____

2. The first question on the math test was ridiculously simple. (brainer)

_____

3. We have a long trip ahead of us. We need to leave now. (hit)

_____

4. Ryan really did more than he should have to help you. (neck)

_____

5. Watching that scary movie made Giselle become extremely frightened. (hair)

_____

Exercise **17.4** **Figurative Language in Poetry**

Now that we understand how figurative language is used in everyday speech, let's see how analogies can be used in poetry.

Directions: Read the following short poem by Robert Frost then answer the questions which follow it to test your *affective comprehension*.

The Road Not Taken

TWO roads diverged in a yellow wood,
And sorry I could not travel both
And be one traveler, long I stood
And looked down one as far as I could
To where it bent in the undergrowth;   5

Then took the other, as just as fair,
And having perhaps the better claim,
Because it was grassy and wanted wear;
Though as for that the passing there
Had worn them really about the same,   10

And both that morning equally lay
In leaves no step had trodden black.
Oh, I kept the first for another day!
Yet knowing how way leads on to way,
I doubted if I should ever come back.   15

I shall be telling this with a sigh
Somewhere ages and ages hence:
Two roads diverged in a wood, and I—
I took the one less traveled by,
And that has made all the difference.   20

1. What do the roads symbolize?

   _____

   _____

   _____

2. The traveler takes one road "because it was grassy and wanted wear."
   What does the poet mean by this description?

   _____

   _____

   _____

3. Why does he conclude that taking the less traveled road "has made all
   the difference"?

   _____

   _____

   _____

4. How does Frost's message apply to your own life?

   _____

   _____

   _____

Reading Comprehension Using Different Forms of Expression

Exercise **17.5**

We can sharpen our affective comprehension by understanding how analogy is used, not only in everyday language, but also in art, song lyrics, and poetry. Let's begin with a visual interpretation by the abstract artist Pablo Picasso.

Selection 1: *Maya in a Sailor Suit* by Pablo Picasso (painting)
Before Reading: Freewrite

Write about how you feel about abstract art. Do you generally like these types of paintings or do they seem complicated or uninteresting?

This portrait, titled *Maya in a Sailor Suit*, was painted by Pablo Picasso in January 1938. The title suggests that it is a picture of the artist's daughter, Maya, who was a little more than two years old at the time.

Examine the picture closely. At first, if you interpret the drawing literally or denotatively, it appears to be nothing more than a brightly colored drawing done by a young child. Certainly, it is not very realistic. Therefore, many observers unfamiliar with abstract art would conclude that the picture is not a very good one.

Take a second look. Try to examine it for its suggested or connotative meaning. The face appears to be depicted full-face and in profile at the same time. Is

Picasso suggesting multiple views instead of just projecting one? The colors are bold and bright, without much shading. What might Picasso's choice of colors suggest about the figure being depicted? The figure dominates most of the page. What is suggested by this choice? What type of personality do you think Maya had at this age? Her ear is represented by a figure-eight, and does not resemble an ear at all. Art historians note that this is a hieroglyph that appears in many of Picasso's works, representing keyholes and infinity. Why do you think the artist chose to place it in this drawing instead of an ear? Finally, even though the title suggests that this is a picture of his daughter, the name "Picasso" is seen on the headband. Picasso himself has hinted that since he often wore a sailor's striped undershirt, the picture is really a self-portrait. How do you explain this?

Write your affective interpretation on the following lines. Do you like this painting? Why or why not? Remember, because an affective response is always personal, there are no wrong answers to these questions.

Selection 2: "Complicated" by Avril Lavigne (song lyrics)

Songs are enjoyed for their sounds but often are also appreciated for the lyrics, words that help the listener connect emotionally. Avril Lavigne's hit song "Complicated" uses figurative language to help the listener respond in a strong affective manner. Examine the lyrics to this popular single to determine just why it appeals to so many people.

Before Reading: Freewrite

Write about how you feel about music. Do the lyrics of a song add to your enjoyment?

Complicated

Uh huh, life's like this
Uh huh, uh huh, that's the way it is

Cause life's like this
Uh huh, uh huh that's the way it is

Chill out whatcha yelling' for?
Lay back it's all been done before
And if you could only let it be
you will see
I like you the way you are
When we're drivin' in your car
and you're talking to me one on one but you've become

Somebody else round everyone else
You're watching your back like you can't relax
You're tryin' to be cool you look like a fool to me
Tell me

Why you have to go and make things so complicated?
I see the way you're acting like you're somebody else gets me frustrated
Life's like this you
And you fall and you crawl and you break
and you take what you get and you turn it into honesty
and promise me I'm never gonna find you fake it
no no no

You come over unannounced
dressed up like you're somethin' else
where you are and where it's at you see
you're making me
laugh out when you strike your pose
take off all your preppy clothes
you know you're not fooling anyone
when you've become

Somebody else round everyone else
Watching your back, like you can't relax
Trying to be cool you look like a fool to me
Tell me

Why you have to go and make things so complicated?
I see the way you're acting like you're somebody else gets me frustrated
Life's like this you
and You fall and you crawl and you break
and you take what you get and you turn it into
honesty
promise me I'm never gonna find you fake it
no no no

Chill out whatcha yelling for?
Lay back, it's all been done before
And if you could only let it be
You will see

Somebody else round everyone else
You're watching your back, like you can't relax
You're trying to be cool, you look like a fool to me
Tell me

Why you have to go and make things so complicated?
I see the way you're acting like you're somebody else gets me frustrated
Life's like this you
and You fall and you crawl and you break
and you take what you get and you turn it into
honesty
promise me I'm never gonna find you fake it
no no

Why you have to go and make things so complicated?
I see the way you're acting like your somebody else gets me frustrated
Life's like this you
You fall and you crawl and you break
and you take what you get and you turn it into honesty
promise me I'm never gonna find you fake it
no no no

Answer the following questions concerning the lyrics you just read.

1. The language in the song "Complicated" reflects the way people actually speak. This language is sometimes called "colloquial." What are some examples of colloquial language found in the lyrics?

_____

_____

2. One of the figures of speech used in the song is "chill out." What is the meaning of this idiom? List other idioms used by Lavigne and their meanings.

_____

_____

3. To whom is the singer speaking?

_____

_____

4. What is the message of the song?

_____

_____

5. How do you feel about the writer's message? Discuss your reaction.

_____

_____

Selection 3: "Success Is Countest Sweetest" by Emily Dickinson

Poems, more than any other art form, make the most use out of figurative language. Here is a famous poem by the poet Emily Dickinson for you to analyze.

Before Reading: Freewrite

Write about how you feel about poetry in general. What, if any, are some of your favorite poems?

Success Is Countest Sweetest

Success is counted sweetest
By those who ne'er succeed.
To comprehend a nectar
Requires sorest need.

Not one of all the purple host
Who took the flag to-day
Can tell the definition,
So clear, of victory,

As he, defeated, dying,
On whose forbidden ear
The distant strains of triumph
Break, agonized and clear.

Emily Dickinson (1830–1886) is regarded as one of the best poets of the nineteenth century. Her poems are noted for their evocative use of imagery, or figurative language. Her themes include death, immortality, and nature. She lived most of her life in seclusion, and almost all of her eighteen hundred poems were published after her death.

Respond to the following questions:

1. What is the literal meaning of this poem? In other words, what happens in the poem?

   _____

   _____

   _____

2. Consider the lines "To comprehend a nectar/Requires sorest need." What does the metaphor symbolize?

   _____

   _____

   _____

3. Reread the final stanza. What is the poem's message regarding success?

   _____

   _____

   _____

Journal Suggestion

With your group, make a list of popular idiomatic expressions (figures of speech). (Check some examples given earlier in the chapter.) Then, each person will write a one-page story or dialogue using at least five expressions. Share your original work with your group.

Collaborative Activity

Practice creating analogies by writing a list of adjectives that describe your appearance, personality, and interests. Exchange lists with your partner and choose at least five of the adjectives to use as analogies. For example, the word "tall" could be made clearer by writing: "Tom is as tall as a pine tree." The word "talkative" could be used in the analogy "Katy is as talkative as a parrot." Share your analogies with your partner.

Look It Up

1. Research information about the painter Pablo Picasso (1881–1973) or another modern abstract painter (Matisse, Chagall, Miro, etc.). Write an extended essay explaining the technique the painter used in his or her art and why the works are appreciated.

2. Find the lyrics to another song popularized by Avril Lavigne or another noteworthy singer. Write a paper in which you examine the meaning of the lyrics and discuss why people may react emotionally to them.

3. Choose a poem by Robert Frost (1874–1963) or another famous modern poet. Analyze each line for analogies to interpret the meaning. Write an essay about your findings.

Getting the Picture

The photo depicts a singer onstage. In detail, describe what you see literally (the person, background). Then, describe what you think the picture suggests. For example, where was the photo taken? What does the expression on her face suggest? Use your imagination to create a short story suggested by the picture.

_____

_____

_____

_____

© Yuri Arcurs, 2010. Used under license from Shutterstock, Inc.

_____

_____

_____

_____

_____

_____

_____

_____

_____

_____

_____

_____

_____

_____

_____

_____

_____

Chapter Highlights

What Have We Learned?

This chapter introduced the concept of **affective comprehension,** which is how writing makes us *feel*. **Analogies** are comparisons that aid in our understanding by comparing one idea to another. **Figures of speech** are analogies we use in everyday language to make the meaning clear. When we read on an *affective* level, we interpret meaning not only in a **denotative** way but also in a **connotative** way, which provides *multiple* interpretations.

Chapter 18

POETIC FIGURES OF SPEECH AND IMAGERY

Now that you understand how analogies help us interpret ideas in an affective way, it's time to focus on ways writers use analogies in literature. Poems usually are good examples of literature that contain analogies and can be interpreted in multiple, or connotative, ways. As an example, take a look at this famous poem by Langston Hughes (1902–1967), a voice for the black experience whose work flourished during the Harlem Renaissance period.

A Dream Deferred

What happens to a dream deferred?

Does it dry up
like a raisin in the sun?
Or fester like a sore—
And then run?
Does it stink like rotten meat?
Or crust and sugar over—
like a syrupy sweet?

Maybe it just sags
like a heavy load.

Or does it explode?

This is a poem about a dream, or an original idea, that has never gone beyond being a dream. It has been laid aside, or *deferred*. This dream is being compared to several things. Analogies are made between a dream and a raisin, a sore, rotten meat, something sweet, and even a heavy load. Finally, if a dream never becomes reality, asks the poet, does it eventually explode (like a bomb)? These analogies suggest new ways we can feel about dreams. "A Dream Deferred" is clearly about different ways we can look at these dreams. It is a poem we need to interpret for *connotative* meaning as we read it again and again.

Lorraine Hansberry (1930–1965) was an American playwright who wrote the drama *A Raisin in the Sun* (1959), whose title comes from Langston Hughes's poem at the beginning of this chapter. The first play written by a black woman to be staged on Broadway, *A Raisin in the Sun* won the New York Drama Critics' Circle Award as the best play of the year. It was later made into a movie starring Sidney Poitier.

Poets, like many writers, use **figurative language,** or analogies, to create different (connotative) images. Let's take a look at a few examples of this method:

1. **Simile**—*a comparison of two things using the words "like" or "as."* For example, this line by the poet Robert Burns uses a simile to compare the woman he loves to a rose:

"My love is like a red, red rose."

Do you think that this is a good analogy? He appears to be complimenting the woman he loves. He might have said, "my love is beautiful," but by comparing her to a rose, he is able to communicate *multiple* meanings. A rose has several positive qualities that appeal to three of our five senses (sight, hearing, smell, touch, taste): it is beautiful to look at, delicate to the touch, and has a fragrant scent. (However, watch out because it may have thorns that can hurt you!) Therefore, Burns is able to convey a great deal through the use of simile.

2. **Metaphor**—*a comparison that does not use "like" or "as."* Let's make a change to the line we just examined:

"My love is a red, red rose."

This image certainly seems to be a stronger analogy than we saw in the simile. We cannot interpret the meaning literally (the poet couldn't possibly be in love with a rose!), but must understand it on a figurative level. It is certainly a greater compliment to say one's love *is* a rose than simply saying that she is *like* one. Take another look at Langston Hughes's "A Dream Deferred." He uses several metaphors to convey his message.

3. **Personification**—*a comparison that gives human qualities to something that is not a human.* To illustrate this point, take a look at the following sentence:

"The sun embraced us with her warmth."

What does this line mean? It suggests that we were warm in the sun. However, by giving the sun *human* qualities, it conveys much more. Like a human, the sun embraces us, an action that suggests that we felt good (the sun throwing darts at us might suggest otherwise!). Furthermore, the sun is pictured as a *female,* indicating a maternal feeling. Again, this figure of speech helps us to better understand the writer's meaning.

4. **Hyperbole**—*a type of simile or metaphor that exaggerates.* The following line is a metaphor that contains a hyperbole.

"There were a million people in the room."

Again, this line cannot be interpreted on a literal level because it would be impossible to fit a million people in a room! Why not just say that there were "a lot" of people in the room? To suggest that there were a million people in the room once again aids our meaning because the number more clearly indicates that there were a *great many* (too many, in fact) people in the room.

Your Turn—What Did You Learn? 18.1 *Exercise*

1. _____ can be interpreted in multiple, or **connotative**, ways.

2. A type of analogy that uses **"like"** or **"as"** in making the comparison is called a _____.

3. A type of analogy **that does not use "like" or "as"** in making the comparison is called a _____.

4. A type of analogy that gives objects **human qualities** is called a _____.

5. A **metaphor or simile that exaggerates** is called a _____.

Exercise 18.2 Identifying Figurative Language

© JupiterImages Corporation

Directions: Write the correct letter(s) identifying the type of figurative language in the following lines. Write the literal meaning on the line provided.

a. simile   c. personification
b. metaphor   d. hyperbole

1. _____ "Life's but a walking shadow, a poor player / That struts and frets his hour upon the stage" (*Macbeth* by William Shakespeare)

_____

2. _____ "Drive my dead thoughts over the universe\Like withered leaves to quicken a new birth!" ("Ode to the West Wind" Percy Bysshe Shelley)

_____

3. _____ "Death be not proud, though some have called thee/Mighty and dreadful, for thou art not so;" ("Death Be Not Proud" John Donne)

_____

4. _____ "I wandered lonely as a cloud" ("I Wandered Lonely as a Cloud" by William Wordsworth)

_____

5. _____ "An hundred years should go to praise / Thine eyes and on thy forehead gaze" ("To His Coy Mistress" by Andrew Marvell)

_____

6. _____ "Whose broad stripes and bright stars thru the perilous fight, O'er the ramparts we watched were so gallantly streaming?" ("The Star Spangled Banner" Francis Scott Key)

_____

7. _____ "Genius is one percent inspiration and ninety-nine percent perspiration." (Thomas Alva Edison)

_____

8. _____ "The pen is mightier than the sword." (Edward Bulwer-Lytton)

_____

Interpreting Poetry

Directions: The following poem by Bonnie Jacobson consists of a series of metaphors, which are numbered here. Next to each number in the answer blanks that follow, write what comes to mind when you picture the image (*affective* interpretation).

On Being Served Apples

(1) Apples in a deep blue dish
    are the shadows of nuns

(2) Apples in a basket
    are warm red moons on Indian women

(3) Apples in a white bowl
    are virgins waiting in snow

(4) Beware of apples on an orange plate:
    they are the anger of wives

                    —Bonnie Jacobson

From On Being Served Apples by Bonnie Jacobson. Copyright © 1981 by Bonnie Jacobson. Reprinted by permission.

© JupiterImages Corporation

1. _____
   _____

2. _____
   _____

3. _____
   _____

4. _____
   _____

Now, try writing your own poem. Choose a particular fruit and place it in four (4) bowls of different colors, then create a metaphorical image for each scene (e.g., grapes in a yellow bowl are hills against the sunlight).

My Poem

1. _____
   _____

2. _____
   _____

3. _____
   _____

4. _____
   _____

Exercise 18.4 Interpreting Figurative Language in Poetry

Directions: Read the following poem by Shirley Russak Wachtel about the feeling one gets right before a snowfall. Identify the types of figurative language then discuss what the poem means to you.

Before the Snow

Is this how it was?
Silence.
The gray-green brushleaf
flickers shadows into
the open air which
ripples its reflections
like an unheeding wave moving methodically
toward the ocean's end
and even the faded images of the stars
are breathless.
The sun too seems
to have lost its luster
and shivers like a
giant metal shield against the sky.
The ground already cracked and
spotted seems reconciled
to its fate.

© JupiterImages Corporation

> *There is*
> *not even a bird or squirrel*
> *in this trembling stillness.*
> *All locked*
> *in an eternity of waiting*
> *for the snow*
> *for the heave of wind*
> *release of single silverdown white*
> *the creaking of a door*
> *the breath against the nape*
> *the sound of two boots marching*
> *toward an unseen gentle spring.*
>
> —*Shirley Russak Wachtel*

Vocabulary*

flickers—flutters, slight back and forth movement
ripples—making little waves
unheeding—not paying attention
methodically—carefully
luster—shine
reconciled—reluctantly agreed
heave—lift with great effort

*Note: *brushleaf* and *silverdown* are words that are created for their sound and have no dictionary definition.

Identify the figures of speech you find in "Before the Snow." There may be a few of each type. The first response is given for you.

1. **simile**: *like an unheeding wave* _____

2. **metaphor**: _____

3. **personification**: _____

4. **hyperbole**: _____

What do you think the poem means? How does it make you feel? (There are no wrong answers.)

_____

_____

_____

_____

_____

Now that you understand how figures of speech are used in literature, analyze the following poems and prose in order to appreciate their meaning.

Exercise **18.5**   **Analyzing Three Poems**

The "rose" has long been a symbol of love and beauty. Read the following three poems that have a "rose" as the topic, then analyze and compare how each uses figurative language to convey a message.

Before Reading: Freewrite
Write about the words that come to mind when you think of a rose.

My Love is Like a Red, Red Rose

O, my love is like a red, red rose,
that's newly sprung in June.
O, my love is like a melody,
that's sweetly play'd in tune.

As fair thou art, my bonnie lass,
so deep in love am I,
And I will love thee still, my dear,
till a' the seas gang dry. (gang = go)

Till a' the seas gang dry, my dear,
and the rocks melt wi' the sun! (wi' = with)
And I will love thee still, my dear,
while the sands of life shall run.

And fare thee weel, my only love! (weel = well)
And fare thee well awhile!
And I will come again, my love.
Tho it were ten thousand mile!

　　　　　　　　　—Robert Burns (1759–1796)

© JupiterImages Corporation

Nobody Knows This Little Rose

Nobody knows this little Rose—
It might a pilgrim be
Did I not take it from the ways
And lift it up to thee.
Only a Bee will miss it—
Only a Butterfly,
Hastening from far journey—
On its breast to lie—
Only a Bird will wonder—
Only a Breeze will sigh—
Ah Little Rose—how easy
For such as thee to die!

—Emily Dickinson (1830–1886)

One Perfect Rose

A single flow'r he sent me, since we met.
    All tenderly his messenger he chose;
Deep-hearted, pure, with scented dew still wet—
    One perfect rose.

I knew the language of the floweret;
    "My fragile leaves," it said, "his heart enclose."
Love long has taken for his amulet*
    One perfect rose.

Why is it no one ever sent me yet
    One perfect limousine, do you suppose?
Ah no, it's always just my luck to get
    One perfect rose.

—Dorothy Parker (1893–1967)

*amulet—a charm that protects against evil or injury

Respond to the following questions:

1. In the first poem by Robert Burns, the poet expresses his love by using various figures of speech. What are some of the things he uses to compare his love to? What comparisons are offered to show how long he will love her?

_____

_____

_____

_____

_____

2. What is the overall tone of the poem?

_____

_____

_____

_____

_____

_____

3. Emily Dickinson presents the rose in a different way. How does she use personification to make her point?

_____

_____

_____

_____

_____

_____

4. What is the meaning of Dickinson's poem? How would you describe the tone?

_____

_____

_____

_____

_____

_____

5. Can you find any metaphors in the poem by Dorothy Parker?

_____

_____

_____

_____

_____

_____

6. Discuss the meaning and tone of this poem.

_____

_____

_____

_____

_____

_____

7. Explain the meaning of the rose in each of the poems.

_____

_____

_____

_____

_____

_____

8. Compare the poets' attitudes toward love. Which poem is your favorite? Why?

_____

_____

_____

_____

_____

_____

Analyzing Figurative Language in Prose   18.6 *Exercise*

Poetry is not the only genre that uses figurative language to make a point. In the next story, "The Hand" by Colette, the "hand" is an "extended metaphor," a comparison that is present throughout the prose. Notice how the author uses figurative language to make her point about marriage.

Before Reading: Freewrite

Write about the concept of marriage. Do you think it serves a purpose in today's society or is it something that has gone "out of style"?

The Hand

He had fallen asleep on his young wife's shoulder, and she proudly bore the weight of the man's head, blond, ruddy-complexioned, eyes closed. He had slipped his big arm under the small of her slim, adolescent back, and his strong hand lay on the sheet next to the young woman's right elbow. She smiled to see the man's hand emerging there, all by itself and far away from its owner. Then she let her eyes wander over the half-lit room. A veiled conch shed a light across the bed the color of periwinkle.

"Too happy to sleep," she thought.

Colette (1874–1963) was a French artist whose themes included love and the role of women in a society dominated by males.

"The Hand" from The Collected Stories of Colette translated by Matthew Ward, edited by Robert Phelps. Translation copyright © 1983 by Farrar, Straus, and Giroux, Inc. Reprinted by permission of Farrar, Straus and Giroux, LLC.

Too excited also, and often surprised by her new state. It had been only two weeks since she had begun to live the scandalous life of a newlywed who tastes the joys of living with someone unknown and with whom she is in love. To meet a handsome, blond young man, recently widowed, good at tennis and rowing, to marry him a month later: her conjugal adventure had been little more than a kidnapping. So that whenever she lay awake beside her husband, like tonight, she still kept her eyes closed for a long time, then opened them again in order to savor, with astonishment, the blue of the brand-new curtains, instead of the apricot-pink through which the first light of day filtered into the room where she had slept as a little girl.

A quiver ran through the sleeping body lying next to her, and she tightened her left arm around her husband's neck with the charming authority exercised by weak creatures. He did not wake up.

"His eyelashes are so long," she said to herself.

To herself she also praised his mouth, full and likable, his skin the color of pink brick, and even his forehead, neither noble nor broad, but still smooth and unwrinkled.

Her husband's right hand, lying beside her, quivered in turn, and beneath the curve of her back she felt the right arm, on which her whole weight was resting, come to life.

"I'm so heavy . . . I wish I could get up and turn the light off. But he's sleeping so well . . ."

The arm twisted again, feebly, and she arched her back to make herself lighter.

"It's as if I were lying on some animal," she thought.

She turned her head a little on the pillow and looked at the hand lying there next to her.

"It's so big! It really is bigger than my whole head."

The light, flowing out from under the edge of a parasol of bluish crystal, spilled up against the hand, and made every contour of the skin apparent, exaggerating the powerful knuckles and the veins engorged by the pressure on the arm. A few red hairs, at the base of the fingers, all curved in the same direction, like ears of wheat in the wind, and the flat nails, whose ridges the nail buffer had not smoothed out, gleamed, coated with pink varnish.

"I'll tell him not to varnish his nails," thought the young wife. "Varnish and pink polish don't go with a hand so . . . a hand that's so . . . "

An electric jolt ran through the hand and spared the young woman from having to find the right adjective. The thumb stiffened itself out, horribly long and spatulate, and pressed tightly against the index finger, so that the hand suddenly took on a vile apelike appearance.

"Oh!" whispered the young woman, as though faced with something slightly indecent.

The sound of a passing car pierced the silence with a shrillness that seemed luminous. The sleeping man did not wake, but the hand, offended, reared back and tensed up in the shape of a crab and waited, ready for battle. The screeching sound died down and the hand, relaxing gradually, lowered its claws, and became a pliant beast, awkwardly bent, *shaken by faint jerks which resembled some sort of agony. The flat, cruel nail of the overlong thumb glistened. A curve in the little finger, which the young woman had never noticed, appeared, and the wallowing hand revealed its fleshy palm like a red belly.*

"And I've kissed that hand! . . . How horrible! Haven't I ever looked at it?"

The hand, disturbed by a bad dream, appeared to respond to this disgust. It regrouped its forces, opened wide, and splayed its tendons, lumps, and red fur like battle dress, then slowly drawing itself in again, grabbed a fistful of the sheet, dug into its curved fingers, and squeezed, squeezed with the methodical pleasure of a strangler.

"Oh!" cried the young woman.

The hand disappeared and a moment later the big arm, relieved of its burden, became a protective belt, a warm bulwark against all the terrors of night. But the next morning, when it was time for breakfast in bed—hot chocolate and toast—she saw the hand again, with its red hair and red skin, and the ghastly thumb curving out over the handle of a knife.

"Do you want this slice, darling? I'll butter it for you."

She shuddered and felt her skin crawl on the back of her arms and down her back.

"Oh, no . . . no . . ."

Then she concealed her fear, bravely subdued herself, and beginning her life of duplicity, of resignation, and of a lowly, delicate diplomacy, she leaned over and humbly kissed the monstrous hand.

Respond to the following questions:

1. This short story does not contain much action, but basically consists of a young woman's thoughts. How would you describe the relationship between the husband and wife?

_____

_____

_____

_____

2. What is the setting for this tale? Why is the setting important?

_____

_____

_____

_____

3. Why is the young wife fascinated by her husband's hand?

_____

_____

_____

_____

4. The hand is an extended metaphor for her marriage. What are some other things the narrator compares the hand to? Are they appropriate?

_____

_____

_____

_____

5. The husband doesn't realize it, but the next morning his wife is changed forever. How is this true? What will marriage be like for this newlywed?

_____

_____

_____

_____

Journal Suggestion

Walk outside and describe what you see, hear, smell, touch, or taste. Write a description of your experience in your journal, using similes, metaphors, hyperboles, and personification (e.g., "the sun smiled warmly," "the breeze whispered through the trees," etc.). Share your descriptions with your group.

Collaborative Activity

Choose a poem by one of the poets mentioned in this chapter. With your group, discuss and analyze the figures of speech and meaning of the poem.

Look It Up

1. William Shakespeare is known for his sonnets as well as his plays. Research information about this prolific writer's sonnets, their themes, and their imagery.

2. Colette's (Sidonie-Gabrielle Colette; 1873–1954) "The Hand" and Kate Chopin's (1851–1904) "The Story of an Hour" (which you read in Chapter 16) are both stories that reveal opinions concerning the role of women in marriage. Write an essay comparing the viewpoints in these stories.

Getting the Picture

The photo represents musical notes. The words to a song are called lyrics. Avril Lavigne, like some other performers, writes the lyrics to her songs. Now that you understand the concept of figurative language, write the lyrics to a song she might sing. Remember to include similes, metaphors, and other types of figurative language. (Write about 20 lines with repeating chorus.)

_____

_____

_____

_____

_____

_____

_____

_____

_____

_____

_____

_____

_____

_____

_____

_____

_____

_____

Chapter Highlights

What Have We Learned?

In this chapter we learned how writers use **figurative language** to convey a clear meaning. Many forms of figurative language often appear in poetry. Some types of figurative language include the **simile**, a comparison using "like" or "as"; the **metaphor**, a comparison without using "like" or "as"; **personification**, a description of a non-living thing by adding human qualities; and **hyperbole**, or exaggeration.

HOW HAVE MY READING SKILLS IMPROVED?

CHAPTER 19 Test-Taking Skills
CHAPTER 20 Creating Your Own Test

Now that you have an understanding of literal, critical, and affective reading skills, it is time to test what you have learned. In the next unit, you will learn some important test-taking skills.

Spotlight on

Martha Stewart (1941–)

Martha Stewart is a renowned business magnate who is also known for hosting her own TV program and publishing a magazine, all of which deal with "gracious living." A former stockbroker, Stewart began a small catering business which led to her one-woman empire. In 1982, her book *Entertaining* was published, and she became a noted expert on cooking, gardening, home decorating, wedding receptions, and various do-it-yourself projects. Her television show, *Martha Stewart's Living* garnered even more success. In 1999, Stewart took her company public, and Martha Stewart Living Omnimedia was listed on the New York Stock Exchange. In 2001, she was named the third most powerful woman in America by *Ladies Home Journal*. However, in 2004, Stewart was convicted of lying to investigators about a stock sale; she spent five months in a West Virginia prison and was released to house arrest in March of 2005. Later that year she began firing potential assistants in *The Apprentice: Martha Stewart*, a short-lived reality show spun off from Donald Trump's hit show *The Apprentice*, and went back into syndicated television with her own daytime talk show. In 2006, her company once again gained a profit. In July 2008, craft items under the names "Martha Stewart Celebrate" and "Martha Stewart Create", two divisions of Martha Stewart Living Omnimedia, premiered in Wal-Mart stores. Household items also appear in Macys stores. In 2006, Stewart donated $5 million to New York's Mt. Sinai Hospital for a center on healthy aging. She has also supported several charities such as Dogs Deserve Better, Parkinson Society Maritime Region, and St. Jude's Children's Research Hospital.

© Lorenzo Ciniglio/Sygma/Corbis

Chapter 19

TEST-TAKING SKILLS

Martha Stewart, like so many of the celebrities featured in this book, knows that preparation and hard work are the keys to success. Let's see how you can be successful as you assess all that you have learned.

Have you ever studied hard and felt certain that you were well-prepared for an exam, only to find that you didn't do as well as you expected? Of course, this situation has happened to almost all of us. Although we may possess all the information, we sometimes lack another very important skill—the ability to successfully answer questions on a test. This is especially true of multiple-choice exams. But don't worry—you *can* learn how to become a better test-taker! Begin by reading the following selection then taking the short multiple-choice reading comprehension test that follows. *Please don't peek ahead for the answers!* When you have completed the test, then review the answers. On those you missed, take careful note of the advice. Then, go on and read the general instructions for scoring well on reading comprehension exams. With these tools in hand, you are sure to become a more confident and better test-taker!

"When can I stop making wild guesses and start making educated guesses?"

© CartoonStock, www.CartoonStock.com

One of Martha Stewart's many skills is organization of the home. In this essay, the *New York Times* columnist Maureen Dowd admits to a problem in this area.

Adieu, Herb Alpert

This is not a simple city.

The more Jimmy Carter shed, from yacht to limo, the less he was respected. Bills about downsizing themselves need downsizing. The capital is more mover than Shaker.

Spartan living is not really a hallmark of my family, either. My sister's philosophy is that if you shop enough, anything you buy will eventually match something you own.

On the rare occasions when I have tried to cut back on clutter, I have lived to regret it. I gave away my platforms and they came back. I gave away all those 70's disco shirts with weird John Travolta collars and they're back.

But I was struck by a recent New York Times article about the hot trend sweeping the country: Voluntary Simplicity. These brave new downshifters are rejecting pushing-and-grabbing to search for a more nourishing way of life.

Elaine St. James of Santa Barbara described how she gave up her real estate job, threw away loads of stuff, moved to a smaller place, cropped her hair and now uses a rubber band around her money instead of a purse. Her closet contains one pair of black loafers, one pair of boots, two skirts, two pullovers, eight T-shirts and six turtlenecks. (Asceticism has its limits. She kept her BMW.)

Since I was moving, it seemed like a fine time to give Voluntary Simplicity a whirl. I wanted New Priorities. I wanted Different Tradeoffs. I wanted to go back to the Land. Well, no, but I definitely wanted to be more like Thoreau, less DKNY.

Feeling virtuous, I began my new relationship with the universe in my kitchen, which had boxes of cookbooks and recipes sent by my mother when she still hoped I would transcend take-out.

When I moved out of her house, she equipped me for modern life with "How to Cook With Budweiser," featuring recipes for "Beef Kidney with Budweiser" and "Chocolate Beer Cake" and tips on pouring: "The best technique is to place the neck of the bottle or lip of the can over the edge of the wetted glass and then tilt the bottle or can by quickly raising its bottom to a high angle. This action causes the beer to gurgle and agitate into the glass until a fine-textured head is created. Allow sufficient space for the foam to rise to the lip."

She also gave me "365 Ways to Cook Hamburger" and "250 Irish Recipes," including Collared Pig's Head. ("Remove the eye from the pig's cheek. Wash the cheek well in cold water, paying special attention to the nasal passages, eye cavity, and round the tongue and teeth, using a pointed knife where necessary.")

She sent me booklets: "Waist Trimmers" from the Florida Celery Exchange, "Confessions of a Kraut Lover" from Empire State Pickling, "50 Wonderful Ways to Use Cheese" from the American Dairy Association, "Exciting World of Rice Dishes" from Minute Rice and "33rd Annual Chicken Cooking Contest" from the National Broiler Council.

I dumped it all in the trash—including the cautionary articles she had clipped ("How to Cope With a Hotel Fire," "Staying Safe in Your Car," "How to Brush Off Gum Disease"). But then I began feeling sentimental and retrieved the cookbooks. Cholesterol is due for a comeback.

Trying harder at voluntary simplification, I turned to my record collection. It was a time for tough choices. The original motion picture soundtracks of "Flashdance" and "Thunderball" and Herb Alpert and the Tijuana Brass had to go. I tossed books on the pile: "Learn to Play Tennis at Home," "How to Write a Romance Novel and Get It Published," a Katy Keene paper-doll book. I agonized about "How to Catch and Hold a Man" but decided that catching and holding was not simple.

More detritus from my years of involuntary complication: a dice clock from Las Vegas, a souvenir fish that says "I was in Reykjavik with Gorbachev and Reagan," crummy presents from old boyfriends (a harmonica from the Great Wall of China and a chunk of meteorite oxide), my early attempts at poetry ("This is the end of my poem, Goodbye, I have to go home!"), old notebooks from Air Force One.

All of this gone, and still no inner peace. Suddenly I realized that simple is empty. Clutter beautiful. It is the stuff of memory, the evidence of an unexamined life that is worth living. I'll do without a BMW, but I want my dice clock back. (Dowd 13)

Reading Comprehension Exam

Please circle the letter next to the correct answer based on the passage you just read. Be sure to mark only **one** answer for each question. Good luck!

1. The author suggests:
   a. Voluntary Simplicity is desirable.
   b. memories are not worth having.
   c. cookbooks should be updated.
   d. clutter can be beneficial.

2. Upon moving to her new house, the author decides to:
   a. collect cookbooks
   b. buy a BMW
   c. throw out some cookbooks and articles
   d. write poetry

3. Maureen Dowd believes that clutter:
   a. is always desirable
   b. may be a good thing
   c. makes people smarter
   d. gives people respect

4. Dowd threw out:
   a. every cookbook she had
   b. every hamburger cookbook she had
   c. some of her original motion picture soundtracks
   d. all of her tapes

5. Dowd finally:
   a. throws her old notebooks in the dumpster
   b. thinks clutter is ridiculous
   c. accepts Elaine St. James's asceticism
   d. received only good advice from her mother

6. The passage suggests that, at first, the author:
   a. hates Elaine St. James because she keeps her BMW
   b. admires St. James because she holds onto important things
   c. admires St. James for her Voluntary Simplicity
   d. has no opinion

7. The purpose of this essay is to:
   a. entertain   c. persuade
   b. argue   d. condemn

8. The gifts that the author's mother gave her concerned:
   a. cooking   c. Las Vegas
   b. cooking and other advice d. writing

9. The author defends clutter because it:
   a. is beautiful   c. may come back into style one day
   b. holds memories   d. all of the above

10. Dowd uses Jimmy Carter as an example of someone who:
    a. sought to eradicate the world's injustices
    b. became simpler and, therefore, less respected
    c. earned the gratitude of a society in turmoil
    d. lavished riches upon himself to the detriment of society

11. According to Dowd, she opposes the trend by becoming:
    a. not uncluttered   c. more respectful
    b. not less tidy   d. humorous

12. The author mentions platform shoes because:
    a. she likes them
    b. she wishes she had saved them
    c. she wishes she threw them away
    d. she loves the 70s

13. The author is all of the following except:
    a. eager to try new ideas   c. talkative
    b. cluttered   d. sentimental

14. Dowd mentions a dice clock because it is an:
    a. example of how clutter serves a purpose
    b. needed in every home
    c. reminder of Las Vegas
    d. oxymoron

15. As used in the passage, *virtuous* means:
    a. tricky   c. stupendous
    b. animalistic   d. well-intentioned

Turn The Page When You Are Finished

Answers and Explanations

1. **d** is the correct answer. While (A) Voluntary Simplicity may, in fact, be desirable, the author's point, or main idea, is that there are times when clutter can be beneficial. Answers A and C are not indicated in the passage.

   TIP—Read all answers before deciding on the correct one.

2. **c** is the correct answer. While (A) collect cookbooks and (D) write poetry may be true, the author throws out some cookbooks and articles upon moving to her new house. Answer B is false, for she does not buy a BMW.

   TIP—Read the question completely, and anticipate the answer.

3. **b** is the correct answer. Dowd accepts clutter, but does not suggest that it is desirable all the time, as in answer A. The author does not suggest that clutter makes people smarter or provides them with more respect. B, therefore, appears to be the most reasonable answer.

   TIP—Avoid absolutes, including words such as *all, always, none, never, every, only, everyone,* and *no one.* Nothing is true all of the time.

4. **c** is the correct answer. While Dowd did throw out some cookbooks and tapes, she did not get rid of all of these things. She did, however, throw out some motion picture soundtracks.

   TIP—Choose qualifiers such as *some, sometimes, many, few, probably,* and *may.* Answers including these words are more probably correct.

5. **a** is the correct answer. There is no indication that the author believes clutter is ridiculous, as in answer B. She never accepts St. James' asceticism as in answer C. It is unlikely that she received only (an absolute) good advice from her mother. While she did not literally take the old notebooks to the dumpster, A is still the most plausible response.

   TIP—Don't overanalyze various responses. Throwing something in the dumpster is another way of saying she got rid of it. While the author personally does not go to a dumpster, she did, according to the passage, throw out some old notebooks. Therefore, this answer is acceptable.

6. **c** is the correct answer. There is no indication that the author (A) hates St. James, even though she keeps her BMW. She does, however, admire her. We do not know if St. James does hold onto important things, as in answer B. But we do know that she practices Voluntary Simplicity. The author admires her, we infer, because she tried to emulate St. James. Answer D is not suggested in the passage.

   TIP—Statements must be true without exception. While St. James MAY hold onto important things, she surely, we are told, practices Voluntary Simplicity.

7. **a** is the correct answer. Answers B, C, and even D call for some action on the part of the reader. It is clear that the passage is not forceful in nature, and serves simply to entertain.

   TIP—Eliminate synonymous responses. Answers B, C, and D are similar. Choose the answer that is different.

8. **b** is the correct answer. C is wrong because the author has a "souvenir" from Las Vegas. D is incorrect because her mother does not appear to have sent her articles on "writing." A seems to be correct, since many of the articles concerned

cooking. However, B is the better answer because the author indicates that her mother also sends her articles like "How to Cope With a Hotel Fire," etc.

TIP—Figure out the difference between similar options. While A is correct, answer B is better because it includes all the items her mother actually did send her.

9. **d** is the correct answer. The passage suggests that, yes, clutter can be beautiful, does hold memories, and may come back into style one day (answers A, B, C). Therefore, "all of the above" must be true.

TIP—If more than one answer is correct, and there can only be one correct answer, use logical reasoning and choose "all of the above" as the correct response.

10. **b** is the correct answer. While answers A and C may, in fact, be true, they are not suggested in the passage. D seems to be false. Dowd clearly indicates that as Carter adopted a simpler lifestyle, he became less respected.

TIP—Choose the obvious answer. While other responses may seem elaborate, pompous, or just "sound good," choose the simplest, most apparent response.

11. **a** is the correct answer. Rephrased, answer A means "cluttered," and answer B means "more tidy." Dowd does Not go against the trend (Voluntary Simplicity) by becoming more respectful or more humorous (answers C and D). Becoming cluttered is the opposite of Voluntary Simplicity and, therefore, the correct answer.

TIP—Simplify double negatives. When presented with confusing double negatives, eliminate both negatives. Therefore, "not uncluttered" is read as "cluttered."

12. **b** is the correct answer. The author states that she "regrets" giving away her platforms, or as B indicates, she "wishes she had saved them." Answers A and D may be true, but are not indicated in the passage. Answer C is incorrect.

TIP—Choose only true responses. Some responses are neither true nor false. B is clearly true, because the author uses the word "regret," which is the same meaning as answer B.

13. **c** is the correct answer. The author admits that she is (A) eager to try new ideas, because she attempts Voluntary Simplicity, (B) cluttered, and (D) sentimental, because she likes "the stuff of memory." Only (C) talkative is not indicated.

TIP—Check all responses for rewording, and read the question carefully. All answers, except for C, are suggested in the passage. By reading the question carefully, we see that the wrong attribute is required.

14. **a** is the correct answer. Answers B and D are not indicated in the passage. While C may be true, A is used to back the author's point. Also, it "fits" grammatically.

TIP—Check for poorly phrased questions. The question ends with the word "an." Therefore, a vowel must follow. Because answer D is not true, the answer must be A.

15. **d** is the correct answer. While the word *virtuous* does not exactly mean well-intentioned, the meaning is appropriate, because the author decides to adopt Voluntary Simplicity. Other answers are totally unsuitable.

TIP—Eliminate absurd responses. The other answer choices offered for this question, *tricky, animalistic,* and *stupendous,* are inappropriate in the context.

Save this page

Now that you have reviewed some specific suggestions, here are some . . .

General Tips for Test-Taking Success

1. Get enough sleep the night before the test.
2. Arrive early for the exam.
3. Listen carefully for instructions.
4. Scan the exam before beginning the test.
5. Stay relaxed during the test, even if it appears difficult.
6. Don't be afraid to take an educated guess.
7. Stay with your first guess, unless you are sure you answered incorrectly.
8. Don't leave any answers blank.
9. Relate as you read, even if the passage seems intricate or boring.
10. Check the time after every few passages; try to leave enough time for review.

When taking any test remember the **3 R's:**

Relax, Relate, Review

And . . . the most important tip:

Be Prepared!!!

The successful student knows the subject well by preparing in advance for the exam. When taking a reading test this means studying the reading skills you have learned, and practicing sample reading tests. Passing those reading exams should not be an intimidating endeavor if you are properly prepared. Now, let's take another reading test.

Getting the Picture

Martha Stewart is a woman who has used her talents to reach the top of the business world. Examine the photo closely. What characteristics about this woman are suggested? What are the specific qualities someone should possess in order to become successful? Do you think that in the 21st century women have attained the same status as men or do they still have a long way to go? Discuss your answers.

_____

_____

_____

© Stephen Coburn, 2010. Used under license form Shutterstock, Inc.

_____

_____

_____

_____

_____

_____

_____

_____

_____

_____

_____

_____

_____

_____

_____

_____

_____

CREATING YOUR OWN TEST

How much do you remember about test-taking skills? Before you take the assessment exam at the end of this text, challenge yourself by reading the following passage; it appears in *Exploring Western Civilization—1600 to the Present* by Thomas J. Kehoe, Harold E. Damerow, and Jose Marie Duvall, a textbook you might find in your history class. The passage is about the women's rights movement. Without the struggle for women's rights, led by such leaders like Betty Friedan, the accomplishments of Martha Stewart and other prominent females would not have been possible. However, even though great strides have been made in the United States and other industrialized nations, several developing countries still have a long way to go. After you finish reading the selection, you be the teacher. Formulate a 15-question multiple-choice exam on the pages that follow, then exchange tests with a partner as you practice what you learned in the preceding chapter. **Remember to concentrate on finding the main idea, vocabulary, and inference.**

The Women's Rights Movement

Women's rights have been an issue for a considerable time. The 1972 publication of Mary Wollstonecraft's *Vindication of the Rights of Women* was mentioned earlier. After World War I, women in Britain and the U.S. obtained the right to vote as a result of the work of suffragettes. Two important works that influenced the women's rights movement were published after World War II. Simone de Beauvoir's (1908–1986) *The Second Sex* was published in French in 1949. De Beauvoir, who was a companion of Jean Paul Sartre, argued that man treats woman as the Other. Man defines woman not in herself but in relation to him. He expects her to be submissive, and she is often complicit. Women have been confined to a secondary position in history, similar to the way Americans have exploited Blacks. Her hope was that modern women would move towards liberation—true equality with men. This would require changes in law, economies, customs, and the whole social context.

Betty Friedan (1921–2006) published The Feminine Mystique in 1963. In this work, she said that psychologists, educators, and advertisers had conspired to emphasize the role of woman as housewife, as if the role promised total fulfillment. She advocated providing women with opportunities in the workplace and elsewhere for fulfillment beyond those provided in marriage and child rearing. Friedan was one of the founders of the National Organization for Women (NOW) in 1966.

The record of success for the women's rights movement is mixed. In highly developed countries, including the U.S., Canada, France, and England, women compose 40 percent or more of the labor force. In Third

© Gines Valera Marin, 2010. Used under license from Shutterstock, Inc.

World countries, particularly Muslim countries, women's participation in the workforce is much less, often 10 to 30 percent. Women are still concentrated in low-status, low-paying jobs, such as teaching, sales, and clerical work. In the U.S., attempts to ratify an Equal Rights Amendment, first introduced in Congress in 1923, failed again in 1982. Yet, recent court decisions have been sympathetic to efforts to compensate for the kind of sexual harassment that was given wide publicity by the allegations raised in the Anita Hill-Clarence Thomas hearings of 1991.

Human rights efforts have gone beyond minority rights and women's rights. In 1948, the United Nations General Assembly adopted a Universal Declaration of Human Rights. In 1975, the Helsinki Accords were signed in Finland by 33 European countries, as well as by Canada and the United States. These accords committed governments to respect such human rights as freedom of thought, conscience, and belief. Organizations like Amnesty International and Human Rights Watch have sought to hold governments accountable for gross violations of human rights.

The United Nations in 1993 and 1994 established war crimes tribunals for the victims of genocide in Bosnia and in Rwanda. While there have been a few indictments, many of the perpetrators of these crimes remain unpunished. (Kehoe et al. 432–33)

Write your exam on the following pages.

1. _____

   a. _____

   b. _____

   c. _____

   d. _____

2. _____

   a. _____

   b. _____

   c. _____

   d. _____

3. _____

   a. _____

   b. _____

   c. _____

   d. _____

4. _____

   a. _____

   b. _____

   c. _____

   d. _____

5. _____

   a. _____

   b. _____

   c. _____

   d. _____

6. _____

   a. _____

   b. _____

   c. _____

   d. _____

7. _____

   a. _____

   b. _____

   c. _____

   d. _____

8. _____

   a. _____

   b. _____

   c. _____

   d. _____

9. _____

   a. _____

   b. _____

   c. _____

   d. _____

10. _____

   a. _____

   b. _____

   c. _____

   d. _____

11. _____

   a. _____

   b. _____

   c. _____

   d. _____

12. _____

   a. _____

   b. _____

   c. _____

   d. _____

13. _____

   a. _____

   b. _____

   c. _____

   d. _____

14. _____

   a. _____

   b. _____

   c. _____

   d. _____

15. _____

   a. _____

   b. _____

   c. _____

   d. _____

Getting the Picture

The photo depicts a woman engaged in the hobby of gardening. Martha Stewart created an enterprise based on a variety of her hobbies, things she loved to do. Today, through her TV shows, magazine, books, and appearances, she teaches others a number of "good things," like cooking, baking, crafts, decorating, and even gardening. People often begin businesses which use their hobbies and talents. For example, someone who likes to write may start a magazine. On the lines below, write a business plan for one of your own hobbies.

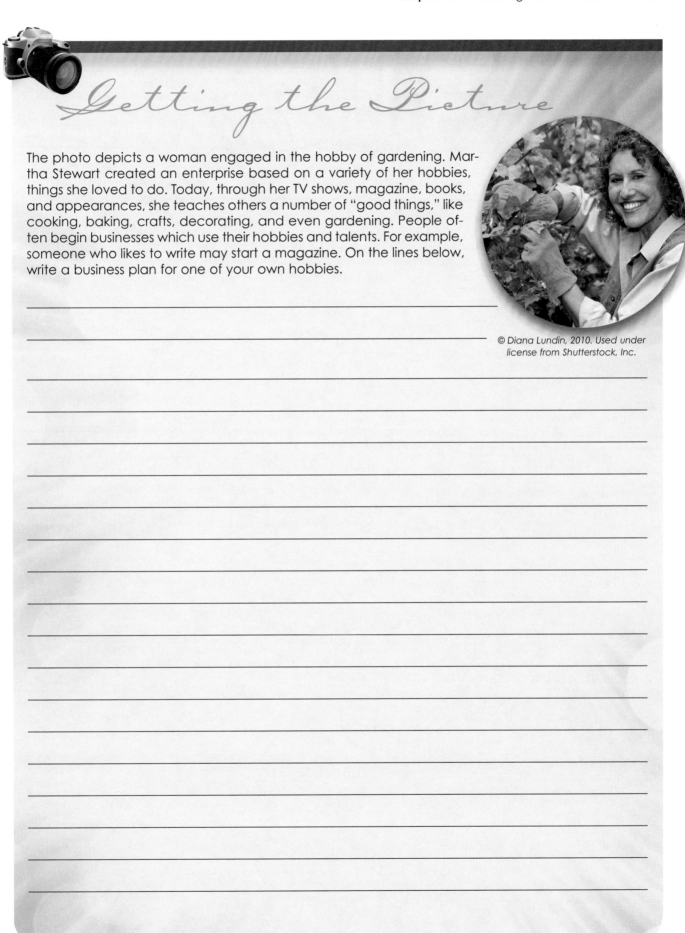

© Diana Lundin, 2010. Used under license from Shutterstock, Inc.

Final Assessment

Textbook Reading Comprehension
Time: Forty Minutes

Directions: This is a test of your ability to comprehend reading passages from textbooks used in a variety of college courses.

First, read each passage carefully. Then answer each question, selecting from the four possible answers the one that is best.

There are six passages and twenty-five questions. Although it is not necessary to finish the entire test to obtain a good score, try to finish the test within the forty minute test time. If you finish before forty minutes have elapsed, reread as many passages as you can and check your responses. Remain seated and wait for further instructions.

Questions 1–7 are based on the following passage.

Because of constant turmoil, rape, pillage, famine, disease, and the lack of a strong central government, the weak sought protection from the strong after the breakup of the Carolingian Empire. During the Middle Ages, three basic classes emerged in society: those who worked (peasants bound to the land), those who prayed (clergy), and those who fought (warriors). The nobles (lords) were the warriors, and they were granted land (fiefs) by a higher noble in return for military service. The lords built fortified castles and manors in strategic locations, such as on a mountain promontory or a river confluence, where as warriors they could fend off attacks and take the peasants (serfs) into their fortress in times of distress.

In these turbulent times, few monetary transactions occurred and land was the primary basis of wealth. A monarch or other lord (duke, count, baron, earl) would grant territory to another lord, who was a member of the same social class (a vassal), in exchange for his services as a warrior. This contractual relationship was called feudalism. The land grant would provide the vassal (the grantee) with the wherewithal (the produce from the land and rents from tenants) to equip his knights with horses, armor, and weapons. Great lords (the grantors) now had armed vassals at their disposal who had sworn personal allegiance and fealty (faithfulness) in return for their land grants.

The formal ceremony whereby the vassal pledged his fealty and loyalty to his overlord was called HOMAGE; at the same ceremony the vassal was "invested" with a clod of earth or a sheaf of grain representing his fief. An oath of loyalty bound the two nobles together until death or mutual dissolution. The vassal promised to be the lord's man, and had the following obligations. He had to fight for his lord, usually 40 days a year, ransom him if he were to be captured, sit at his court in order to hear criminal and civil cases, provide hospitality and entertainment for a specified number of days each year, and give generous gifts upon the knighting of the lord's eldest son or the marriage of his oldest daughter. Customarily, in a system called primogeniture, the vassal's eldest son inherited the land, the title, and the privileges and obligations of his rank. (Kehoe et al. 315–316)

1. The topic of this selection is:
   a. the vassal system.
   b. the feudal system.
   c. the Homage.
   d. the tenant system.

2. The passage suggests that during the Carolingian Empire, the central government was:
   a. weak.
   b. stable.
   c. strong.
   d. divided.

3. According to the passage, the feudal system:
   a. existed before the Middle Ages.
   b. existed after the Middle Ages.
   c. existed during the Middle Ages.
   d. was never successful.

4. During the Middle Ages, the three classes in society were:
   a. peasants, fiefs, nobles.
   b. peasants, nobles, serfs.
   c. peasants, clergy, warriors.
   d. serfs, clergy, fiefs.

5. In the sentence, "The lords built fortified castles and manors in strategic locations, such as on a mountain promontory or a river confluence, where as warriors they could fend off attacks and take the peasants (serfs) into their fortress in times of distress," the word "promontory" means:
   a. cave
   b. valley
   c. a high ridge of land jutting out into a body of water
   d. oasis

6. In the sentence, "The lords built fortified castles and manors in strategic locations, such as on a mountain promontory or a river confluence, where as warriors they could fend off attacks and take the peasants (serfs) into their fortress in times of distress," the word "confluence" means:
   a. flood
   b. the meeting of two or more streams
   c. drought
   d. obstacle

7. The basis of wealth in the feudal system was:
   a. trinkets.
   b. animal skins.
   c. money.
   d. land.

Questions 8–11 are based on the following passage.

"I trust you have not had an unpleasant journey here," says Frau Danhaus, bending slowly to pour the tea into little cups of china. The appearance of this frail woman matches that of her home. She appears to be in her eighties. Her hair, a pure white, is loosely piled on the back of her head and fastened with an onyx comb. She wears no makeup except for two lines of pink rouge painted on her cheekbones. She is attired in a tangerine-colored suit with huge round buttons, and as she pours, I can smell cheap German cologne. I am humbled that she considers my visit an occasion for formality. Overall, Frau Danhaus reminds me of a small sparrow, so quick are her movements. Even her voice has a chirping quality.

8. The main idea of the selection is:
    a. Frau Danhaus is old.
    b. Frau Danhaus is a strange woman.
    c. The visitor has respect for Frau Danhaus.
    d. The visitor distrusts Frau Danhaus.

9. The overall organization of the passage is:
    a. description
    b. illustration/example
    c. definition
    d. cause/effect

10. In the sentence, "The appearance of this frail woman matches that of her home,"the word "frail" means:
    a. neat
    b. fantastic
    c. fragile
    d. old

11. In the sentence, "I am humbled that she considers my visit an occasion for formality," the word "formality" means:
    a. a tea party
    b. questions and answers
    c. a visit
    d. correctness

Questions 12–14 are based on the following passage.

The Jarabe Tapatío, or Mexican Hat Dance, is a piece of music and a dance that have come to be regarded as the national dance of Mexico. The music is a compilation of traditional Mexican folk tunes fashioned into a unified composition in the late nineteenth century by Mexican composer Jesús Rubio. The music is most frequently performed by a mariachi band, a combination of trumpets, violins, and several sizes and varieties of guitars, including a very large one that serves the function of a bass. Mariachi music originated in the Mexican state of Jalisco as did the Hat Dance. The word "tapatío" in the name refers to Jalisco as the place of origin.

While not tied to any particular celebration, the Mexican Hat Dance may be heard, and seen, at any public celebration in Mexico throughout the year. The most widely known Mexican celebratory event is Cinco de Mayo, Fifth of May, which has come to be known around the world as a celebration of Mexican traditions and ethnicity. It is at events like this, as well as at smaller celebrations like weddings, that the Mexican Hat Dance is often performed. The name, Mexican Hat Dance, is a reference to the part of this courtship dance where the man throws the large wide-brimmed hat that he is wearing, a sombrero, to the ground for the woman to pick up, thus sealing their union in love. (Chiego 154)

12. The pattern of organization in this passage is:
    a. definition
    b. compare/contrast
    c. sequence of events
    d. illustration/example

13. The main idea of this passage is:
    a. music is a part of all Mexican traditions.
    b. the Mexican Hat Dance is an important part of Mexico's tradition.
    c. Jesús Rubio is a famous composer.
    d. dances for courtship are popular in Mexico.

14. The purpose of this passage is to:
    a. entertain
    b. inform
    c. praise
    d. satirize

Questions 15–18 are based on the following passage.

Obesity in children has become a major problem in the United States and needs to be confronted immediately. Instead of getting exercise by playing team sports or simply running around outdoors, youngsters are content to spend their time playing video games or watching TV. Furthermore, the availability of "fast food" hinders attempts to make more nutritious choices. Parents should assume the greatest blame for this problem because they fail to educate the younger generation on the consequences of poor food choices or a sedentary lifestyle. Besides, the parents themselves usually serve as poor role models.

15. The overall tone of the passage is:
    a. ironic
    b. persuasive
    c. sad
    d. informative

16. The organization of the passage is best described as:
    a. descriptive
    b. cause/effect
    c. compare/contrast
    d. illustration/example

17. The main idea of the passage indicates:
    a. Parents should take the blame for child obesity.
    b. Children need to exercise more.
    c. Parents must make better food choices for their children.
    d. A number of factors are responsible for child obesity.

18. In the sentence, "Parents should assume the greatest blame for this problem because they fail to educate the younger generation on the consequences of poor food choices or a sedentary lifestyle," the word "sedentary" means:
    a. athletic
    b. inactive
    c. solitary
    d. inadvisable

Questions 19–21 are based on the following passage.

Most fears and phobias are learned through the process of classical conditioning. The famous experiment of John B. Watson and Rosalie Rayner (1920) demonstrates how fears and eventually phobias are easily learned.

An eleven-month-old boy named Albert was classically conditioned to fear a variety of furry things. Before the experiment, Albert enjoyed playing with a white rat. One day as the rat was handed to Albert, the experimenters made a loud terrifying noise that startled Albert and made him cry. They continued to do this six more times, until Albert showed a strong fear of the rat, crying and shrinking away whenever the rat was placed near him. As the experiment continued, the experimenters presented Albert with other objects that were similar to the white rat, such as a white stuffed animal, a furry white blanket, and a Santa Claus mask. To their surprise, Albert showed the same fear response to the different furry objects as he did the white rat. This process is called stimulus generalization. A day later, Albert was released from the hospital where the experiment took place. So, if you are walking down the street one day wearing your white fur coat and a seventy-year-old man starts yelling and running the other way, say, "Hi Albert." Albert should have gone through a reconditioning process called desensitization in order to extinguish him of the fears.

Classical conditioning helps explain the formation of fears, attitudes, prejudices and feelings that may seem quite irrational. For example, you don't understand why you have such an uneasy feeling around your red-haired boss. You can't think of any logical, rational reason for this feeling. You have also noticed that you feel uneasy around other red-haired individuals. One day while you were reminiscing about elementary school, you remembered that your second-grade, red-haired teacher slapped your hands with a ruler every time you made a mistake. At this time, this was a very painful, embarrassing experience to be hit in front of all your friends. This one early experience that you repressed is still having an effect upon your present life, especially your interactions with red-haired individuals. Prior to second grade, you liked people with red hair, but since this one experience, red-haired individuals have become the conditioned stimulus for your fear (uneasy feeling), the conditioned response. Have you ever had an experience like this? (Walker 123–124)

19. The topic of this passage is:
    a. desensitization.
    b. stimulus generalization.
    c. classical conditioning.
    d. Albertization.

20. The pattern of organization in the last paragraph is:
    a. definition
    b. compare/contrast
    c. sequence of events
    d. illustration/example

21. This passage suggests that:
    a. most fears and phobias can never be overcome.
    b. irrational feelings are learned.
    c. all fears and phobias are learned.
    d. it is impossible to "unlearn" feelings.

Questions 22–25 are based on the following passage.

Researchers have suggested a variety of personal factors as reasons why individuals go into business. One that is often cited is the "entrepreneurial spirit"— the desire to create a new business. Other factors, such as independence, the desire to determine one's own destiny, and the willingness to find and accept a challenge certainly play a part. Background may exert an influence as well. In particular, researchers think that people whose families have been in business (successfully or not) are most apt to start and run their own business. Those who start their own businesses also tend to cluster around certain ages—more than 70% are between 24 and 44 years old. Women own 4.8 million businesses and are starting new businesses at twice the rate of men.

Finally, there must be some motivation to start a business. A person may decide she has simply "had enough" of working for someone else. Another may lose his job for some reason and decide to start the business he has always wanted rather than seek another job. Still another person may have an idea for a new product or a new way to sell an exciting product. Or the opportunity to go into business may arise suddenly, perhaps as a result of a hobby.

22. Surprisingly, one reason not at all stressed for going into business is:
    a. the "entrepreneurial spirit."
    b. to control one's destiny.
    c. to make a lot of money.
    d. the role of family history.

23. The best title for this selection would be:
    a. Getting Rich in Your Own Business
    b. Getting Started in Your Own Business
    c. The Psychology of Success in Small Business
    d. Why People Start Their Own Businesses

24. According to the selection, women usually:
    a. own more businesses than men.
    b. are more successful than most men in business.
    c. are acquiring more new businesses than men.
    d. are much younger than men in small businesses.

25. The pattern of organization in this article is:
    a. definition
    b. compare/contrast
    c. sequence of events
    d. illustration/example

Works Cited

Diagnostic Test

Feldman, Robert S. *Essentials of Understanding Psychology.* 2nd ed. New York: McGraw-Hill. 1994. Print.

Hales, Dianne. *An Invitation to Health.* 6th ed. Benjamin-Cummings. 1994. Print.

Pride, William M. et al. *Business.* 4th ed. Boston: Houghton-Mifflin. 1993. Print.

Chapter 1

Bandler, Grinder, and Grinder. *Fastrak Consulting.* Web.

Learning Disability Forum. "Famous People—Learning Disabilities." n.d. Web.

Nicholl, Malcolm J., and Colin Rose. *Fastrak Consulting.* Web.

Chapter 2

Hales, Dianne. "Dependence on Nicotine." *An Invitation to Health.* Belmont: Wadsworth/Cengage, 2009. Print.

Long, Elizabeth Cloninger. *Resources for Writers.* Longman, Print.

Rudell, Martha Rapp. *Teaching Content Reading and Writing.* Allyn & Bacon, 1993. Print.

Chapter 3

Ellison, Brooke. *Miracles Happen: One Mother, One Daughter, One Journey.* New York: Hyperion, 2001. Print.

Lahey, Benjamin B. *Psychology: An Introduction.* McGraw-Hill Primis, Print.

Parks, Alice. "Stem Cell Research: The Quest Resumes." *Time* 29 Jan. 2009. Print.

Reeve, Christopher. *Still Me.* New York: Random House, 1998. Print.

Chapter 4

Belton, John. "Genre and the Genre System." *American Cinema/American Culture.* 2nd ed. New York: McGraw-Hill, 2005. Print.

Lahey, Benjamin B. *Psychology: An Introduction.* McGraw-Hill Primis, Print.

Long, Elizabeth Cloninger. *Resources for Writers.* Longman, Print.

Chapter 5

Gray, W. S. *On Their Own in Reading.* Chicago: Scott, Foresman, 1946. Print.

Henricks, Mark. "Success and Its Discontents." *American Way* 1 Feb. 2001: 87;pl. Print.

Stewart, Jon. "Local News." *Naked Pictures of Famous People.* New York: HarperCollins, 1998. Print.

Chapter 6

Kent School District. http://www.kcnt.k12.wa.us/KSD/MA/resources/ greek_and_latin _roots/suffix.html;mt. Web.

Merriam-Webster Online. Merriam-Webster, 2009. Web.

Schaefer, Richard T. *Sociology: A Brief Introduction.* 6th ed. Boston: McGraw-Hill, 2004. Print.

Stewart, Jon. "Local News." *Naked Pictures of Famous People.* New York: HarperCollins, 1998. Print.

Chapter 7

Adams, Laurie Schneider. *Art Across Time.* 3rd ed. Boston: McGraw-Hill, 2007. Print.

Baran, Stanley J. *Introduction to Mass Communication.* 5th ed. McGraw-Hill, 2008. Print.

Brinkley, Alan. *American History.* 12th ed. Boston: McGraw-Hill, 2007. Print.

Costanzo, William V. *The Writer's Eye.* New York: McGraw-Hill, 2008. Print.

Di Scala, Spencer M. *Twentieth Century Europe.* McGraw-Hill, 2004. Print.

Divine, Robert A., et al. "The Terrorist Within." *America Past and Present.,* 5th ed. Pearson/Addis. Print.

Forster, E. M. "What I Believe." *Two Cheers for Democracy.* London: Hogarth Press, 1939. Print.

Futrell, Charles M. *ABC's of Relationship Selling Through Service.* 8th ed. New York: McGraw-Hill, 2005. Print.

Gregory, Hamilton. *Public Speaking for College and Career.* 8th ed. Boston: McGraw-Hill, 2008. Print.

Griffith, W. Thomas. *The Physics of Everyday Phenomena.* 5th ed. Boston: McGraw-Hill, 2007. Print.

Insel, Paul M., and Walton T. Roth. *Core Concepts in Health.* 10th ed. McGraw-Hill, 2008. Print.

Joyner, David. *American Popular Music.* 2nd ed. McGraw-Hill, 2003. Print.

Kaplan, Paul S. *A Child's Odyssey.* 4th ed. Kendall-Hunt, 2008. Print.

Mader, Sylvia S. *Human Biology.* 10th ed. McGraw-Hill, 2008. Print.

Martin, Andres. "Tattoos Today." *The Decorated Body.* Ed. R. Brain. New York: Harper & Row, 1979. Print.

McConnell, Campbell R., and Stanley L. Brue. *Economics.* McGraw-Hill, 2008. Print.

Mencher, Melvin. *News Reporting and Writing.* 11th ed. Boston: McGraw-Hill, 2008. Print.

Passer, Michael W., and Ronald E. Smith. *Psychology.* 3rd ed. Boston: McGraw-Hill, 2007. Print.

Pearson, Judy C., et al. *Human Communication.* 2nd ed. McGraw-Hill, 2006. Print.

Quindlen, Anna. "Aha! Caught You Reading." *Loud and Clear.* New York: Random House, 2004. 239–40. Print.

———. "A Shock to the System." title from "The Last Word." *Newsweek* 25 Aug. 2003. Print.

Schiller, Bradley R. *The Economy Today.* 10th ed. McGraw-Hill, 2006. Print.

Shaw, Ines Senna. *The Collective Pursuit of Gender Equality Around the World.* Dubuque: Kendall-Hunt, 2008. Print.

Teague, Michael L., et al. *Your Health Today.* McGraw-Hill, 2007. Print.

Williams, Yohura, et al., eds. "The Impending Crisis and the Challenge to Slavery (1850–1860)." *A Constant Struggle—African American History.* Kendall-Hunt, 2005. 365–66. Print.

Wilson, Edwin. *Theater Experience.* 10th ed. McGraw-Hill, 2007. Print.

Wong, Elizabeth. "The Struggle to Be an American Girl." *Los Angeles Times* 7 Sept. 1980. Print.

Chapter 8

Avison, David, and Guy Fitzgerald. *Avison-Fitzgerald Information Systems Development.* 4th ed. McGraw-Hill, Print.

Britt, Suzanne. "Neat People vs. Sloppy People." *The Bedford Reader.* Eds. X. J. Kennedy, Dorothy M. Kennedy, and Jane E. Aaron. Bedford/St. Martin's, 2009. 233–35. Print.

Catton, Bruce. "Grant and Lee: A Study in Contrasts." *The American Story.* Rpt. in *Steps to Writing Well* by Jean Wyrick. Wadsworth, 2003. Print.

Feldman, Robert S. *Essentials of Understanding Psychology.* 6th ed. New York: McGraw-Hill, 2004. Print.

Goodman, Ellen. "The Company Man." *Washington Post* 1 Jan. 1981. Print.

Mader. *Human Biology Manual.* 9th ed. McGraw-Hill, Print.

Chapter 9

Editorial. *Los Angeles Times. Viewpoints.* 3rd ed. Ed. W. Royce Adams. Houghton-Mifflin, 1998. Print.

Gonzales, John. "College Brings Alienation." *Viewpoints.* 3rd ed. Ed. W. Royce Adams. Houghton-Mifflin, 1998. Print.

Wellborn, Stanley. "Birth." *Viewpoints*. 3rd ed. Ed. W. Royce Adams. Houghton-Mifflin, 1998. Print.

Chapter 10

Conti, Edmund. "Pragmatist." 1985.

Crane, Stephen. "A Man Said to the Universe."

Moore, Janice Townley. "To a Wasp."

Quindlen, Anna. "Death Penalty's False Promise." *New York Times* 23 Dec. 1979. Print.

Rozin, Skip. "Big White." *Harper's Magazine* Jan. 1975. Print.

Sullum, Jacob. "Capital Punishment: Yes." *Reason* June 1990. Print.

Swift, Jonathan. "A Modest Proposal." 1792.

Wheelock, John Hall. "Earth." *The Gardener and Other Poems*. Simon & Schuster, 1961. Print.

Chapter 11

Breen, Steve. Cartoon. *San Diego Union-Tribune* 22 Sept. 2005: Print.

Cayton, Andrew, Elisabeth Israels Perry, and Allan M. Winkler. *America: Pathways to the Present*. Saddle River: Prentice Hall, 1995. Print.

Coffee, Peter. "There's a Bad Example on Every Desk." *eWeek* 15 Apr. 2002. Print.

Divine, Robert A., et al. *America—Past and Present*. 7th ed. Pearson Longman, 2005. Print.

Goldsborough, Reid. "For Love of the PC." *Community College Week* 24 June 2002. Print.

Parker, Jeff. Cartoon. *Detroit News* 22 Sept. 2005. Print.

Chapter 12

Klassen, et al. "Illyusa.com" and "LeBeers". Advertisement. *Ad'Mat*. Kendall Hunt, 2009. Print.

Trump, Donald. "Be a General." *How to Get Rich*. New York: Random House, 2004. Print.

Sherry, Mary. "In Praise of the F Word." *Newsweek* 6 May 1991. Print.

Volvo Gran Turismo. Advertisement. Volvo Cars of North America. Feb. 1964. Print.

Chapter 13

"Army Replacing Steel Helmet." *New York Times* 1 Dec. 1982. Print.

Halpern, Jake. "Stardust: The Talk of the Town." *New Yorker* 26 Dec. 2005. Print.

Jacobs, Andrew. "Rural China's Hunger for Sons Fuels Traffic in Abducted Boys." *New York Times* 4 Apr. 2009: A1. Print.

Littlejohn, Georgina. "The Ugly Truth about This Badly Drawn Boy." *Metro* 6 June 2002. Print.

Radosta, John. "Red Wings Defeat Islanders." *New York Times* 9 Dec. 1982. Print.

Chapter 14

Frisch, Laurie. "'Fast Track Adoption' Ends in Suicide." *PRWeb*. Web.

Gammage, Jeff. "Adoptive Parents Tell It Like It Is—and with Love." *Philadelphia Inquirer* 14 Feb. 2005. Print.

Hax, Carolyn. "Tell Me about It: Boyfriend Tricked Her, Fed Her Beef." *Washington Post* 20 Nov. 2005. Print.

"NYC Billboard Rules Don't Violate First Amendment, 2nd Circuit Says." *Associated Press*. 4 Feb. 2010. Print.

"Religion, Science and Civility." Editorial. *Chicago Tribune* 12 Dec. 2005: 22. Print.

Chapter 15

Barrie, James M. "The Flight." *Peter Pan*. Henry Holt, 1987. Print.

Jackson, Shirley. "Charles." *The Lottery and Other Stories by Shirley Jackson*. 1948. Print.

Chapter 16

Chopin, Kate. "The Story of an Hour." *The Complete Novels and Stories.* The Library of America, 2002. Print.

Poe, Edgar Allan. "The Tell-Tale Heart." *The Complete Stories of Edgar Allan Poe.* International Collectors Library, 1966. Print.

Wachtel, Shirley Russak. "Darkness Falls." *The Story of Blima—A Holocaust Survivor.* Townsend Press. 2005. Print.

Walker, Alice. "Flowers." *In Love and Trouble—Stories of Black Women.* Harcourt Brace, 1973. Print.

Williams, William Carlos. "The Use of Force." *The William Carlos Williams Reader,* ed. M.L. Rosenthal. New York: New Directions Publishers, 1984. Print.

Chapter 17

Dickinson, Emily. "Success is Countest Sweetest." Print.

Frost, Robert. "The Road Not Taken." *The Poetry of Robert Frost.* Henry Holt, 1969. Print.

Lavigne, Avril. "Complicated." Alfred Publishing. 2002.

Picasso, Pablo. *Maya in a Sailor Suit.* 1938. Oil on canvas. Museum of Mod. Art, New York.

Chapter 18

Burns, Robert. "My Love is Like a Red, Red Rose." *Selected Poems of Robert Burns.* Penguin, 1993. Print.

Colette. "The Hand." *The Collected Stories of Collette,* Ed. Robert Phelps. Farrar Strauss & Giroux, 1983. Print.

Frost, Robert. "The Rose Family." *The Poetry of Robert Frost.* Henry Holt, 1969. Print.

Hughes, Langston. "A Dream Deferred." *The Collected Poems of Langston Hughes.* Ed. Arnold Rampersand and David Roessel. Alfred A. Knopf, 1951. Print.

Jacobson, Bonnie. "On Being Served Apples." *On Being Served Apples.* 1981.

Parker, Dorothy. "One Perfect Rose." *The Portable Dorothy Parker.* Viking Penguin Press, 1954. Print.

Wachtel, Shirley Russak. "Before the Snow."

Chapter 19

Dowd, Maureen. "LIBERTIES: Adieu, Herb Alpert." *New York Times* 22 Oct. 1995: 13. Print.

Chapter 20

Kehoe, Thomas J., Harold E. Damerow, and Jose Marie Duvall. "The Women's Rights Movement." *Exploring Western Civilization—1600 to the Present.* Kendall Hunt, 1999. Print.

Final Assessment

Chiego, John J. *The Musical Experience.* 2nd ed. Kendall Hunt, 2010. Print.

Kehoe, Thomas J., Harold E. Damerow, and Jose Marie Duvall. "The Women's Rights Movement." *Exploring Western Civilization—1600 to the Present.* Kendall Hunt, 1999. Print.

Walker, Velma. *Becoming Aware.* 11th ed. Kendall Hunt, 2010. Print.